Table of Contents

Preface – 7

Area Map – 9

Prince George and its outdoors – 11

Awakening – 14

Inside the City – 15
    Gunn Trail – 18
    Citywide trails – 19
    Urban walkabout – 20
    Lunchtime walk – 24
    Doug Little's legacy for Prince George's outdoors – 26
    Forests for the World – 28
    Moores Meadow – 34
    McMillan Creek and two-viewpoints walk – 36
    Ferguson Lake Nature Reserve – 37
    Otway ski centre – 39
    Wildlife in the city – 40
    Cranbrook Hill Greenway – wilderness in the city – 42
    Heritage River Trail – 44
    Other in-town trails – 46
    Christmas Bird Count – 47

North – 48

History – 50
Off road – 51
Huble Homestead and Giscome Portage Trail – 52
Summit Lake – 54
Teapot Mountain – 54
Coffeepot Mountain – 55
Crystal springs – 59
Crooked River Provincial Park –59
North to the Pine Pass – 62
Gateway to Northern BC – 65
Wokkpash and Stone Mountain – 66

East through the Rocky Mountain Trench – 75

Green Mountain – 76
Tabor Mountain – 77
Moose viewing area – 80
Willow Canyon and demonstration forest – 80
Purden Lake – 82
The Bowron Valley – 82
Entering the Rocky Mountain Trench – 82
Sugarbowl Grizzly Park – 83
Grand Canyon of the Fraser – 85
Sugarbowl and Viking Trails – 105
Dave King – 113
Grizzly Den and Raven Lake – 118
Interior rain forest – 122
Driscoll Ridge – 124
The Longworth Lookout – 130
More communities of the Trench – 134
Ptarmigan Creek – 134
Erg Mountain – 139
Robson Valley – 142
The National Hiking Trail – 142
Rainbow Falls – McBride and Teare Mountains – 147
Paradise Ridge – 148

Holliday Creek and Stone Arch – 150
Holmes River – Beaver River – 151
Dunster – 152
Mount Terry Fox – 157
Mount Robson Park – 162
Beyond Robson – 163

East to the McGregor and Rocky Mountains – 165

Aleza Lake Research Forest – 165
Skiing the McGregor Mountains – 167
Deep snow at The Farm – 169
Evanoff Provincial Park – 172
Golden Eagle – 175
Upper Herrick Valley – 176
Kakwa – 184

South – 197

Blackwater Road – 197
Fort George Canyon Trail – 197
Baldy Hughes – 199
Punchaw Lake – 200
Nuxalk Carrier Grease Trail – 200
The Telegraph Trail – 201
Blackwater River – 201
Blackwater south to Quesnel – 202
Wells and Barkerville – 202
Cariboo getaway – 204
Fire lookout open to the public – 205

West – 207

Otway – Miworth Roads – 207
Eskers Provincial Park – 211
Bobtail Mountain – 216
Vanderhoof – 218
Fort St. James and Pope Mountain – 219
North to the Nation Lakes – 221
Fraser Lake – 223

History in Prince George – 229

Mountain named for woman adventurer – 229
Pioneer packer – 231
New Rivers of the North – 232
1927 journey of Prentiss Gray from the Peace to the Fraser – 234
Passing of Pierre Trudeau – 236
Murder at Swift Current Creek – 238
John and Cyril Shelford – Burns Lake pioneers – 239
Japanese Canadians in wartime Prince George – 241

Centre for caving – 244

Redemption is near – 244
One chance for young cave birds – 249
Caves of Prince George – 250

Encountering bears – 252

First experience – 252
Up close – 254
Demonstration of power – 255
Territorial habits – 255
Bear safety – 256
Face to face – 261

Readiness for the outdoors – 262

Preparedness – 263
Assessing the situation – 265
Leadership – 266
Technology in the backcountry – 268
Preparing for the backcountry – 269
Food and food dehydrating – 269

Northern Light – 271

Index – 274

About the author – 280

Preface

We joined the semicircle of cars and pickup trucks that were enveloped in a drifting cloud of exhaust gases, condensing in the early winter air. I wasn't sure whether the engines were kept running to keep the occupants warm or to facilitate a quick getaway, but we followed suit. The object of our attention reacted angrily to the snowballs being thrown at it by a lone figure standing inside the arc of vehicles. The first attempt to tranquilize this snared bear had failed, and the biologist was testing its reactions.

Not wanting to administer an overdose but finding it still very much awake, he waited another 15 minutes before firing a second dart at it. This time the bear went down. It was weighed and tagged, blood and tooth samples were taken, and its enormous paws were draped around the shoulders of the attending RCMP sergeant's visiting relatives for a souvenir photograph. I volunteered to help lift the animal into a vehicle for transport down the coast. A biologist warned us to be alert. "You stay alive in this work by learning to have a lot of respect around polar bears," he said. This one was a 275-kilogram sow, and with its winter fat it was like trying to lift a colossal lump of jelly. Leveraged up in one place, it flopped down somewhere else, eventually requiring five men to lift it, half a bear at a time. Despite many later black bear and grizzly bear adventures that I would have in the outdoors of Prince George and Northern B.C., my most intimate bear encounter was this one, with *Ursus maritimus,* on the shores of Hudson Bay, 18 months before I moved to British Columbia.

It was October 1976 and I had flown from Toronto to Winnipeg to take the train north to Churchill, Manitoba. It was an opportunity to see the country at close quarters, to share stories with people whose pace of life we have nearly forgotten. As we rolled north, Winnipeg commuters gave way to rural folk, then to northern resource workers, and finally to First Nations people. A trapper got on and slung his load in the overhead rack across from me as the apparently endless taiga forests were slowly replaced by tundra. Arriving at the mouth of the Churchill River, it was too late in the season to cross the estuary to Fort Prince of Wales—the fort had been built during the period 1732 to 1771 and was visible, low on the opposite shore. Instead, I rented a car with two people whom I had met on the train and we drove down the coast looking for polar bears.

Buoyed by this journey, I undertook another train ride the following spring that was to lead, more than a quarter of a century later, to this book. In May 1977, I flew to Edmonton and took the train west to Prince Rupert. En route, we pulled into Prince George and with an hour to wait, I disembarked and strolled down First Avenue where, unknowing what the future would hold, I saw the Nechako cutbanks for the first time. The train left Prince George with just a handful of passengers, and I stood on the open balcony of the last car watching the Nechako River wind past as we threaded our way through Miworth. In the afternoon we stopped in Smithers for two hours. I walked around a fairy-tale town clad in the fresh greenery of spring and overhung with the snow and ice of Hudson's Bay Mountain. Sailing south from Prince Rupert the following day, the weather was clear along the Inside Passage for the first time in a month, and salmon leapt in abundance around the boat. I was the only passenger braving the chill wind on deck when I heard a knock on the glass behind me and was invited onto the bridge to listen to the captain's tales of B.C.'s northern coast.

North and Central British Columbia had captivated me, from the Coast to the Interior Plateau to the Rocky Mountains, and a year later I moved to Prince George right in the centre of it all. There, I was quickly drawn to the scenic backdrop of rivers, treed escarpments, and green spaces. I marvelled at the endless forests, and during the spring and summer of 1978 began to explore the surrounding trails. Snowfall was heavy during my first winter in Prince George and the temperature dipped to minus 40 degrees Celsius. Shovelling snow off the roof of the house until it piled up to the eaves was hard work but fun, although climate change has lessened the need for the task in recent years. It was dry snow, without the drifting or the piercingly damp winds that I had been accustomed to from the Great Lakes when I lived in Ontario. I found unlimited cross-country skiing close to home, and the surrounding area was well-endowed with ski hills and mountain backcountry. The key to living here I realized, was to get outside and use the winter. The combination of a nearly ideal climate, the central location, buoyant economy, numerous amenities, rich culture, affordable housing, and proximity to some of the best outdoor environments in the world, makes Prince George an exceptional place in which to live.

The Prince George Area

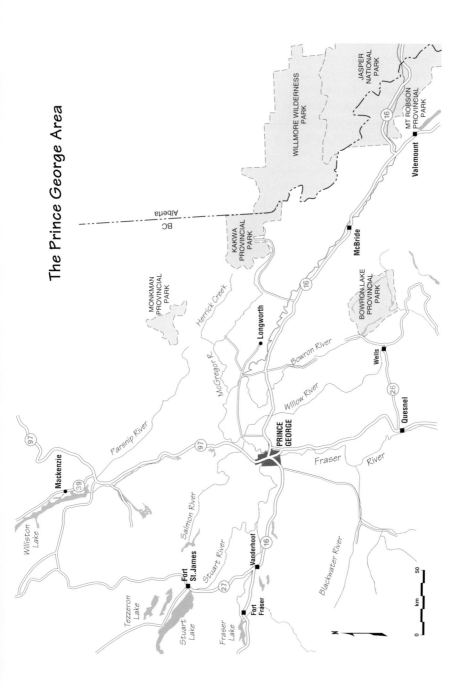

Acknowledgments

I would like to acknowledge all those who have contributed to this book. Some are mentioned in the text, but there are many others who will recognize places and events described. First, I would like to recognize Catherine J. Johnson for her professional, insightful, and supportive editing of the manuscript during several weeks of intense, but always fun, back and forth discussion. I wish to thank Jack Boudreau for helping to find information on the Grand Canyon area and on wartime internees, Roy Howard for information about the National Hiking Trail and the Raush Valley, and Mike Murtha for his historical inspirations about Wokkpash, Kakwa, and the journeys of Prentiss Gray. I would like to thank my wife, Judy Lett, for her support during the writing of the book; my parents Nina and Stuart Nash for introducing me to the outdoors as a child, and the late George Evanoff for being my principal inspiration and mentor in the Prince George outdoors. I also wish to acknowledge those who have published my works, notably *Prince George This Week* and its editors, and I would especially like to thank all the readers who have encouraged me to keep on writing. When I began, I thought that I would quickly run out of material, but as most writers will attest, that doesn't easily happen. There is always something new to discover, from the polar bear on the shores of Hudson Bay to the halls of a new northern university, and the endlessly varied Prince George outdoors.

Mike Nash
January 2004

Disclaimer

There are inherent risks associated with any outdoor activity, and readers of this book must exercise their own best judgement in the outdoors and use the information contained in the book entirely at their own risk. The author and publisher disclaim liability for injuries, damages or other consequences suffered by anyone using the outdoors. Knowledge, combined with planning, preparation, practice and common sense are keys to having a safe and enjoyable outdoor experience.

Prince George and its Outdoors

Prince George lies close to the geographic heart of British Columbia, where major north–south and east–west road and rail corridors intersect. It is a provincial transportation hub, and one can travel in any direction without being constrained by borders or shoreline. It has a strong resource base, and is an important centre for regional government, health, education, and industrial and retail supply. The College of New Caledonia (CNC) and the University of Northern British Columbia (UNBC) have helped to diversify its economy and have added significantly to its cultural and academic life. Prince George is an easy one-day drive from Edmonton, Calgary, Vancouver, or Prince Rupert, yet is far enough away to have a unique identity. It is less than two hours drive from the Rocky Mountains and only half a day from Jasper and Banff National Parks. It is surrounded by wilderness where it is still possible to explore untrodden ground within a short distance of home. The remaining pieces of untouched interior rainforests of the Rocky Mountain Trench and the Cariboo Mountains are only an hour away, and are part of a rich ecosystem that is unique on the planet. Prince George is a city of about eighty thousand—an ideal size. People get involved, and the city has an excellent reputation for raising a family. Sports and outdoor recreation opportunities abound in the city, and there are many outdoor opportunities available in the surrounding backcountry and mountains.

This combination was brought home to me one fall day when, with one companion, I drove out to the Rocky Mountains northeast of the city and saw several bald eagles and moose in the morning light along the way. Leaving the vehicle, we began our approach hike and soon encountered a moose, a deer, and a black bear as we pushed through dew-laden vegetation. Climbing in the midst of an ancient forest, we emerged into alpine meadows set against glaciated mountain and green valley backdrops. There we saw a grizzly bear, a golden eagle, and later,

The author on a horse packing trip in 1995 into the wild Anzac valley before it was logged. Courtesy of Big Game Guide Ken Pickering.

met a group of caribou cows with their calves. We arrived back in town with time to enjoy a leisurely supper, then a dressy concert. My thought as I listened to music played by one of Canada's best regional orchestras, was where else could one find this mix of wilderness, culture, amenities, and community? And because of its location in the geographic heart of the province, Prince George is also a great staging place for remote wilderness trips into Northern British Columbia.

In the 1990s I started writing about my outdoor experiences in Central and Northern B.C. for national and provincial newsletters, magazines, and local newspapers. From feedback received, I realized that collectively some of this material would be a resource for people wishing to discover the best that this area has to offer. I have loosely organized the essays into geographic areas, with additional sections on safety, history, and other topics. This book is mostly about outdoor activities that can be done on foot. That being said, the country around Prince George offers many other recreational opportunities such as river and lake canoeing, mountain biking, climbing, caving, and snowmobiling. I have included directions and maps to help the reader locate the places described, but this is not a guidebook in the usual sense—the accent is on self-discovery. I offer you my vision of why Prince George and its surrounding area is special, perhaps to inspire you to explore and seek experiences similar to those that are described in the book. There is something here for everyone, and as for those places that you can't physically get to, I invite you to enjoy them vicariously.

Since arriving here in 1978, the natural attributes of Prince George seem not to have changed much at all; especially the scenic beauty of its surrounding treed escarpments that are now protected by city bylaw. Yet during that quarter-century, I have seen the building of a university, a library, a civic centre, the Two Rivers Art Gallery, a multiplex arena, a second swimming pool, three bridges, an outstanding railway and forestry museum, and many parks, trails, and athletic facilities. Other major additions have included a courthouse, a jail, two theatres, and major expansions of the College of New Caledonia, UNBC, the Fraser–Fort George Regional Museum, and the Regional Hospital. And lately, a new northern medical program is under development at the university and at the expanded hospital. The courthouse is an architecturally splendid building whose rotunda has served as a fine venue for the B.C. Festival of the Arts, and whose sidewalks now provide a community focus for the summer-long Saturday farmer's market. Its location is the hub of revitalization for Prince George's downtown, where new sidewalks, trees, and decorative lamps are being installed as this book goes to press.

The forest industry, long the mainstay of the Prince George economy, continues to face significant challenges, but it is likely here to stay, as despite recurrent mountain pine beetle infestations, the region very possibly has the strongest forestry potential in British Columbia. To the north, oil and gas reserves are both under development and in production, while undeveloped resources may exist in the Nechako Basin west of the city. Also an economic boon, the University of Northern British Columbia is attracting worldwide interest, and on the outskirts of the city large retail stores have been built to serve Northern B.C.

An important consideration for the future is Prince George's potential to feed itself by utilizing large areas of underdeveloped agricultural land, especially in the surrounding river valleys. As well, prospective developments at the Prince George Airport will open the community to international shipping and tourism. A proposed new casino will offer entertainment to rival major centres, while two live theatres and the Prince George Symphony Orchestra continue to provide the mainstay of cultural life. Cinema CNC regularly brings in the latest and best arts films from international festivals, which play to sold-out audiences in the college lecture theatre from September to April. As many have already discovered, Prince George is an ideal place in which to live, work, and play. It is poised to reap the advantages of the new century with its resources, infrastructure, location, culture, and entertainment, and as this book will show, its outstanding outdoors and open spaces.

Awakening

A mark of Prince George is the intensity of the seasonal change that we experience here. Spring may be slow in coming to the north, but then it quickly makes up for lost time, carrying with it the fulsome promise of a long summer and fall to come.

The sun's northward race past the equinox
  Foreshadows the burst of a boreal spring.
Glimpses, this week, of the explosion soon to come.
Hints of green and subtle wisps of fragrance
  tease the senses.

Snow, two weeks late leaving our yards,
  one lawn green,
  the other not yet clear of the leftovers of winter.
But the trees aren't late—they know
  the time to renew.

Distant mountains white against the changing valleys
  experience a different kind of spring.
Deep snows reach their seasonal peak
  and begin the frantic transmutation
  to the waters of life.

As we join this fevered cycle of change
Between cleanup, renovations and new horizons,
will we pause
  to rejoice in each flower and each insect
  as they awaken?

Inside the City

There is no better or healthier way to experience a community than to explore it on foot, and one of the most useful possessions that a person can have upon arrival in a new town is a pair of walking shoes. While this book is largely about the countryside around Prince George, most visitors and new arrivals to B.C.'s self-ascribed northern capital will spend at least some of their time in the city, and will therefore have the opportunity to discover what it is all about, up close and personal.

A good starting point is to walk around the roughly four square kilometre downtown, beginning at the Civic Centre Plaza, around which are located the civic centre, the Bob Harkins Library, Two Rivers Art Gallery, Four Seasons Pool, Coliseum, and city hall. From there, a short walk along historic George Street, with its interesting retail shops and cafes, brings you to the modern, architecturally impressive courthouse. Take a look inside its rotunda entrance before turning west along the newly revitalized Third Avenue, then south along Victoria Street to the downtown shopping centre at Parkwood Mall. Return to your starting point via Connaught Hill Park, where it towers above the library and Patricia Boulevard. Summertime flower displays and views of the city there are a must for a first-time visitor to Prince George. If you wish to continue farther, descend Connaught Hill on its southeast side to Queensway, from where it is only a few minutes walk southeast to Fort George Park, situated on the banks of the Fraser River. There, you can visit the Fraser–Fort George Regional Museum, the miniature railway, First Nation burial ground, and summer concerts in the park at the Fort George Band Shell.

From Fort George Park, if you feel energetic, the 11-kilometre Heritage River Trail loops past the confluence of the Fraser and Nechako Rivers, Cottonwood Island Nature Park, the railway and forestry museum, Nechako riverside, then via Carney Street to the Prince George YMCA. Across the road from the 'Y' is the popular

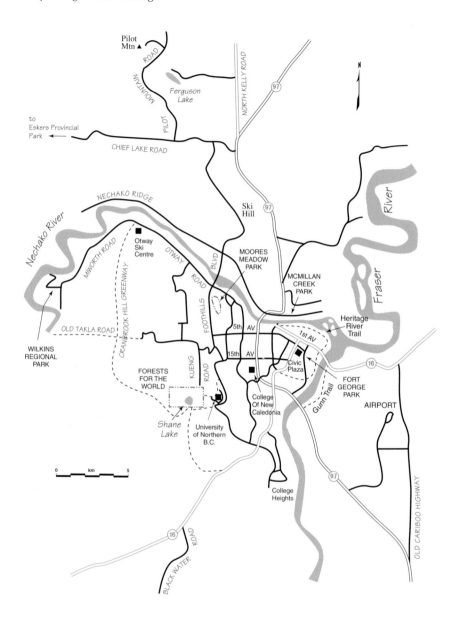

Prince George Farmers Market in the Courthouse Plaza.

walking track at Massey Stadium (originally built to host the B.C. Summer Games), as well as several playing fields and a skateboard park. Return to Fort George Park on the Heritage River Trail as it winds through Carrie Jane Grey Park, Strathcona Park, and the Hudson Bay Slough. Alternately from Fort George Park, the nine-kilometre Gunn Trail loop can be walked by crossing the Yellowhead Highway bridge to connect with the three-kilometre rustic trail along the top of the treed Fraser cutbanks, before returning on the other side of the river through historic South Fort George.

When you have exhausted the downtown, take a city transit bus, or car, to the University of Northern British Columbia via 15th Avenue and University Way. First look around the impressive campus with its themes of wood and stone, and the superb views across the city to the Rocky Mountains, and then take a walk on the nearby Cranbrook Hill Greenway trail to what is perhaps the city's best outdoor area at Forests for the World.

Finally, consider visiting some of Prince George's varied urban and rural residential areas, with surrounding parks and greenbelts. These and other places to see inside the city are described in the first section of the book. But beware! As you get to know the city better, and especially as you begin to explore the surrounding countryside, you might be drawn to the conclusion that Prince George is a desirable place to call home.

Gunn Trail

The Gunn Trail follows the wooded edge of the Fraser River escarpment between the Yellowhead Bridge and Simon Fraser Bridge. Three kilometres long, it winds steeply through a forested area that affords spectacular views over the Fraser River and Prince George. The mix of surrounding forest directly overlooking the heart of the city recalls the intimate association between Stanley Park and the downtown area of the City of Vancouver to the south. Sponsored in the 1990s by the City of Prince George through its Rivers Committee and by BC Rail who provided the right-of-way, this trail was a model of community involvement. An outdoorsman and friend who had great influence on me during my first 20 years in Prince George managed this volunteer project and did a lion's share of the work. A bronze plaque at the trailhead now stands to the memory of George Evanoff.

The easiest access to the trail is at L.C. Gunn Park situated at the end of Guay Road. The park and the trail are named after Luther Collins Gunn, head surveyor of the Grand Trunk Pacific Railway Company in Prince George in the early years of the twentieth century. Take the first road on the right after driving or walking across the Yellowhead Bridge heading east on Highway 16. Walk through the park to the first viewpoint and then follow the trail south along the escarpment. For safety, stay well away from the edge along the steep sections, and supervise children there. The first part of the trail from the parking lot is almost flat and within reach of anyone; after that it climbs steeply to the middle section of the route where the best views are.

My favorite Gunn Trail walk is a round trip from Fort George Park. Follow the Heritage River Trail north from the northeast corner of the park along Taylor Drive and walk across the Yellowhead Bridge. Take the shortcut trail that leads south from the east end of the bridge into Gunn Park. Follow the Gunn Trail south to the Simon Fraser Bridge, and after recrossing the Fraser River walk back to the starting point through historic South Fort George. Stay as close to the river as you can on this return section to include such riverside opportunities as Paddle Wheel Park. The loop takes up to two hours at a steady pace, or longer if you stop to enjoy a picnic at one of the viewpoints. It is a perfect walk on a weekend afternoon or a long summer evening, and depending how late it is, you might catch a northern sunset over Prince George and Cranbrook Hill. One can also tie this walk in with a visit to the Fraser–Fort George Regional Museum or one of the many outdoor concerts held during the summer in Fort George Park.

Citywide trails

In 1998 the City of Prince George unveiled its master plan for a new citywide trails system. When completed, it proposed to add over 130 kilometres of new trails to those already existing, to give Prince George over 200 kilometres of non-motorized, multi-use trails. For the most part, the trails would be built and maintained to certain standards, while some would be designated low maintenance rustic trails located in natural areas with greenbelt on either side. The plan was commissioned by city council following a 1997 survey that placed trails at the top of the list of leisure facilities used in Prince George. According to that survey, there were over seven hundred thousand visits per year, with more than 67 per cent of households using trails. Today, when people seek a town to visit or to live in, the existence of a good trail system is one of the things they look for. In the past, while cities have spent mere thousands of dollars annually on trails — often with donated money, or goods and services in kind — they have invested many millions of dollars in other facilities. Prince George is no exception to this trend, with the result that today we have the many fine civic facilities described earlier. The citywide trails plan, when actualized, will bring outdoor trails to the fore and help to complete a well-rounded recreational infrastructure.

The citywide trails plan builds on the Heritage River Trail's 1984 and 1992 master plans. Like its precursors, the 1998 plan is a vision that is intended to guide the development of the trail system during succeeding years. It overlays the official community plan and ensures that advantage is taken of opportunities as they arise. Having the plan helps the city secure key trail connections by approaching third parties during development planning. Around the same time that this plan was being developed, the Cranbrook Hill Greenway Society brought a dream of an urban greenway to reality. According to one chairperson of the society, the city's vision "...will be tempered by the hard reality on the ground and we will end up with something uniquely Prince George."

Underlying the plan is the realization that trails are high on the list of recreational needs in Prince George. And the movement of people away from cars to self-propelled means of getting to work will have health benefits as well as help Canada to meet its commitment to mitigate the effects of climate change. The emphasis on crosstown connectors and neighbourhood walkways supports the original design ideas for Prince George. In short, this is an important step toward ensuring a healthy and ecologically-sound community for the twenty-first century.

Urban walkabout

Continuing the theme of citywide trails, an "urban walkabout" is taking the time to explore and enjoy the city on foot, by piecing together a mix of trails, parks, streets, refreshment stops, and other interesting places and events along the way. One can begin over breakfast or the evening before with a map of the city and a list of community events taken from a recent newspaper, making a rough plan of your urban adventure, allowing room for spontaneity. Looking at the Prince George map, there are many parks and linear green spaces to choose from that link interesting street walks— you are only limited by your ingenuity. Some examples are the Lakewood, Rainbow, and Harry Loder chain of parks; the Massey Drive green space, with its school grounds, parks, recreation facilities and link to the Heritage River Trail; and the Connaught Hill and Patricia Boulevard green space. Add in a mix of rustic trails such as the Gunn Trail, or a section of the paved Heritage River Trail. Plan one or two well-timed stops at patio coffee shops or eating establishments. And lastly, work in some summertime events such as the Fort George Park festive activities, the railway and forestry museum, the farmer's market, a community ball game, or any of the myriad things going on all over town on a typical summer weekend.

The following story describes such a walk around the city on a warm, sunny day in August. You could retrace all or part of my route, or create an urban walkabout of your own, and you may find, as I did, that your daylong journey gives a different sense of Prince George. When I look around at what we have, I am reminded of a comment made a few years ago by a resident of Dome Creek, east of the city. When asked by a worldly tourist who was passing through the tiny community whether he had done any travelling, the resident quipped, "I never needed to, I was born here!"

It was a warm, sunny Sunday and I packed a few snacks and water and set out on what would become a marathon 36-kilometre, eight-hour circumnavigation of the city bowl. For those not familiar with the term, the "bowl" is the natural depression that makes up much of the city of Prince George. It has been carved out of the Interior Plateau, over time, by the Fraser and Nechako rivers. About to embark on an urban version of an Australian aboriginal walkabout, I had no definite plan, but I would live partly off the land by stopping at strategic places of refreshment, travel light, and experience the moods and spirit of the city.

I began and ended my trek at Moores Meadow Park in the northwest corner of the bowl. Leaving this large natural park, I crossed First Avenue and followed the linear greenway leading

Fur brigade arrival at Fort George (now Fort George Park) – reenactment August 1985.

into Heritage Park and then out to Foothills Boulevard via Killoren Crescent. There I picked up one of the countless mountain bike trails that have sprung up all over town, and in this case it climbed steeply through the bush of Cranbrook Hill. Emerging from the trees at the top, a half-hour walk along Kueng Road brought me to Forests for the World and to a viewpoint overlooking the city and the distant Rocky Mountains. After a snack, I headed down past Reflection Lake toward the University of Northern British Columbia. The vegetation and wildflowers were luxuriant thanks to a wet spring and early summer. Much of the cow parsnip west of Shane Lake had reached its full potential of three metres in height. Leaving the lake at the beaver dams, I joined the Cranbrook Hill Greenway where it twists and turns between Forests for the World and UNBC. This one kilometre section is not unlike walking through a tropical forest in the summer, full of birds and lush undergrowth.

Bypassing the attractive campus of UNBC, I started down University Way looking for the old trail that used to connect Shane Lake to Ferry Avenue. I hadn't used it since the university was built and I wanted an alternative to the long walk down the hill and along 15th Avenue. I found the trail a short distance before the road starts downhill—inevitably it had been well-used by mountain bikes. A short, steep descent brought me to the grassy area below the site of the old Ben Ginter mansion. Jan-Udo Wenzel's biography, *Ginter,* offers a fascinating insight into aspects of Prince George and Ginter's role in its colourful past.

Ben Ginter was a self-made man who arrived in Prince George with almost nothing, and who at his peak employed about ten thousand people in the development of highways, pulpmills, and other infrastructure in the interior of B.C. His reach eventually extended across Canada, its decline only coming about after he acquired the brewery in Prince George and took on Canada's national beer barons. From the site of the now demolished Ginter mansion, a trail leads down through the tall grass to Pinewood Avenue, which I followed across Ospika Boulevard. Turning left on Vanier, I discovered for the first time sizeable Lorne Park that took me through to the Pine Centre shopping mall. Thus far I had been in natural surroundings for most of the way and was ready for a little urban walking.

As I crossed the street, the driver of a car waiting to exit the mall parking lot leaned out his window and waved, "Hi, Mike," and I was reminded of what it means to live in a not too-large city. I followed the green space along Massey Drive, then dropping down from Prince George Secondary School, I paused to watch an adult soccer game before entering Massey Stadium. There I walked a half-lap of the popular rubber-surfaced track originally built for the B.C. Summer Games. Passing the 'Y' where I had once taught Iyengar yoga, I followed wooded trails past apartment buildings to 15th Avenue and Parkwood Place. There I took a well-deserved break at a favourite coffee shop to enjoy a latte.

Massey Stadium on Massey Boulevard, one of the many linear green spaces in the city of Prince George and a popular walking area. The Prince George 'Y' and the city skate board park are in the background.

On the road again, I walked south down Spruce Street, past cheerful improvements of decorative sidewalks, lamps, and signs—the "Gateway" area along 20th Avenue and Victoria Street was a foretaste of the renewal that would later take place downtown. Continuing on Spruce Street to Strathcona Avenue, I passed the community gardens, a reminder of the "garden allotments" of Europe, whereby urban residents are provided with access to a plot of land for growing vegetables and flowers. Hopefully this would be a harbinger of more such projects to come. Prince George's potential to feed itself could help curb the absurd use of resources that I had observed the previous day in the form of organic tomatoes flown in from Europe.

In front of me was nearly half a kilometre of grass between Pearson Avenue and Diefenbaker Drive. Together with nearby St. Laurent Avenue I was reminded that Prince George had not yet named a street for another of Canada's deceased, yet well-known prime ministers, Pierre Elliott Trudeau. Short jogs south on Victoria, east on Pearson, and south on Pine brought me to the Simon Fraser Bridge, where the four-minute crossing on the unprotected sidewalk was the least pleasant part of the entire trip. Widening this bridge is one of the top infrastructure priorities for Prince George, as it is the last of the city's four highway river crossings with only two lanes. Below me, the turbid chocolate-coloured water of the Fraser River carried enormous amounts of silt and debris from a week of rain in the mountains. On the east bank, the towering pinnacles of the Fraser cutbanks beckoned me away from the traffic.

Dropping off the south end of the bridge, I was quickly re-engulfed in forest as I followed the three-kilometre Gunn Trail leading to L.C. Gunn Park. This forest had a different smell to it—drier than Cranbrook Hill. The trail was developed as a multi-use segment of the river trails system. Multi-use is a key element of today's urban recreational infrastructure, but well-used, soft-surface trails like this one will eventually require maintenance, as mountain bike wheels accelerate the erosion of mud holes and exposed roots. Pausing at a viewpoint halfway across, I enjoyed a cool soft drink while gazing across the city to fully absorb the magnitude of my walk. The landscape has an entirely different feel when traversed on foot as compared to by vehicle.

Crossing the Yellowhead Bridge with its four lanes and lower traffic volume, the protected walkway and downhill grade was a much more pleasant experience than its downstream counterpart. Nearly across, I paused to watch the boils, whirlpools, and back currents where the Nechako and Fraser flood waters meet at the westernmost bridge abutment. If one were caught here in a canoe in conditions like this, it could mean serious trouble. Goat Island was nearly submerged, and

I found all the paths into Cottonwood Island Park barred by flood waters. The river was repairing the damage inflicted on it in the early spring by vehicles driven over its exposed bed. Detouring around River Road gave me a chance to check out the railway and forestry museum, without a doubt one of the best exhibits in Prince George.

A variety of watercraft passed me as I walked along the pleasant Nechako section of the Heritage River Trail, the occupants experiencing the city in a different way. Prince George is built on two rivers, and we sometimes overlook the opportunity to see it from a Venice, Italy or San Antonio, Texas perspective. Leaving the river, I was ready for a patio supper at a pub-restaurant where copious glasses of water instead of beer would do for much needed re-hydration.

A postprandial pace found me wandering more leisurely along 5th Avenue across to Dezell Drive and out to Ospika via the walkway on Radcliffe Drive, typical of many neighbourhood links in Prince George. Dropping down to Wilson Park, I rejoined the Nechako River and, walking into the evening sun, made my way back through Moores Meadow to my starting point. I reflected on what a magnificent day it had been, and why a person might be prompted to ask, "Why do I need to travel, I already live here?"

Lunchtime walk

A problem faced by some people in northern climates is seasonal affective disorder, or SAD, caused by insufficient exposure to natural light during the winter months. It is also known as cabin fever syndrome. Often, people deal with this by flying south for a mid-winter break, a strategy that works if you have the time and can afford it, but which is not strictly necessary. Unlike coastal areas of the province or large parts of the Okanagan and Southern Interior, we in Prince George are fortunate to receive generous amounts of winter sunshine. The key is simply to make the time to go outside. The problem is that during mid-winter it's dark when most people go to work and dark again when they return home. For indoor-workers it is therefore possible to go from one weekend to the next without seeing much sun, and if it is cloudy on the weekend, life can get a little depressing. Our bodies need sunlight, and the low-angle winter sun with its low UV rating is just right.

Some years ago, a group of employees at a local forest company, including myself, solved this problem for ourselves by walking each day at lunchtime. On most workdays between noon and 12:30 pm, small groups of people could be seen walking what affectionately became known as "the loop." Starting from the company administration

Connaught Hill park in the centre of downtown Prince George offers fine views of the city for visitors and lunchtime walkers alike – looking west towards Cranbrook Hill.

building near Canadian Forest Products' Northwood Pulpmill, the 2.5-kilometre loop can be walked in either direction. It begins with a short stretch of forest service road, and continues past the J.D. Little Forest Centre on Landooz Road until turning south to rejoin the main road and back to the office. One winter during a minus 20-degree Celsius cold snap, up to a dozen people continued to do the walk; coming around the northwest corner to head directly into the winter sun was the crux of what it was all about. Despite the industrial setting, the walk has a rural flavour, and it is not uncommon to see moose, deer, fox, bear (in season), eagles, and on occasion, a cougar. Some years, the company supported this walk through its employee health committee, offering prizes for activity points earned and on one occasion, providing refreshments for those on the loop. Several years later, I still enjoy my two denim "Healthstyles" shirts that I earned in this way. Other Prince George organizations have at one time or another offered similar incentives for their employees to undertake health breaks during the workday.

Working in another industrial area south of the city for a few months, I found several walks in natural surroundings where it was still possible to encounter wildlife there as well. It is surprising how many interesting walks can be found even at the height of winter almost anywhere in the city. So, why not try it where you work and see what a difference a short daily walk in the sun can make?

Doug Little's legacy for Prince George's outdoors

The J.D. Little Forest Centre just referred to in "Lunchtime walk" was established by then senior vice-president of forestry operations for Northwood Pulp and Timber Limited in the 1980s, and was later named in his memory. At the 8th annual Doug Little Memorial Lecture held at UNBC in October 2003, Walter Matosevic, general manager of forestry and environment for Canadian Forest Products who subsequently acquired Northwood, spoke about Doug Little's legacy, telling the audience that Doug was a true family man, a great forester, and a real statesman for the forest industry. Doug, along with his wife Sheila, raised a large family of six children. He worked in the sector for 44 years, with a career that ranged from assistant ranger with the B.C. Forest Service in the Kootenays, to timber cruising and logging on Vancouver Island. Returning to the Interior, he was instrumental in establishing and growing a company that eventually became known as Northwood. He was responsible for acquiring the timber quota and building the roads and bridges needed to access it. Doug was a great leader and a strong advocate for forest policy change. His broad and fair perspectives were always well respected by his peers. In 1986 he received the Distinguished Forester Award from the Association of B.C. Professional Foresters, as the association was known at the time. Through his vision, Northwood became a leading company in the development of sustainable forest management standards, long before B.C.'s forest practices code or forest certification standards became a reality, and many of his ideas can be recognized in the current forest policies of our province. Doug also had an untiring devotion to forestry education, serving on many boards and committees such as the College of New Caledonia and the Forest Education Foundation of B.C. His dream was to see a university of the north, and while he didn't live to see the infrastructure of UNBC as it exists today, his vision and dedication lives on there through the Doug Little Memorial Lecture.

Doug Little actively supported fish and wildlife enhancement projects such as the fish hatchery at Penny, as well as some of the recreation initiatives in the backcountry that are described in later sections of this book, particularly those east of Prince George. For example, he supported the construction and maintenance of recreation campsites on Northwood's Tree Farm License 30, northeast of Prince George, as well as maintenance on the alpine cabins at Grizzly Den and Raven Lake (later becoming the Sugarbowl-Grizzly Den Provincial Park). The suspension bridge over the McGregor River, that backcountry recreationists have used for decades to access the

McGregor and Rocky Mountains was, according to Walter Matosevic, one of Doug's "pride and joys" as the man behind the project, and as a keen outdoorsman.

When I first got involved in the public land use planning processes of the early 1990s from a recreational perspective, I was working for Northwood in a non-forestry field. Feeling a little unsure of my ground, I went to Doug Little and asked him if I had a conflict. We had occasionally chatted in the corridor about issues such as higher elevation logging in the mountains, and I, like anyone who came into contact with him, knew him on a first name basis. When I posed my question, Doug replied, "Mike, you've got a head on your shoulders. If I hear anything from my people that I don't like, I'll let you know, and if I hear anything about them I don't like, I'll let them know."

In the ensuing 10 years, I was involved in many public processes and advisory committees, including the Herrick Creek Local Resource Use Plan, Prince George's Rivers Committee, B.C.'s Commercial Recreation Policy development, and later, the Prince George Land and Resource Management Plan, all while employed with Northwood. During that time, I frequently received support, and never experienced any pressure from anyone in the company even when we differed on issues. I attribute at least part of that to Doug Little, and to the influence that he had on people around him during his career. If he had taken a different tack with me, for example, I could not have been as effective in my ensuing public participation roles that led, in 2002, to a three-year appointment as a lay member of the Council of the Association of B.C. Forest Professionals.

On another occasion, I approached Doug Little and asked him if I could borrow the negatives of a couple of historic logging photographs that were hanging on the wall outside his office, in order to make prints. He was busy at the time, and as I left his office, I wasn't entirely sure that he had registered my question. A month later, he walked unannounced into my office with a large cardboard box containing his entire collection of historic prints and negatives. He entrusted them to me for several weeks to look through and select what I wanted. Today I have good memories of reviewing those fascinating images of early forestry in the Prince George area, and I now have a framed picture on my dining room wall of a horse-logging show in the Sinclair Mills area printed from one of the negatives. There was, as it turned out, considerable drama in this for me, as during the printing process, somewhere in their Canada-wide processing plant in Winnipeg, the photographic company lost the two negatives I had left with them. I hadn't realized they were sending a custom black and white print job like this out of town. Twice in my life I have telephoned presidents of national companies. This is not something you can get away with lightly or too often, but I felt that this situation warranted it. The result was that I got serious action, and the Winnipeg facility was searched during the annual maintenance shutdown that followed the Christmas rush. Happily, the negatives were found, in perfect shape, behind a machine.

At Doug Little's funeral in 1993, so many people attended the church ceremony that an overflow hall had to be used with a closed circuit TV feed. A forester who delivered one of the eulogies mentioned that Doug had once said something to him about coming back as a raven. Later at the reception, another forester who was not given to superstitious thought, turned to me and quietly said that he would never look at a raven in the forest the same way again. This small incident somehow spoke to me about the man that we had lost—that a common symbol of respect for the natural world among many indigenous peoples of British Columbia, was also a symbol of respect for Doug Little.

Forests for the World

One of the best places for walking within Prince George is the city's provincial centennial project, Forests for the World. The most direct access to the area is via Cranbrook Hill Road, which climbs southwest from Foothills Boulevard between 5th and 15th Avenues. At the top of the hill, turn left and follow Kueng Road south to the Forests for the World parking lot. Alternately, one can access Forests for the World on foot from the UNBC campus at the top of University Way, either via the water tower cutline that starts near the enhanced forestry laboratory, or from the terminus of the Cranbrook Hill Greenway trail located southwest of the student residences. The Greenway trail has at least three connections to Forests for the World as it skirts the site to the south.

Forests for the World offers a wide range of walks, and it is nearly impossible to tire of the area. Options range from a short, flat, "special needs" accessible trail to the viewing platform at Shane Lake, to hours of rugged loop-trails around the perimeter, some with interpretive signs. The most common large mammals seen in the area are moose, beaver, and black bear, but cougar have also been seen there. Other features of Forests for the World are its outstanding views across Prince George toward the Rocky Mountains; its lush natural second-growth vegetation; its isolated fragments of giant Douglas fir trees; and various successional stages of managed forest plantations. In recent years, it has become a handy research site for students and faculty of UNBC's College of Science and Management.

A favourite place for a nature walk, picnicking, or ice skating in the winter, Prince George's second largest lake, Shane Lake is the centrepiece of Forests for the World.

It is rare to find the parking lot empty, and the trails are so well used that they remain packed and accessible on foot throughout most of the winter months.

Fall

October is the beginning of the shoulder season for outdoor enthusiasts where, at some point, there is too much snow to walk comfortably in the bush or the mountains, and not enough snow, or perhaps enthusiasm, to begin skiing. Instead, it is time to think about get-togethers, concerts, films, and slide shows. But it can also be a time to hang onto the last vestige of summer by seeking sunny, low elevation walks endowed with fall colour; perhaps even to squeeze in a last few days of wearing hiking shorts. There are many natural trails inside the city, and Forests for the World is high on the list. Established in 1986, this area has developed slowly and relentlessly into a maze of nature walks and forest-related interpretive opportunities.

One of the more challenging Forests for the World trails is a two-kilometre loop signed *Who's Home?* To locate this loop, follow the perimeter trail west from the parking lot as it climbs toward the main viewpoint. Take the trail to the right (west) of the hill leading up to the viewpoint. After a few hundred metres, watch for a rustic trail to the right beneath two large cottonwood trees. Follow this trail up the hill that heads toward the giant Douglas fir trees, and watch for the above mentioned sign. In other words, keep to the right all the way from the parking lot to the *Who's Home?* sign. The side trail soon descends a steep hill and loops through mature, mixed forest with five elaborately carved interpretive signs about squirrel, beetles, colonizing fungi, moose, and bear. Tread softly on this half-hour long trail and you might see a moose as I did on my first walk there. Entranced, I returned the following day and hiked the loop in the reverse direction to get an entirely different perspective. From the main parking lot, the distance is about five kilometres, requiring one to two hours, and from UNBC it is 10 kilometres, requiring two to three hours. Add in some of the other loops and a portion of the Greenway trail and you could easily spend an entire day at Forests for the World. And if you leave your car in the bowl area of the city near 15th Avenue and Foothills Boulevard, then walk up the hill to access Forests for the World via the university, it is almost as good as a daylong mountain hike.

November evening

One voting day, leaving the polling station mid-afternoon, the lure of the blue sky and sun over Cranbrook Hill were irresistible. Heading straight up to Forests for the World, I found the trails mostly clear of snow. Treading lightly on the still unfrozen forest floor was an uncommon treat for late November. The sun shone nearly horizontally through the trees, hinting at the coming sunset. Back through the stand of old Douglas fir trees I reached the viewpoint as the alpenglow hit Tabor Mountain to the east of Prince George. Even farther to the east, a 15-kilometre wide column of falling snow was lit up, the shadow of Tabor Mountain slowly projecting onto this red curtain of sky. The dips and bumps of Tabor's familiar profile came into clear outline, then slowly ascended until lost in the rising shadow of the earth itself. Red was reflected into the waters of the Fraser River as the lights of industry came on. A nearly full moon backlit the cumulus clouds like the Baily's beads of a solar eclipse. Jupiter was above, and Saturn to the left, almost in conjunction, while to the north, the Rocky Mountains caught the last rays of the sun—a "northern light" that is uniquely Prince George.

Winter Solstice

It took effort to collect up the outdoor clothes and cross-country ski equipment, then venture out of a warm house into the cold, dark fog. It was December 21st, the night of the winter solstice and the first day of winter. Two or three weeks would go by before we would notice an increase in daylight, but this day marked an important psychological time for northerners even in the relatively low latitude of Prince George. It is easy to see why people have celebrated the "return of light" throughout human history.

We drove up to Forests for the World, climbing from a thick bowl of fog into clear night air under a full moon. On this night, according to the radio, the moon would be at its brightest in 133 years. Three celestial events would occur within a three-hour window around midnight—a full moon, the winter solstice, and lunar perigee (the closest approach of the moon to the earth in its monthly orbit). As well, the earth was only a few days away from perihelion, its closest approach to the sun. As if that weren't enough, we were treated to the spectacular conjunction of Saturn and Jupiter. Throw in a shooting star or two and nearly ideal skiing conditions, and that is what greeted us on the hill. There was so much scattered light that it wasn't even dark in the shadows.

At Shane Lake, we caught up with several members of the Prince George Naturalists Club. They, like us, were there for the celestial display, but they were also hoping to hear some owls. To help matters along, one person had a tape recording of owl calls—useful for identification, as well as for encouraging the owls to respond. Another person lent me her binoculars and I was able to clearly see Jupiter and three of its largest moons. With a little imagination I fancied I could also see the rings of Saturn.

Leaving, we toured first to the lower viewpoint and then around the far end of Shane Lake where the city had recently assessed the structural integrity of a beaver dam there, and had subsequently begun maintenance. The beavers, it seemed, could no longer be trusted to fulfil their age-old responsibility of maintaining their own dams and it was time for human engineering to take over. At first, this work caused consternation to some users of the area. But the stepped beaver dams at the outflow of Shane Lake hold back the second largest body of water in the city and there is some concern that, over the long term, there will be a major flood event similar to others that have happened in the past. The beavers in the lake have exhausted their readily available food supply of aspen trees and the lake is becoming less viable as a natural beaver habitat. Outwash fans such as the large one beneath the site of the old Ben Ginter mansion in the city bowl below, tell a story of similar events in the past. The beavers move on; their dams eventually fail; the forest matures and inevitably burns; new aspen trees spring up, bringing back the beavers; the dams are rebuilt. At least, that's how it used to be.

At the main viewpoint, the fog below us was lit a fluorescent orange by the city lights beneath. In the distance, two islands of luminous cloud betrayed the presence of the pulp mills below: these mills have been the economic engines of the community for nearly 40 years. The sky was bright, and only the main constellations shone faintly through—a night for romantics, not for astronomers as we glided effortlessly and quietly back to the car.

Inspiration in the outdoors

Jean-Jacques Giguère is an artist with two masters degrees, who exhibited around the world before choosing to make Prince George his home. He developed a form that explores colour harmony, not only in art but also in the environment, living spaces, sports, and interactive media. I met Jean-Jacques for a three-hour walk through the woods of Forests for the World. It was a chance to hear him explain the influence of the natural landscape on his work and ideas. He talked about the harmony of our spiritual being when we come into the world, and the stresses that result from disharmony in the man-made world. He talked a lot about colour. How the simple choice of colour on either a canvas or a structure can invite us into the artwork or into the building in a way that helps to reduce the stress of everyday living, and at the same time stimulate creativity. For example, Jean-Jacques designed a sculpture placed outside a Quebec hospital that invited people to enter the building, the theme being subtly picked up again inside.

In many large art centres around the world, people are lost in straight lines, angles, walls, and competing colours that unconsciously drain, rather than supplement, our energy. Prince George lies close to a vast natural landscape, so instead of copying what's current in New York or other meccas of art, there is a chance here to do something different. As Jean-Jacques explained to me, there is opportunity to bring the sense of harmony that we experience in the outdoors into our art and everyday living.

"Look at the edge of that forest," he said as we walked across the frozen surface of Reflection Lake. "It has depth and colour that makes it soft and inviting." During our long walk, he gave voice to aspects of our environment that I knew of instinctively but hadn't necessarily given expression to. We moved from place to place, passing through scenes of more and then less light according to the type of forest cover we were in, and from there into open spaces, all the time considering the effect of these experiences on the mind. Jean-Jacques likened this to moving into a room, and from there envisaging a universe of possibilities opening beyond that.

Official opening ceremony for the new viewing structure at Prince George's Forests for the World in the fall of 2003.

Viewpoint

When a need arises in a community, one way to respond is to get involved and to have fun making something happen. This is what a group of individuals and companies did in 2003 when they applied their initiative, enthusiasm, and hard work to replacing Prince George's best-known viewpoint at Forests for the World.

The lookout at Forests for the World was originally funded by the forest industry and was designed to last up to 15 years. Having served Prince George well for its planned lifetime, it was demolished in 2002 for safety reasons. Users of the area lamented the loss of what was undoubtedly the best view of the city, set against the backdrop of the river valleys and the Rocky and Cariboo Mountains. For many, the viewpoint had always been a highlight of a visit to Forests for the World. City hall began to receive inquiries and requests to replace the structure. A community newspaper ran an account by a man who had been married on the lookout platform in 1994. And another Forests for the World user, Ken Bilski, approached me in a downtown coffee shop and asked me if I knew of any plans to rebuild the observation platform. I didn't, but as soon as I got home I penned a story, "What's happening at Forests for the World?" which ran locally on December 15, 2002.

A few days after the article appeared, I received a phone call from a contracting supervisor with Blackwater Construction, a major local forestry contractor. The company's owner had given him a copy of the story and asked him to look into whether Blackwater could do anything to help by using old bridge timbers they had in their yard. Although weathered on the outside, the timbers were still sound and could be refinished. In an action reminiscent of when the forest companies got behind the original Heritage River Trail in the 1980s, Blackwater's Russ Polsom offered the company's help, and said that he would also see what other interest he could stir in the business community.

Over the next several months, Blackwater Construction and several other local businesses and individuals, notably Ken Bilski, worked with city staff to bring the project to a successful conclusion. At a ribbon-cutting ceremony held on October 9, 2003, Mayor Colin Kinsley noted the significance of the viewpoint project to the city of Prince George, and thanked all the project's participants and sponsors for their leadership and work in making it happen. The viewpoint can be accessed via a 10-minute walk from the Forests for the World parking lot, taking the trail that heads uphill in a westerly direction. The view there is confirmation that Prince George is a satisfying place to call home, and the viewpoint structure is an inspiration to become involved in enhancing the community.

Moores Meadow

Moores Meadow is one of the largest natural parks within the city of Prince George. Its location in the city bowl area means that it is highly accessible, both from a parking lot on Foothills Boulevard, north of First Avenue, and from Dornbierer, Corless, and Claire Crescents west of Tabor Boulevard. Although completely surrounded by roads and residential areas, a walk along the east ridge trail on a quiet Sunday morning, looking across the meadow toward wooded slopes that blend into the backdrop of Cranbrook Hill, can give one the impression of being in a remote wilderness setting. Birds and other wildlife such as black variants of the red fox are common, and a wide range of plants take advantage of the meadow's microclimate. With the building of Foothills Boulevard in the early 1980s, Moores Meadow began to suffer the impacts of its new accessibility. I decided to get involved, and with a small group of concerned residents from the immediate neighbourhoods, formed the Moores Meadow Park Association. We got the attention of city hall, and achieved prompt action that far exceeded our initial expectations. This came about partly through presentations to city council, but mostly through the goodwill earned by a massive volunteer cleanup of the park after calling in every IOU we could think of in the community. This was an extremely satisfying project that has led me to many other public involvements since.

The meadow is a glacial kettle left by a piece of melting glacier ice at the end of the last ice age. The ridge above it, to the east, is an esker built of rocky debris deposited by a glacial river. The park is the easternmost representation of the Stuart Eskers complex that appears west of Garvin Creek on the north side of the Nechako River and comes into its full glory in Eskers Provincial Park northwest of the city. Once proposed as a city garbage dump—a natural hole waiting to be filled—the depression and surrounding woods were preserved thanks to the foresight and efforts of a local naturalist, Mary Fallis.

Mary had observed many unique features of the park, including a rare orchid that is sensitive to human disturbance, which she monitored every year as an indicator of the health of the city. After her retirement in 1972 as a college teacher, Mary Fallis took up nature photography, which she used to political effect in seeking the preservation of both Moores Meadow and Cottonwood Island Park. Her interest in photography began much earlier in Vancouver, and for a number of years she was photographic chair and later, national archivist for the Alpine Club of Canada. The ACC subsequently made her a life member. Following Mary's death, her collection of 5,400 photographic images was given to the newly established Northern B.C. Archive at UNBC in November 2000, and later, a UNBC scholarship was established in her name. During our 1980s presentations by the Moores Meadow Park Association to city council, the mere presence of Mary Fallis in the public gallery, as well

West through the lower meadow of Moores Meadow Park.

as her ever-present support outside of meetings, gave a tremendous boost to our efforts.

Popular at any time of the year, Moores Meadow Park is a favourite place for residents to walk, run, cross-country ski, and to exercise their dogs in one of the city's off-leash areas. Park users have repeatedly expressed the desire that, except for unpaved trails and signage, the core of the park should be kept in a natural state. Although the park is little more than a kilometre in length, it has over seven kilometres of trails. As evening approaches, cold air settles into the depression of the meadow and a thin ghostly mist may form a few feet above the ground. One cold January morning, I took a thermometer to the ridge trail overlooking the meadow where I measured minus 39 degrees Celsius. Scrambling a very short distance down the slope to the meadow, I repeated the procedure and measured minus fifty degrees Celsius—a difference of 11 degrees! This was a dramatic illustration of the effect of cold air pooling, and allowed me to experience the breath-crackling temperatures that used to be normal in January in Prince George and that are seldom felt here any more.

McMillan Creek and two-viewpoints walk

A favourite, yet easily overlooked walk inside the city, is McMillan Creek Regional Park, located on Hoferkamp Road east of the Hart Highway, a kilometre north of the Nechako River. McMillan Creek is a fish-bearing tributary of the Nechako River that winds through the north side of the city, and it has been the subject of stream conservation work in recent years. A short distance along Hoferkamp Road, a large paved parking lot and an information sign mark the trailhead. After a short drop through the trees, the trail joins Hoferkamp Road to cross over McMillan Creek before climbing away from the road at a small parking space reserved for service vehicles. There are three short, forested trails leading to viewpoints overlooking Prince George from atop the Nechako cutbanks. The middle trail is the easiest, and after the first short climb, it is flat all the way to a grassy picnic area and viewpoint equipped with interpretive signs. For someone preparing for backcountry travel, this is a great spot to practice map and compass skills, as there are many triangulation targets within sight. All one needs are a compass and the 1:50,000 national topographical map sheet for Prince George, 93 G/15. There are two other trails leading to the same viewpoint, climbing high above the first trail, one on each side. These trails give a different perspective of the park, especially the west trail that winds through remnants of an old-growth forest. A loop walk of the two high trails

McMillan Creek Park offers one of the best views of Prince George from atop the Nechako River cutbanks. The Heritage River Trail runs along the far bank of the Nechako River.

provides a good cardiovascular workout of 20 to 30 minutes in a natural setting overlooking the city.

A longer option, the "two viewpoints walk" starts at either McMillan Creek Regional Park or Gunn Park and connects the two via the old wooden Nechako River Bridge at the west end of River Road, then onto the Heritage River Trail, Cottonwood Island Park, and the Yellowhead Highway Bridge. There is as yet no trail from the wooden bridge to McMillan Park, so you can either scramble up the treed cutbanks across from the bridge, or walk up the highway to Hoferkamp Road. Options range from leaving a vehicle at each end and walking it one way only, to walking the route both ways, or doing a half-day loop of the Gunn trail, historic South Fort George, and the entire Heritage River Trail.

Ferguson Lake Nature Reserve

One kilometre along North Kelly Road from Highway 97, and four winding kilometres west on Ferguson Lake Road, is the largest lake within the city of Prince George. A small parking lot accommodates four vehicles, while nearby are tables and a canoe launch that make a great three-season picnic site. The Ferguson Lake Nature Reserve is accessible all year round, and the winter trail encircling the lake is usually well-packed from people walking and skiing.

The area's name goes back to 1919 when William Ferguson acquired a 120-acre parcel of land there. The remains of Ferguson's first trapper's cabin can still be found by the lakeside, along with that of a larger cabin built in 1928. In 1946, Ivor Killy built a bush sawmill on the site, and the remains of its sawdust pile still stand next to the parking lot. Later, the Killy family donated the reserve to the Nature Trust of British Columbia — a charitable, non-profit corporation dedicated to the conservation of areas of ecological significance. The Killy family remained actively involved with Prince George's recreational trails during the 1980s and early 1990s, with George Killy being an enthusiastic member of the city's Rivers Committee, and later providing a key referral to BC Rail that led to the acquisition of the Gunn Trail right-of-way.

Organizations contributing to the development and maintenance of the Ferguson Lake Nature Reserve have included the Prince George Naturalists Club, the City of Prince George, and the Downtown Rotary Club. Fishing may be allowed in the lake, although boat motors, including electric, are not. Because it is a nature reserve, no horses or motorized vehicles of any kind are allowed, and dogs must be kept on a leash. The trail around the lake takes about half to three-quarters of an hour to walk, ideal for an occasional back-to-nature lunch break if you work in the northern half of the city. Interpretive signs discuss the history of the area: its plants, its wildlife, and forest succession from past timber cutting with a remnant patch of climax forest on the far side of the lake.

Ferguson Lake, the largest lake within the city of Prince George is a nature reserve suitable for canoeing and walking. Pilot Mountain in the right background. Although this is inside the city, an interior plateau grizzly bear wearing a satellite collar denned for at least one winter near this lake in the early 2000's.

The treed slopes of Pilot Mountain provide a scenic backdrop to the lake from the trailhead. There are abundant opportunities to experience local natural history, and the trail's long stretches of slowly sinking boardwalk through swampy vegetation are sure to appeal to kids in the spring, summer, and fall. Unlike other natural areas in Prince George, the Ferguson Lake trail is nearly flat, and although not accessible by wheelchair, it is suitable for almost anybody on foot. Only a short drive within the city, the Ferguson Lake Nature Reserve is worth a visit any time of the year.

Otway Ski Centre

One of Prince George's grassroots success stories is the Caledonia Nordic Ski Club. By the year 2000, the club had grown to 1000 members and had developed a lighted cross-country ski facility on the Otway Road at the western boundary of the city. The track is used by mountain bikers in the summer and is the northern terminus of the Cranbrook Hill Greenway trail. By early December each year, the Otway Ski Centre is transformed into a haven of daytime and evening winter fitness fun.

It doesn't take much snow for the club to begin operations, needing only 10-centimetres to set a track for skate skiing, and another five-centimetres for traditional track skiing. Apart from the club's state-of-the-art grooming equipment, some of the reasons for their ability to open on next to no snow are the big work parties that are held each summer to pick rocks as small as five centimetres. This ensures that the trails through the pine forest, as they slowly grass over, are as smooth as possible. With the warmer winters that we have been experiencing in recent years, the club may begin skiing by the end of November at Crooked River Provincial Park, an hour north of the city at Bear Lake. Then, within a couple of weeks, there is usually enough snow at Otway to begin operations there. Some who just can't wait until November or December for the cross-country ski season to begin, seek out the white stuff as early as October in the McGregor, Rocky, and Cariboo Mountains east of town, while others roller ski on roads, or run with ski poles in Eskers Provincial Park.

The ski club usually holds an early November registration for the Jackrabbits kid's program. This program typically meets twice a week and may include some two hundred children. The annual membership pass gives almost unlimited skiing for the season and access to a number of social events at the track clubhouse. Taking out a membership is an important part of supporting a club that has significant upfront operating costs each year for insurance, lighting,

Otway ski centre on the road to Miworth is the northern terminus of Cranbrook Hill Greenway.

and grooming equipment. But for those who would just like to try out the Otway track, or who have out-of-town visitors, or only ski occasionally, there is also an option of a drop-in fee.

Wildlife in the city

Periodically I remind myself how fortunate we are to enjoy the benefits of an urban area that is located close to some of the best wilderness in the world. I remember watching a large black bear chase a rival up a 30-metre high aspen tree just outside of my office window. Once, while walking up the hill along University Way, I stopped to watch a red-tailed hawk land in a tree below, and soon realized that a black bear was lying beneath the tree. I wouldn't have seen the bear if the hawk hadn't flown in. The next day during a lunchtime walk in greenbelt near an industrial site, I became aware of two deer only a few metres away. They had been watching me approach for some time, and I didn't see them until one of them moved. How often do we miss seeing things because we are focussed on something other than our immediate surroundings?

A favourite summertime activity in Prince George is to canoe down the Nechako River from Miworth (described later in the book). During the three hours it took me to travel the 25 kilometres on one occasion, I observed a great blue heron in a side channel, watched several ospreys fishing the main river, and saw numerous ducks, assorted hawks, and a bald eagle along the way. Near the confluence with the Fraser, we paddled by an immature bald eagle that was sitting on a rock in the middle of the river, royally ignoring the harassment of a flock of crows. Earlier, we had passed two black bears a few kilometres apart, ambling along the rocky shores. As we passed the second bear feeling secure that we could outpaddle it, I shouted "Hello," and received what appeared to be a look of consternation back from the animal. Later, in Miworth at dusk, a black fox with a white patch on its tail watched us secretively as we returned to retrieve the vehicle.

Fall is a great time to explore the trails and waterways of the city. The water may still be warm enough to swim in, the colours begin to appear, and the mosquitoes, black flies, and caterpillars are gone. By moving quietly and being alert to the surroundings, and without expectation of seeing anything, one can experience a walking or paddling meditation. My bet is that you will return feeling calmed, refreshed, and a lot closer to the things that are important in life.

Wildlife encounters can happen in town even in winter, as in the case one February when my wife and I were completing a long walk around Forests for the World on newly packed trails following a heavy snowfall. As we came around a bend only 200 metres from the parking lot, we found the narrow trail ahead blocked by two moose. The animals, a cow and a calf, looked sleek and healthy as they munched on twigs beside the trail. As we approached, the calf moved into the trees out of sight, but the cow saw no reason to interrupt her feeding. After enjoying the sight for a few minutes, we felt it was time for her to allow us past. She disagreed. Aware of how dangerous these animals can be close up—people have been stomped to death by antler-less cow moose—we weren't going to push the issue, but the trail wasn't wide enough for us to slip past. Keeping a respectful distance, I asked the moose if she would kindly move. Nothing doing. So I made myself larger by waving my arms and shouting, "Shoo!" This time I had her attention. She stopped eating, turned in the narrow track to face us, let out a big yawn, and fixed me with a long stare. "OK," I said. "Have it your way. We'll go back and find another route." This decision was not made lightly, as it was late in the day, we were tired after trudging through snow for two hours, and the car was almost in sight. But there was another trail 100 metres behind us that eventually led to the parking lot. As we backed away, my wife said, "Look there's another one!" I looked but saw only a large moose-like shadow cast by some branches. Discounting my skepticism born of years in the bush, she assured me that she knew the difference between a moose and a shadow. Sure enough, a few metres away, just off the trail was a third moose—a larger animal that was most likely a bull that had recently thrown its antlers. We were bracketed between the three animals just metres from the parking lot, with thigh-deep snow limiting our off-trail options.

It's exciting to know that we have such magnificent animals close to town in a popular walking area, and then to experience them there. But moose must be respected. It was only a year earlier that a woman had a dangerous encounter with a moose close to UNBC—possibly one of these same animals. And a few months after our experience, a series of encounters with an aggressive cow moose in the area prompted wildlife officials to post warning signs. In our case, the bull partly resolved our dilemma by moving back into the bush, although not very far. Slowly, we eased our way past as he watched intently from the trees. Perhaps his willingness to give ground was because he had just arrived on the trail behind us, whereas the cow had been there for some time and felt more ownership.

Moose aren't the only large animal one might encounter at Forests for the World—black bears are common as well. And a few years ago, a man jogging alone at dusk rounded a corner in the trail and nearly ran into a large cougar walking in the same direction. The jogger exercised discretion and returned quickly the way he had come. By visiting places like Forests for the World often enough, and especially by keeping dogs on a leash, one is sure to have experiences like these. I have seen moose there on many occasions, including an amazing total of six during a 30-minute walk to the viewpoint and back early one morning. Around dawn or dusk is the best time, and if you treat moose with the respect that any wild animal deserves, you should have a safe, and definitely memorable, experience.

Cranbrook Hill Greenway – wilderness in the city

The centrepiece of the Cranbrook Hill Greenway is an 18-kilometre, non-motorized, multi-use trail crossing Cranbrook Hill from the Otway Cross-country Ski Centre (on the road to Miworth), to Forests for the World and to UNBC. An additional seven-kilometre extension runs from Forests for the World to Highway 16 West, making this one of the longest urban greenway trails in Western Canada. This remarkable project was accomplished by a group of volunteers beginning in 1994, ably led by Prince George resident Robin Draper. A number of people had considered the possibility of such a trail on Cranbrook Hill for many years, but it took the work and perseverance of Robin and his team to guide the project to its conclusion. In 2003 Robin Draper received a Citizen of the Year nomination as recognition for this work. The project was accomplished through much negotiation over access, and with financial help secured from the community and from three levels of government. And importantly, the undertaking included creation of a program for ongoing upkeep and maintenance. Young people found employment and valuable life experience in actually building the trail, and many more have benefited from using it.

One way to sample the trail is to take what I feel is the nicest short walk in Prince George from the Greenway parking lot at UNBC to Shane Lake in Forests for the World. To walk the full length of the Greenway trail is not as daunting as it may seem; no special equipment is required, and for a person of average fitness, it can be covered in four to five hours. The trail is in good condition and is well marked throughout its length. If you are concerned about being in the woods for so long a distance, get some friends together and walk it as a group, or join the annual fundraiser walk that is held in the fall. One can avoid the hours and many kilometres of driving that are usually necessary to access the backcountry, yet still experience the feel of wild forestland along the western edge of the city. There, it is possible to get a sense of what the area must have been like in the fall of 1807 when Simon Fraser established a post at the confluence of the Fraser and Nechako Rivers and named it Fort George in honour of the reigning King George III. The trail can, of course, be walked in either direction, each giving a different sense of the country through which it passes. My preferred hiking direction is to start at the Otway Ski Centre and walk south to UNBC or to Forests for the World. This means going generally uphill, which provides a little added exercise by gaining 240 vertical metres in a slow easy grade during both the first and final few kilometres. On skis or mountain bike, I prefer the downhill direction, starting at UNBC.

The northern end of the trail begins at the Otway Ski Centre parking lot, and winds through delightful pine flats for the first kilometre, before beginning its climb just past the Biathlon Shooting Range. There, a few years ago, a local man out for a run had entered the warm-up cabin and, to his surprise, found a lynx inside. As he described it, the trapped animal began "bouncing off the walls" as the man entered, and both he and the lynx were happy to make their respective escapes. From this point, the Greenway leaves the ski trails and enters the lush, wetter forest of predominantly old spruce. The undergrowth is thick with devils club and other tall shrubs that give it a primitive feel. I had once encountered a brown-coloured black bear along this section of trail. My wife, who had dropped behind for a few minutes, was quite excited to see a large head and set of claws coming through the bush in her direction. But the animal was probably just foraging for berries and small critters, and we learned later from a regular trail user that it had been resident all summer.

A little over seven kilometres from its northern end, the trail crosses the unpaved Takla Road, affording either an alternate route or an option to walk just half of the trail. A kilometre or so farther south, the trail reaches its halfway point, where a picnic table is located next to the nine-kilometre sign overlooking the beginning of a long, exposed gully system. This is the perfect spot for lunch. From here, the open trail picks up lots of sun on a clear day as it trends gradually east toward UNBC. Three side trails offer a choice of routes into Forests for the World or you can continue to the UNBC trailhead.

As the *Stop and Think* signs say along the way, the Cranbrook Hill Greenway is a little more serious than a walk in the park, and one should be prepared accordingly. Yet, walking "The Greenway" is an activity that I highly recommend every able person try at least once. And you can support the trail and reward yourself further by attending the principal annual fund raiser, the Banff Mountain Film Festival World Tour, or by "purchasing" a popular metre of trail.

Heritage River Trail

Back in the city bowl, the Heritage River Trail offers some of the most accessible and pleasant in-town walks, especially along the Nechako River between Cottonwood Island Nature Park near the confluence of the Nechako and Fraser Rivers, and Carney Street. This is particularly enjoyable on a long summer evening with the sun setting to the west over the Nechako River.

Prince George's Heritage River Trail project began in 1984 with the aim of protecting and rehabilitating natural areas along the city's rivers and creeks. Since much of the prime riverfront was industrial, the involvement of several forest companies was crucial to the plan's success during the early years, and their legacy is still evident in the landscaping and trail right-of-ways along the Nechako River section and along River Road. A "Riverfront Park and Trail System Master Plan" was commissioned by the City of Prince George through its Rivers Committee in 1984, and an update was produced in 1992 at a time when I had the privilege of chairing the committee. The long-range vision of the two plans included tying together existing and future riverfront destination parks, riverfront trails, river valley escarpments, crosstown trail connections, heritage structures, as well as commercial and residential areas. In addition to the existing anchors of Fort George and Cottonwood Island Parks, the riverfront plan envisioned future connectors with Parkridge Creek on the Fraser River below College Heights; Wilson Park and Fish Traps Island on the Nechako River between Ospika and Foothills Boulevards; and with

*The walk west along the Nechako River from Cottonwood Island Park
is the nicest stretch of the Heritage River Trail*

Moores Meadow Park. The plan also foresaw the currently proposed Nechako Ridge Trail from McMillan Regional Park at Highway 97 to the proposed Nechako River Park just north of the Otway Ski Centre, as well as connectors to the Cranbrook Hill Greenway.

Principal access points to the Heritage River Trail are at the north end of Carney Street; at the River Road Boat Launch; from two access points to Cottonwood Island Park; from Fort George Park, and at the intersection of Carney Street and Massey Drive near the YMCA and Massey Stadium. By including the crosstown connector along Carney Street between the Nechako River and the 'Y' on Massey Drive, the Heritage River Trail can be looped for a total of 11-kilometres. Again, this is a wonderful summer evening walk or run that can be followed by much earned refreshments at a patio-restaurant or pub.

The centrepiece of the Heritage River Trail is undoubtedly Cottonwood Island Nature Park, located at the confluence of the two big rivers. There, one may still have a sense of what the country was like 200 years ago when Fort George was first established, and when many of the giant cottonwood trees that are presently in the park were just seedlings. Wildlife in the park includes beavers, owls, and a bald eagle's nest that has produced chicks annually for at least the last 25 years. A major project undertaken in the park in recent years has been the three-stage Cottonwood Island side-channel rehabilitation. One of six original province-wide projects, the Fraser Basin Program included the cleanup and restoration of the park's side channels to provide important resting habitat, and a safe haven from peril, for young salmon on their journey to the Pacific Ocean.

Other in-town trails

At the city's western boundary, near the Otway Ski Centre, there are rustic trails that can be explored in the undeveloped parkland lying between the Otway Road and the large north-facing meander of the Nechako River: the proposed Nechako River Park. There is potential for this area to be part of a connection between the Cranbrook Hill Greenway and the Heritage River Trails via a pedestrian river-crossing to the North Nechako area. The North Nechako Ridge trails are user-developed rustic trails that run along portions of the northwest trending ridgeline above the Nechako River and North Nechako Road. Most of the recreational use of the ridge trails is currently taking place in the Pidherny Road area, and it is unofficially referred to as the Pidherny Recreation Area, with trails being used for a variety of purposes.

In 2003, a society was formed in an effort to formalize a recreational trail corridor along the entire Nechako Ridge. It would be centred on the existing Pidherny Recreation Area, with connectors to the Heritage River Trails, the Otway Ski Centre, and the Cranbrook Hill Greenway. The proposed corridor would extend from McMillan Regional Park, across the Hart Highway, onto the ridge above North Nechako Road, and then northwest along the ridge past Foothills Boulevard to the city limits near Garvin Creek. Organized along the lines of the Cranbrook Hill Greenway project, the long-range vision is to connect the corridor via its centrepiece, a pedestrian suspension bridge to the Nechako River Park. It could then be linked with the Caledonia Nordic Ski Centre and the Cranbrook Hill Greenway. Organizers also believe there might be an opportunity to connect the trail with a future regional district recreational corridor from the city limits, west to Eskers Provincial Park.

There are also extensive trails that can be accessed where residential areas abut Prince George's plentiful greenbelt. In fact, wherever there is greenbelt in the city, a look around will generally reveal a variety of official and unofficial trails. In College Heights, for example, a first-class paved trail leads from Jean de Brebeuf Park to Gladstone Drive, just east of Simon Fraser Avenue. A little farther south, numerous unpaved trails radiate out from Latrobe Park, some of them extending to the Fraser River through remnants of old-growth forest, such as those found at the mouth of Parkridge Creek. As in other cities, the popularity of mountain biking in recent years has resulted in many new unofficial trails being developed. And wherever there is a perceived need, there is usually a way. For example, from the southeast corner of the main UNBC parking lot, an unofficial trail leads through the trees and under the University Way road bridge with its spectacular graffiti art. From there it leads down through the old escarpment forest to either 22nd Avenue or, by branching right down a steep and rough side trail, past the ghosts of the Ginter mansion (between the ends of Massey Drive and Ferry Avenue). Once you have descended this trail and learned where it comes out, you will have discovered a new access to UNBC, the Cranbrook Hill Greenway, and to the high point of Prince George's trail systems, Forests for the World.

Christmas Bird Count

There is another opportunity to explore this unique city that must be mentioned—more an event than a place— the annual Christmas Bird Count is open to anyone with an interest in birds. More than a century ago, ornithologist Frank Chapman organized a North America-wide count of birds as an alternative to the hitherto popular Christmas pastime of shooting them. The first count was held on Christmas Day 1900, and involved 27 people in 25 locations stretching from Toronto, Ontario to Pacific Grove, California. Known today as the Christmas Bird Count, it has grown to include over eighteen hundred locations throughout North and South America, involving more than fifty-two thousand people. More importantly, it has become the source of an inventory that provides an indicator of the state of the planet's environment: an ultimate "canary in a coal mine." The long-running Christmas Bird Count provides conservation biologists and researchers with a huge annual database of early winter bird populations. It helps determine which populations are stable, increasing or declining, and the data is useful for developing winter range maps for birds. It puts the spotlight on conservation issues affecting birds that winter in both North and South America—and it is a fun event!

In Canada in 2003, the Christmas Bird Count was coordinated by Bird Studies Canada in partnership with the National Audubon Society. The data is available on the Internet by going to the National Audubon Society's Web site. Locally, the Prince George Naturalists Club organizes the Christmas Bird Count each year within a 12-kilometre radius of the Prince George Regional Hospital. This is an event that the club takes so seriously that in late November, or early December, they hold a practice bird count, then discuss their results over a potluck supper. By becoming part of the annual Christmas Bird Count, you can enjoy a fun experience, see different parts of the city, learn more about bird identification from the experts, and contribute to an important inventory.

North

Climbing north away from Prince George, on Highway 97, also known as the Hart Highway, you gain the northeastern corner of the Interior Plateau. This region is a vast expanse of mostly low relief highland, stretching west between the Rocky and Coast Mountains and south to the United States border. It encompasses the Salmon River Valley, 24 kilometres north of the city, and reaches the Arctic Pacific Divide at Summit Lake, 48 kilometres north of Prince George. Highway distances in this section of the book are measured north from the intersection of Highway 97 (Central Street) and 5th Avenue in Prince George. From just south of Summit Lake, the historic Giscome Portage trail extends nine kilometres in a southeasterly direction from the highway to Huble Homestead Regional Park on the Fraser River, above Giscome Rapids. North from Summit Lake, there are many recreational opportunities along Highway 97, most of them relating to water, such as canoeing on the Crooked and Parsnip Rivers, and boating and fishing on the many lakes that dot the highway corridor.

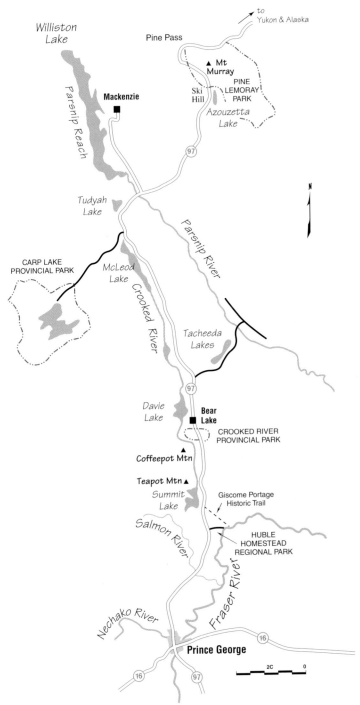

to
Yukon & Alaska

Williston
Lake

Pine Pass

▲ Mt
Murray

PINE
LEMORAY
PARK

Ski
Hill

Mackenzie

Azouzetta
Lake

Parsnip Reach

97

Tudyah
Lake

Parsnip River

CARP LAKE
PROVINCIAL PARK

McLeod
Lake

Crooked River

Tacheeda
Lakes

97

Davie
Lake

**Bear
Lake**

CROOKED RIVER
PROVINCIAL PARK

Coffeepot Mtn ▲

Teapot Mtn ▲

Summit
Lake

Giscome Portage
Historic Trail

Salmon River

HUBLE
HOMESTEAD
REGIONAL PARK

Fraser River

Nechako River

16

Prince George

2C   0

16   97

49

History

The journey north from Prince George is also a journey back in time to B.C.'s earliest colonial history. The post-1940s highway closely parallels the Crooked River as it continues to McLeod Lake, where in 1805, Fort McLeod was established by Simon Fraser as the first non-native settlement in British Columbia. This small community soon became a gateway to the lands of New Caledonia and its capital of Fort St. James on Stuart Lake, and in recent years there have been suggestions to reconstruct the historic trail between these two outposts. The McLeod Lake Indian Band, part of the Sekani First Nation, was in the forefront of recent treaty negotiations in British Columbia as they sought to become part of the historic "Treaty 8," one of western Canada's oldest settlements dating back to the late nineteenth century. "Sekani," sometimes spelled "Tse'Khene" or "TseK'hene," means "People of the Rock," referring to the northern Rocky Mountains that make up a large part of their traditional territory.

When I first arrived in Prince George in the late 1970s, Highway 97 was as crooked as the river that it followed and was notorious for accidents, especially in the wintertime. In the past 25 years, however, it has been rebuilt and improved all the way through Pine Pass in the Rocky Mountains, northeast of Mackenzie. Before the 1940s highway construction, freight was moved first by road to Summit Lake, and then by riverboat up the Crooked and Parsnip Rivers to the forks of the Finlay and Peace Rivers. Historic black and white and early colour

Canoe tripping down the Parsnip River.

films made by Prince George pioneer Ted Williams, just before and after the Second World War, show riverboat traffic on the Crooked and Parsnip Rivers and at the forks where the Finlay and Parsnip Rivers once flowed into the Peace River. Today, the "Forks of the Finlay" as they were once known, are under the waters of man-made Williston Lake. The lake was created to feed B.C.'s largest hydro electricity plant at Hudson's Hope on the Peace River. It is held back by the W.A.C. Bennett dam that, along with dinosaur exhibits found in the area, is a great tourist stop for visitors to Hudson's Hope. The lake was named after a member of Premier W.A.C. Bennett's cabinet, Ray Williston, whom I had the pleasure of meeting in September 2002 at the opening of the University of Northern B.C.'s new science building. In a dinner event appropriately titled "UNBC North to the Future," Williston, then nearly 90 years old, delivered a powerful speech that left me wondering what he must have been like in his prime. He related how a young forester had walked into his office in the Victoria Legislature and persuaded him that wood waste in the north could be utilized in the manufacture of pulp. This was the pivotal event that led to development of the Prince George area as we know it today—none of it would have happened quite the way it did if it wasn't for the man before us. The standing ovation that he received was a fitting end to a milestone-day in the life of one of Canada's brightest, young universities.

Off road

A look at the *British Columbia Road & Recreational Atlas*, or any forest service map, will show that the backcountry in B.C.'s interior and north country is riddled with unpaved back roads and forest roads. Anyone using these roads must be self-sufficient, as there are generally no services, and there may be road blockages, washouts, fallen trees, deactivations, and closures. When forest roads are open and in active industrial use, there are traffic rules that should be observed, including the use of two-way radios and other protocols. From these forest roads, there are countless deactivated side roads, tracks, and skid trails providing opportunities for exploration on foot or other off-road means. One such starting place is the Salmon Valley Forest Service Road, leading west from its Highway 97 junction, just 34 kilometres north of Prince George. You can find abandoned, overgrown routes there, leading to wild sections of the Salmon River, home to such large animals as moose and plateau grizzly bears. The latter belong to a population that travels widely over the Interior Plateau and intermingles with the Rocky Mountain grizzlies northeast of the Parsnip River. Going off-trail has its risks as well as rewards, and anyone trying it should have the experience and equipment appropriate to the situation. This means having the ability to navigate in the bush using a good old-fashioned map and compass, without being totally dependent on satellite technology, and having some wilderness first aid and survival skills. Leave details of your route and destination with someone you can trust, and preferably, do not travel off-trail alone.

Huble Homestead and Giscome Portage Trail

Thirteen kilometres north of the Salmon River highway bridge, or 38 kilometres from Prince George, is the access road to the Huble Homestead Historic Site and the south end of the Giscome Portage historic trail. This site, operated as a regional park, is Prince George's equivalent of Barkerville, with historic buildings and "period" activities. During the late spring, summer, and early fall months, watch for announcements in the local media advertising the many interesting costumed events that are held there. Even when there are no organized events taking place, there are year-round easy walks and ski routes around the homestead and along the banks of the Fraser

Huble Homestead in the final stages of restoration in the fall of 1986.

Fraser River in the winter – just downstream from the Giscome Portage.

River. The other feature of the area is the historic nine-kilometre long portage trail that leads out to a parking lot on the highway just south of Summit Lake. Having two vehicles allows the trail to be walked in only one direction over this low divide between the Arctic and Pacific watersheds. First Nations people were the first to use the portage trail as a trade route—probably the people of the L'heidli T'enneh Nation, or Fort George Band. The portage is first mentioned in the journals of Simon Fraser in 1806. Then, during the 1860s, gold was found on Germansen and Manson creeks northwest of Prince George, sparking the Omineca gold rush, and soon afterward, a native guide led Jamaican miner, John Giscome, over the trail. The government built a wagon trail over the newly named Giscome Portage, and improved the navigation on the Crooked River north from Summit Lake. Later, at the beginning of the twentieth century, a small community was developed on the banks of the Fraser River to service the portage trade, and became known as the Huble Homestead. Use of the portage slowed down during the First World War, and finally came to an end after the construction of a road between Prince George and Summit Lake in 1919. The open fields leading to and around the Huble Homestead are now part of a community pasture, and the public is asked to observe and respect any signs that are posted there in order to protect the cattle.

Summit Lake is a popular place in winter for ice skating, skiing, and snowmobiling. Photo: J. Lett.

Summit Lake

There are two approaches to the small community of Summit Lake, located 46 and 50 kilometres north of Prince George respectively. This four-kilometre paved side road is part of the original Hart Highway and affords an idea of what the entire winding route used to be like. Summit Lake is notable today for its old-style potluck dinner-dances in the spacious community hall there. A beautifully refinished wood floor is a striking interior feature. Some annual events worth noting are the cross-country ski social, close to Valentines Day; a Labour Day end-of-summer dance; and the very British Guy Fawkes bonfire and dance on the closest weekend to the historic fifth of November. Long-time Summit Lake residents Hilary and Floyd Crowley have been instrumental in organizing and maintaining these traditions, and they are the best contact for information about them. The Summit Lake community does include a small boat launch, but the best access to the lake is attained by continuing north on Highway 97 to Talus Road (described next).

Teapot Mountain

Just north of Summit Lake, or 51 kilometres from Prince George, Talus Road leads west from Highway 97 to the main Summit Lake campground and then to the very popular hiking trail on Teapot

Mountain. Follow Talus Road for 900 metres, and turn right onto the Caine Creek Forest Service Road. A farther 3.3 kilometres (passing the lakeside campground on the left) brings you to the bridge-crossing of the Crooked River just past its outflow from Summit Lake, and to the Teapot Mountain parking lot. From there, a short, steep 200-vertical metre hiking trail to the top of the volcanic outcropping affords a superb view of the surrounding countryside, including the start of the Crooked River and the Arctic watershed.

Teapot Mountain

Activity Hiking
Rating 1 to 2 hours round trip
Distance 3+ km round trip
Principal Elevation Gain 200 m
Map 93 J/7 Summit Lake
Details Follow Talus Road and the Caine Creek Forest Service Road to the trailhead. A clearly marked, but steep trail, with loop trail and pleasant site for a picnic on the summit.

Coffeepot Mountain

A twin, flat-topped volcanic outcropping to the north of Teapot Mountain is harder to access but similarly rewarding. As the book goes to press in the spring of 2004, there are as yet no trails on Coffeepot Mountain. But for those who are willing to bushwhack up this prominent steep-sided hill, Coffeepot affords good views of the Interior Plateau. The summit is 100 vertical metres higher than Teapot Mountain by virtue of the rising topography of the surrounding plateau, but the approach from the northeast is more gradual. The flat summit is much larger than Teapot, and hides an unusual geographic feature—a steep-sided lake on top of the mountain. Currently, the best access to Coffeepot is the Davie Lake Forest Service Road west from Highway 97, and 65 kilometres north of Prince George. If you don't have a two-way radio, and if log hauling is in progress, follow a vehicle that is radio-equipped. Take great care approaching the one-lane bridge over the Crooked River on this main industrial forest road. Two kilometres from the highway, turn left on the 603 Road (Davie Teapot Forest Service Road) and immediately branch right onto the 6503 Road. Four kilometres west on the 6503 Road brings you to a block that was logged a few years ago and has a direct view of

Coffeepot Mountain

Activity Hiking
Rating 2 to 4 hours round trip
Distance 3 km round trip, plus road walking as necessary
Principal Elevation Gain 125 m, plus road walking as necessary
Map 93 J/7 Summit Lake
Details Davie Lake and 6503 Forest Service Roads. Bushwhack from the highest point of the road on the northeast side. Easy bushwhacking around the summit with good views.

Coffeepot, now only 3.5 kilometres away. This is the point from which I used to access Coffeepot by starting through the cutblock, crossing a beaver-dammed swamp, and bushwhacking along two kilometres of old forested pine, spruce, and interior Douglas fir slopes. In the summer of 2003, a new logging road was built that skirts the swamp to the north and has spur roads on the northeast side of Coffeepot Mountain. To what extent it will be possible to drive this road will depend on the season, ongoing forestry operations, and future road deactivations—but it will certainly afford easy walking access to within a few hundred metres of the summit for many years to come. Coffeepot is an obvious place on which to build a hiking trail similar to that on Teapot, but it is also nice to have a few places that afford a sense of exploration, and a destination that fewer people get to.

Even without a trail, bushwhacking around the approximately one hundred-hectare, table-like summit of Coffeepot is easy. There are dramatic views and dropoffs, with the approach from the northeast being the easiest. Wherever you choose to ascend, however, watch for loose rocks, and people above or below you as you scramble up the final slope. Thick lichens and mosses still cover the rocks and attest to the relatively untouched nature of the summit. In one location below the westerly bluffs, a debris field is coated with pale green lichens, while on either side of it are rock fields that appear to be of a similar age but are lichen-free, with no obvious difference between these proximate micro-sites. Artifacts from past human activity on the top of Coffeepot Mountain include the remains of an old helicopter platform from the 1960s, and a stove and chimney pipe, both near the south point of the peak. Covering the entire top of Coffeepot are old stumps—evidence of 1930s or 1940s winter logging of small-diameter trees, many with an old-style, 45-degree angled cut. Until recently, it was a mystery to me why these trees were cut and what they were used for, since clearly they were not removed from the top of the

Northeast side of Coffeepot Mountain from the beaver dammed swamp 2 km away.

mountain, and yet there is no sign of a structure there. Perhaps a cabin burned down and the remains lay buried beneath the moss. No one I talked to about this who currently lives in the Coffeepot area had an explanation for the stumps, despite one man who reported seeing them there half a century ago. It began to appear that the reason for the stumps might have been lost in the mists of time. Then, in the fall of 2003, a professional surveyor who was out for a hike on the hill with his son, noted that Coffeepot had once been an important survey point. In the days before widespread use of photogrammetry in mapmaking, prominent hilltops such as this were used as ground survey stations. Good sightlines would have been needed from a single location, and it is likely that much of the top of Coffeepot Mountain would have been cleared of its trees for that purpose.

There is abundant sign of moose on Coffeepot, the animals presumably accessing the top via the relatively easy northeast slope. And according to local people, mountain caribou were seen there 50 years ago. In late October 2003, Prince George naturalist Sandra Kinsey observed spruce grouse, pine grosbeak, golden-crowned kinglet, red-breasted nuthatch, black-capped chickadee, and common raven, with a woodpecker cavity spotted in a blowdown. There was a suggestion that the lake on the south–central top of Coffeepot is spring-fed via an old volcanic vent. This could be consistent with other spring activity in the area, notably Livingstone Springs to the north (discussed later in this section). On a trip in the fall of 2003, we did locate a sizable outflow creek from the lake, but it was brackish in colour, indicating that the lake was being fed by seepage from the surrounding hilltop, rather than by a spring. Walking around the top of Coffeepot, there was abundant water in numerous small, swampy ponds, sufficient to account for the lake and its outflow. These ponds included a black spruce swamp and sphagnum moss bogs. A visit in the midst of a dry summer might tell a different story.

Despite having apparently similar volcanic origins, Coffeepot Mountain differs from Teapot to the south in that it appears to be largely made up of basaltic columns. It isn't clear why there is this difference between Teapot and Coffeepot, which are otherwise similar looking geological features. On the west edge of the hill, the tops of columns are clearly visible in the fractured bedrock at one's feet. The columns were formed in the cooling lava of the intrusive body—that later became Coffeepot Mountain—from a type of shrinkage similar to the formation of cracks in drying mud. They generally form hexagonal patterns, but can sometimes have four or five sides owing to cooling irregularities. Such columns may then break into variable-length sections (transverse joints). This process is very much in evidence on Coffeepot where the columns readily break down, resulting in the fields of strewn rubble below.

One of the cutblocks planned for logging in 2004 to access mountain pine beetle-killed trees will go quite high on the northeast slope, and has raised questions and concerns given the significance of Coffeepot as a local landmark. Forest managers have the challenging task of balancing economic, forest health, and timber supply needs, while meeting the spirit of the 1999 Prince George Land and Resource Management Plan objectives and strategies for recreation and visual quality. A general management strategy for the entire Prince George planning area is to: "Avoid square or rectangular cutblocks and linear boundaries to minimize visual impacts on dominant views and within scenic areas." In order to assess the visual impact of the proposed cutblock on Coffeepot Mountain, and to reassure concerned members of the public, a computer-generated visual simulation was created from a viewpoint on the highway. This is one of the tools now available to manage non-timber values on the landscape, and in this case it showed just the top of the block visible from the highway, with an irregular shaped edge that seemed to blend well into the countryside. By 2005, we will be able to see how well this projection matches the reality on the ground.

Tourism is unlikely to displace forestry as the main economic driver of this area. However, as the forest industry comes under increasing pressure from long-term declines in timber supply (resulting from the mountain pine beetle epidemic), recreation and tourism will take on increasing economic importance to Prince George. It is important that, even as we respond to the mountain pine beetle and other issues, we continue to do everything we can to ensure good landscape esthetics that will support new economic opportunities. Apart from the spirit of goodwill that comes from operating and living in a community, today's companies need to have the public behind them for their forest certification programs (the present marketplace demands forest products that are certified to have been produced responsibly and sustainably). And as company foresters have stressed repeatedly to people over the years, "If you've got a concern, come in and talk to us - the coffee's always on." Through good communication early in the planning process, and willingness by all parties to be flexible and to respect each other's interests, we can keep a wide range of opportunities open for the future.

Crystal springs

Just before the access to Coffeepot Mountain, 63 kilometres from Prince George, a standpipe gushes spring water year round. Across from the spring is a small pull-off for vehicles to park in order to access the supply that is also used by Summit Lake residents for their drinking water. This spring is indicative of the many spring-fed lakes in the area, such as those found in Crooked River Provincial Park (described next). One kilometre north of the roadside spring is an unmarked gravel road leading east to Crystal and Emerald Lakes. The clear spring-fed lakes in this area fluctuate more according to water table levels governed by annual snowmelt cycles in the Rocky Mountains, than by local precipitation.

Crooked River Provincial Park

Crooked River Provincial Park is situated on Highway 97 less than an hour north of Prince George. Best known for Bear Lake, with its outstanding sandy beaches, picnic areas, and campgrounds, this park also contains nature trails that are a worthy destination in their own right. Entering the park, 70 kilometres north of Prince George, you'll find Hart Lake, a small, easily accessible lake, popular for fishing, to the east of the highway. One kilometre north of Hart Lake, the main paved access road heads west into the park. On the left is a large paved parking lot adjacent to the main day-use area, equipped with

Livingstone Springs in winter.

change rooms, many picnic tables, and a good-sized sandy beach on the clear waters of Bear Lake. On a hot summer day, this is perhaps the nicest beach in the Prince George area, but beware of the waterfowl-borne parasite that causes "swimmers itch" in the early summer. This problem can usually be avoided by towelling off as soon as one leaves the water.

As the paved access road curves around Bear Lake, watch for a small parking lot on the right, just before the camping area. From there, a wide, easy trail takes off along the edge of a swampy area extending west of Bear Lake. Follow the trail signs to another small lake, where there is a dock, a fish-cleaning table, and a rustic trail around the shoreline. The surrounding woodlands comprise mostly pine trees on sand flats that are thick with low-bush blueberries in the fall. Be alert, as I have seen the berry-laden scats of both black bear and grizzly bear in the area.

As you retrace your steps from the lake, the trail crosses a sandy access road. Continue west along this road until it drops along a dip in the land, and watch for a faded sign to Livingstone Springs on the right. Livingstone Springs is not usually identified on the park map signs seen earlier in the walk, perhaps because of its fragile nature and its location on the edge of the park. This is, however, one of the interesting natural features of the Prince George area and is definitely worth a visit. The trail meanders through pine forest before dropping down to the springs next to an old log cabin. Built in 1945, this served both as a trapper's cabin and a residence. Be ready for an unusual sight—Livingstone Springs is not just a trickle—it gushes out of the ground to form a fair-sized river within a short distance of only 100 metres. As is typical of the springs that feed lakes in the area such as Bear Lake and Crystal Lake, the springs are not hot. But the water temperature is above freezing all year round, which helps to maintain the open stretches of water on the Crooked River that serve as wintering grounds for trumpeter swans. Livingstone Springs is especially worth a visit in the winter on skis or snowshoes—lush, green, aquatic vegetation provides a colourful relief to the surrounding snowpack.

Returning along the sandy access road, the walk can be completed with a 30-minute loop to the south that climbs gently up to a view trail above the Crooked River. Leaving the sandy pine flats behind, the forest cover quickly changes to the sub-boreal forest that is more typical of this area. Looking southwest across the Crooked River, there is a clear view of Coffeepot Mountain a short distance to the southwest. There are several exits from the Crooked River viewpoint trail. The first one returns to the small parking lot at the swamp, while the others detour through the camping area. There are several nice spots for a picnic lunch throughout the walk, or you may choose to visit the day-use picnic area and sandy beaches at Bear Lake.

North to the Pine Pass

From the community of Bear Lake, there are many other recreational areas to explore: north along the sparsely populated Crooked River; east to the Parsnip and Anzac Rivers; west to Davie Lake and to Carp Lake Provincial Park; and north through the town of Mackenzie. Highway 97 then climbs northeast from the Highway 39-Mackenzie Junction (at the Parsnip River Bridge) into the Rocky Mountains, where it reaches a maximum elevation of 933 metres near the Powder King ski hill. North of Azouzetta Lake, it swings northwest to enter Pine Lemoray Provincial Park before completing a wide U-turn around the northern tip of the park and continuing east toward Chetwynd. The Pine Pass, as it is known, is the easiest, and one of the most important, transportation corridors through the Rocky Mountains, comprising a highway and a railway, as well as major hydro electricity, and oil and gas transmission lines. It is also home to the Mount Murray trail, one of my favourite local hikes, one that I pioneered in 1982 and 1983.

Directly above, and to the east of the highway through the Pine Pass, lies the spine of the Rocky Mountains, an area consisting of open ridges, lovely alpine meadows and lakes, wildlife, and, according to reports, caves and hot springs waiting to be rediscovered. Historically, the ridgetop was accessed by bushwhacking from the highway via

Hikers approach alpine camp below Mount Murray.

Azouzetta Lake and Pine Pass from the top of the Powder King ski hill.

a steep, open gully just north of Azouzetta Lake. Then in 1982, I went looking for a route up Mount Murray, nine kilometres north of Azouzetta Lake where the topographical map showed an interesting-looking area of lakes and alpine meadows. Picking the ridgeline northwest of the mountain's main drainage gully, and after fighting my way up a steep cutbank, I found a route on and off game trails that was easily bushwhacked. Animals prefer easy paths through the bush just as people do, and if you pick a route carefully, it's common to find well-used game trails already there. The alpine area that I found and explored that day exceeded my expectations, and the following year a rough hiking trail was developed by the Caledonia Ramblers Hiking Club of Prince George and added to the club's popular trail guide.

Pine Pass

Activity Mountain Hiking
Rating 1 to 3 days
Distance 8 km round trip to alpine lake campsite
Principal Elevation Gain 820 m to the alpine lake
Map 93 O/7 Azouzetta Lake
Details A moderately steep trail to treeline starts on the northeast side of Highway 97, nine kilometres north of Azouzetta Lake. From treeline, a poorly marked route contours southeast to the pass above the alpine lake campsite. There are many unmarked alpine routes possible

Alpine tarn below the summit of Mount Murray in the Pine Pass.

Since then, the trail and area have received light but steady use by people both from Prince George and the Pine Pass area. It is suitable for day and overnight trips, with superb alpine flower displays and good wildlife viewing. In the late 1990s, the area became part of Pine Lemoray Provincial Park.

The start of the Mount Murray trail is located on Highway 97, roughly two to three hours driving time north of Prince George. Continue past the Powder King mountain ski resort to the small lodge at the north end of Azouzetta Lake, and drive north for a further nine kilometres or so, watching for a small gravel road leaving west off the highway and crossing the Pine River. This is about one kilometre before the railway on the east side of the highway enters a tunnel.

There is good parking at this side road, and the ribboned trail starts on the opposite (east) bank of the highway. After a brief treed section, the trail crosses the railway tracks and climbs steeply to the right of a cutbank. After its short, precipitous beginning, the trail gentles out to ascend a pleasant ridgeline above and north of a steep-sided gully all the way to treeline. Before leaving the trees, it is important to make a careful note of the return entry-point, as it is easy to lose the route in the open meadows, especially if clouds or mist roll in. Once above the trees, a poorly marked route contours right (south) to the pass above the gully, where it enters a beautiful alpine bowl containing the area's main lake. From there, many scenic routes await you on surrounding peaks, ridges, alpine meadows, and around tarns, where you may be fortunate enough to see moose, caribou, elk, grizzly bear, black bear, hoary marmots, and wolverine. In spring, flower displays are abundant, including the unusual yellowish hues of the normally red-coloured Indian Paintbrush.

In 2003, six members of the Caledonia Ramblers returned to Mount Murray for an overnight stay. It was the twentieth anniversary of the trail, and for me, the twenty-first anniversary of my first exploratory bushwhack there. At the trailhead we met three men from the Pine Pass area who were on a day hike. It was hard not to be caught up in their enthusiasm and enjoyment for what they were doing, especially when, during a rest stop halfway up, they told me this story: Two of them had been smokers for much of their lives until just 18 months earlier. They had not only quit the habit then, but had put the money they saved into outdoor activities such as hiking, skiing, and ice climbing. Their story was an inspiration that it is never too late to make a significant lifestyle change, and demonstrated one way to have fun doing it. Equipped with light daypacks, they pulled ahead of us and headed directly for the north summit, while our party traversed from treeline into the natural amphitheatre with its lakeside camping area. After setting up tents, we climbed out of the basin and wandered north among spectacular wildflower displays. These grew amid alpine pools dotted between hills and ridgelines, and were more beautiful than any man-made garden I have seen. Among the wildlife that we saw that afternoon were numerous ptarmigan with chicks, five elk, and three hoary marmots. Threatening weather accompanied us back to camp, but despite distant thunder, only a few sprinkles of rain were felt during a long, leisurely evening around the campfire. A resident duck population woke us at 4 am the next morning with a cacophony of territorial-sounding calls. Then it started to rain, pouring heavily for several hours before easing off and leaving us blinded by dense cloud and intermittent drizzle. This was the other side of mountain weather that one must be prepared for at any time of the year. We waited until 10 am, then abandoned our intended side trip down the ridge, packed up wet tents to start down early, and stayed close together in the mist until we reached treeline. Despite conditions, the mountains took on a new beauty, with the terrain shrouded in ever moving cloud, and flowers appearing even more colourful in the grey light.

Gateway to Northern B.C.

I will conclude this section on the north, by taking an excursion 1,000 kilometres north of Prince George to describe one of the best (and lesser-used) backcountry hikes in the world. This is a trip of an altogether different magnitude than the day trips described thus far, and is also well outside the geographical area that is mostly covered by this book. However, I have included the 70-kilometre loop trek through Wokkpash and Stone Mountain Provincial Parks, as the trip can be staged from Prince George, and it highlights the many superb wilderness opportunities available in Northern B.C.

Wokkpash and Stone Mountain

The Wokkpash and Stone Mountain loop hike is equal to anything in the national parks, with the added lure of solitude and, at the time of writing, fewer regulations. Twenty kilometres back from the highest point of the Alaska Highway and tucked away behind Stone Mountain Provincial Park lies the Wokkpash Valley. People driving north to hike in the Yukon often overlook the Wokkpash despite its many outstanding and accessible features.

Circle tour

The Wokkpash can be reached with a single, but long day's drive north from Prince George, returning via the same route, or it can be combined with a 2,500-kilometre "Circle Route" to the Yukon. In the latter case, the outbound Alaska Highway is completely paved, while the return leg down the Stewart–Cassiar Highway is over 80 per cent paved, and the rest is mostly good quality gravel. Stone Mountain, the starting point for the Wokkpash hike, is 1,000 kilometres by road north of Prince George. Staging options are to stay overnight in a cabin or campground at Summit Lake in Stone Mountain Provincial Park, or to stay in Fort Nelson and drive the remaining distance early the next day.

My first walk through the area was with one friend, and although we started at the height of the summer season on the August civic holiday weekend, we saw no other people during our eight-day trek. Our companions were the caribou who approached close on several occasions, the chipmunks busy harvesting seeds from mountain avens plants, and a larcenous porcupine who tried to take our stove at midnight at Forlorn Gorge. Awakened by a loud clatter just metres from the tent, I grabbed the bear spray and charged outside to face whatever was there. Relief flooded over me as I realized it was only a porcupine, attracted no doubt, by the smell of white gas. The prickly thief had already dragged the stove over to some nearby bushes, and was about to disappear with it. The animal's teeth had punctured the carrying bag but had fortunately missed the stove's gas line, and my

Wokkpash / Stone Mountain

Activity Backpacking
Rating 6 to 10 days
Distance 70 km loop
Principal Elevation Gain 632 m Wokkpash Lake to Last Call Lake
Maps 94 K/10 Mount St. George, 94 K/7 Wokkpash Lake
Details At the time of writing, registration is still voluntary. Usage statistics are uncertain, but 40 to 60 hikers are estimated to use the area each year. Horse-packing, especially for hunting, may push the numbers up in the fall. The Wokkpash / Stone Mountain trek requires good planning and previous backpacking and route finding experience. The route is largely unmarked and there are, as yet, no developed campsites, which is part of its charm. However, there are good trails most of the way, as well as a number of old horse camps. The side road that leads down to the ford at the start of the Churchill Mine Road is located 16 kilometres west of the community of Summit Lake, a collection of buildings and a motel just east of the lake itself. The exit point (and alternate starting point for the MacDonald Creek trail in Stone Mountain Park) described in the stories above, is nine kilometres west of the community of Summit Lake. The route that I took on both of my trips ended with an easy ford of MacDonald Creek where it is heavily braided as it approaches the highway. But there may be another option that stays east of the creek and that avoids fording altogether. Allow one or two days of extra food and slack in your schedule for some of the side trips discussed, and the possibility of delays as creeks become difficult to ford after periods of rain.

quick, if reckless exit from the tent had saved the night. After having chased it off, the porcupine soon returned, and this time I pursued it up a young tree where I gave it an exciting ride for several minutes as it clung to the top of the swaying crown. It was enough of a scare to send it packing for the rest of the night. We were even on the "fright scale," and I had learned an important lesson about storing stoves and fuel, as well as food, out of reach of wildlife.

With no set campsites along the way, we enjoyed the freedom of nomadic life, stopping when we were ready and had found a suitable place. After fording MacDonald Creek where we left our vehicle, we spent a long day walking up the abandoned, but scenic, Churchill Mine Road to Wokkpash Creek. Starting with heavy packs weighing over 25 kilograms, this was a comfortable way to break into the trip

Wokkpash Lake in morning light.

with steady, even-grade walking in outstanding countryside. For the next three days we worked our way slowly up the Wokkpash Valley, each day bringing new challenges and surprises. The weather was kind to us, and the northern latitude meant long days.

One of the highlights of the trip was the famous Wokkpash Gorge with its thousands of spectacular hoodoos and impossibly balanced capstones along a five-kilometre canyon—one of the best such displays anywhere. After the Wokkpash Gorge comes the large, glacial blue Wokkpash Lake. Surrounding the lake are the peaks of the Muskwa Ranges that make up the northern end of the Canadian Rockies. Glaciers and classic 2,700-metre peaks such as the White Tower, North Bastion Mountain, and Mount St Sepulchre make up this backdrop. At the halfway point in our trip we took a rest day, spending two nights at the gravel outwash of Plug Creek near the south end of Wokkpash Lake. This allowed us to recuperate after four days of carrying heavy packs, and to eat two more days of food weight before tackling the alpine section of the route. It also provided a chance to relax and enjoy short side trips. It was during one of these excursions, as we were quietly eating lunch by a sandy beach, that we heard a noise. A large bull caribou, with antlers in the velvet, splashed along the lakeshore and stopped a short distance in front of us. He tested the air for awhile before he caught our scent, turned, and was gone as quickly as he had appeared.

From the south end of Wokkpash Lake, we climbed the 630 vertical metres to starkly beautiful Last Call Lake. The silence of the evening at this place contrasted with the previous five nights of sleeping with the sound of running water. Sometime during the night the clicking heels of a lone caribou betrayed its presence near our tent. The alpine in the far north of B.C. is quite different from what we are used to around Prince George—it is covered by scrub birch, known to the locals as "shin tangle" or "buck brush." We used the maze of caribou trails to pick our way through this vegetation. The next day brought us to the headwaters of MacDonald Creek and a two-day trek back to the Alaska Highway along a well-used horse trail. We had enjoyed eight days of mostly sun and blue skies, while the rest of the province was experiencing its wettest summer in years. Our main concern was whether we had enough sunscreen to last the trip.

Opting for a circle tour, we continued on to the Yukon, stopping in Watson Lake for an oil change before starting down the Stewart–Cassiar Highway. Improvements to roads, vehicles, and tires in recent years have had a corresponding deleterious impact on the vehicle repair trade. The garage had a *For Sale* sign on the front, and our mechanic lamented that they used to employ three people full-time just to change tires, while now they're lucky to get one tire job in two weeks. Some things stay the same, though; the sign by the cash register read: *We don't care what you pay at home—this ain't home!*

There were many highlights on the return drive, including a lot of fine scenery, although cloud, rain, and smoke from forest fires in

Upper Wokkpash River above Wokkpash Lake. Looking south towards its headwater glaciers.

Lake St. Sepulchre, east of the Wokkpash Valley and Plug Creek.

the Northwest Territories had moved in to blanket much of B.C.'s northwest. We took the side trip past Bear Glacier to Stewart B.C. and its sister frontier town of Hyder, Alaska. And just before joining Highway 16, our final side trip was to the unspoiled native village of Kitwancool, which has the best collection of totem poles that I have seen, with local people who were delighted to explain them to us.

Return to Wokkpash

I returned to the Wokkpash in 1999, five years after my first trip. It had then recently been upgraded from a Wilderness Recreation Area to become part of the 665,709-hectare Northern Rocky Mountains Provincial Park that had just been established in the Muskwa-Kechika Management Area. Together, the Wokkpash Valley and Stone Mountain Park offer a wonderful 70-kilometre loop trek, with many off-trail possibilities that could easily expand a week-long stay into a month. Except for a ranger cabin at the south end of Wokkpash Lake, there were no facilities when we were last there. Backpackers must be self-sufficient and prepared to deal with wet creek crossings and flash floods, as well as with all the usual challenges of travel in the mountain backcountry. Although we enjoyed exceptional weather during both of my visits, the area is prone to heavy rains that can last for days, and come straight down off the limestone mountainsides to flood creeks quickly. The good news is that the creeks subside equally fast, within hours of the rain ending.

On my second visit I had two companions, and the trip was again made in a counter-clockwise direction, starting with the 17-kilometre walk up the abandoned Churchill Mine Road that heads southwest from the highway, 16 kilometres west of the community of Summit Lake in Stone Mountain Park. This route direction allows you to put off the main climb until packs are lighter, and it provides better options for fording MacDonald Creek later in the trip in the event of high water. It is sometimes possible to get across the creek at the start of the old mine road with a high clearance vehicle, but having walked this road twice, I found its easy grade and pleasant scenery a nice way to ease into the trip.

A good trail leaves the old road and follows the pine forests along the northeast side of Wokkpash Creek. The river flats in the lower valley are well-suited to informal camping, and caribou are often seen close by. After nine kilometres, the lower end of the Wokkpash Gorge is reached and it is definitely worth stopping here to fully appreciate the feature the next day. For five kilometres the river cuts through a canyon containing thousands of erosion pillars that line each wall. I have looked at geological reports and spoken to experts, but the origins of these formations do not seem to have been definitively addressed. They appear though, to have originated from a combination of geological and glacial events that left a layer of ancient limestone blocks on top of much younger glacial conglomerates. These harder rocks form capstones that preserve pillars of erodible debris underneath.

In the Wokkpash, one spectacle follows another, and at the head of the main gorge, Forlorn Creek has cut a 150-metre deep slot canyon into the mountainside. To those interested in slot canyons, Forlorn Gorge is perhaps a more impressive feature than the main Wokkpash Gorge, and it is definitely worth at least a half-day to explore both from above and below. Entering Forlorn Gorge is akin to a caving experience, a similarity that may extend to its original formation. Caution is needed if going beyond a short distance into the canyon to avoid being trapped by a flash flood. Just past Forlorn Gorge, the six-kilometre expanse of Wokkpash Lake suddenly opens up. Early morning is a good choice for walking the lakeshore trail to the next camping area at Plug Creek, and in August 1999 we disturbed a large bull caribou halfway along the lake. Rather than make his escape through the woods, he chose to swim the kilometre-wide glacial water. For 20 minutes we sat and watched his antlers bobbing as he swam steadily on, occasionally glancing over his shoulder. When he emerged on the far shore, he shook himself off and wandered into the trees as if nothing had happened, leaving behind a wake in the glassy water that was nearly two kilometres wide.

When I first investigated this area, I was curious about the unusual number of names on the Wokkpash Lake map sheet. Most of them were British, with military and London, England connotations. I obtained a copy of a report titled: *The Royal Fusiliers (City of London Regiment) Canadian Rocky Mountains Expedition 1960*. Its historic and entertaining reading adds significantly to the enjoyment of a hike through the area. Captain M.F.R. Jones commanded a small team of men comprising two commissioned officers, four NCOs and two retired Canadian liaison personnel. Only the two British officers had prior climbing experience and the team members' ages ranged from 19 to 78 years. The narrative marks the expedition's formal start: "On 8th July 1960, in pouring rain, we left the Tower and drove to Euston. "The Tower" refers to the Tower of London, which was the Regimental HQ and harbinger of the raft of Wokkpash names to-be. For example, Tower Mountain now overlooks the south end of Wokkpash Lake, North Bastion Mountain and South Bastion Mountain stand sentinel farther back, and the beautiful 2,730-metre White Tower could almost be mistaken for Mount Robson. In his report, Captain Jones muses: "The Bloody

Fusilier Glacier: Historic photograph of Corporals Rogers and Hassett on Fusilier Glacier during the Royal Fusiliers Canadian Rocky Mountains Expedition of 1960.

Tower has not yet lent its name to a peak, although there are several that would undoubtedly qualify." Some features were named after the expedition's British sponsors and supporters, notably Mercers Peak, Merchant Taylors Peak, and Lord Mayor Peak at the south end of the valley. One can only wonder about this profusion of more than 30 officially sanctioned names, after the difficulties of finding just one mountain to honour former Prime Minister Pierre Trudeau. In a letter to Captain Jones dated 23rd October 1959, Colonel G.S. Andrews, Surveyor General for the Province of British Columbia, gives an interesting insight into the politics of the day as he offers guidance on the naming of features. "We are in favour of one theme being carried out in a mountain group where feasible - for example, in parts of the Province names from Norse and Greek mythology have been applied to mountain groups. However, we would not favour an enlargement of the Churchill-Roosevelt-Stalin theme; in other words, we do not want to have the whole British war cabinet perpetuated in that area and, needless to say, the Russian theme is not at all popular."

During their six weeks in the Wokkpash, the officers taught their men glacier and climbing skills, and together they recorded 13 first ascents, including Fusilier Peak and Mount Stalin. They explored the middle and upper Wokkpash Valley, obtained wide photographic coverage of the surrounding area, produced a 16-mm colour film titled, *The Ascent of Fusilier Peak*, and made a collection of 177 plant and 67 rock specimens. Meanwhile, retired 66-year old Canadian Lieutenant–Colonel S.W. Archibald and his Cree survey assistant, Sam Chappise, provided liaison and logistical support, and they spent much of their time surveying the area from high vantage points including Red Ridge. Two years after his successful Wokkpash expedition, Captain Jones died tragically in an avalanche in Northern Kashmir in a joint Pakistani–British forces expedition attempting the first ascent of 7,852-metre Mt. Kinyangchish.

During my second sojourn in the valley, we crossed Wokkpash Creek at the south end of the lake where 19 braids in the channel made fording quite easy. Hiking partway along the lake on a good horse trail, we climbed up Fusilier Creek into a very beautiful hanging valley, one of several such places along the west side of the Wokkpash. Above the valley we could see Fusilier Glacier where the expedition had honed their ice skills, and above that a snowclad peak that became their first successful summit and which they named, you guessed it, Fusilier Peak. Leaving Wokkpash Lake, there is then a 600-metre climb on a good trail on the north side of Plug Creek that takes you into the high alpine. Alternatively you can do as we did in 1999 and opt for a combination of old horse trails and bushwhacking on the south side of Plug Creek in order to spend a night or two at Lake St. Sepulchre. This lake, and mountain above, were named for the Fusiliers' regimental chapel in London. From this camp, options are to explore the extensive upper valley of Plug Creek, wander among the tarns of the curved hanging valley below Mount St. Sepulchre, or scramble to the top of Mount St. Magnus. Travelling north through the U-shaped valley between Whitestone Ridge and Mount St. Magnus, small groups of caribou can often be seen. Last Call Lake is definitely worth a couple of nights stay in order to explore the lovely hanging valley behind the lake, and to make an easy ascent of either Angel Peak or Kiwi Mountain for the outstanding view back over Wokkpash Lake and the Tower of London Range. From here, it's mostly all downhill, first crossing into Stone Mountain Park and then beginning the long easy descent of MacDonald Creek back to the Alaska Highway. Another good horse trail begins on the east bank and affords easy passage through the endless maze of ever taller scrub birch. As we approached a ford halfway down MacDonald Creek, first one, and then a chorus of young wolves started calling from nearby. We set up camp and relaxed over supper as an alpenglow deepened on the slopes behind us. Once again the wolf pups joined in their serenade to the wild as we contemplated where we were, what we had experienced, and those who had gone before us.

East through the Rocky Mountain Trench

The drive east of Prince George on the Yellowhead Highway affords hundreds of kilometres of first class, lightly used pavement, leading into the progressively higher mountains and spectacular scenery of the Rocky Mountain Trench and the Robson Valley. Both the Yellowhead Highway and the community of Tête Jaune Cache are believed to have been named after Pierre Bostonais, an Iroquois who worked for the North West Company and the Hudson's Bay Company in the early nineteenth century. The Rocky Mountain Trench, extending from southeast British Columbia to the Yukon where it connects with the Tintina Trench, is the second longest such feature on earth after the Great Rift Valley in east Africa—and it is the longest that is wholly on land. But unlike its African counterpart, the Rocky Mountain Trench is not a rift valley. The northern part, which includes the section described in this book, is a strike-slip fault, where the southwest side of the trench has moved some 750 kilometres in a northwesterly direction relative to the other side of the valley. After passing through the communities of McBride, Dunster, and Tête Jaune Cache, the eastward journey from Prince George culminates in a stunning drive alongside the headwaters of the Fraser River, past Mount Terry Fox, and toward the imposing southwest face of Mount Robson. Its 3,000 metres of vertical relief is comparable to anything in the world, even the difference between Mount Everest's base camp and its summit. And, if having all this on one's doorstep isn't enough, a few more kilometres brings you into Rocky Mountain National Park at Jasper—all within half a day of Prince George. After a quarter of a century of driving this highway, my sense is that we have a richness of outdoor opportunities near a city the size of Prince George that is unsurpassed anywhere in the world. In the spring season, Highway 16 east can seem like a game reserve with all manner of wildlife seen along its freshly vegetated roadside. Animals that I have seen there include moose, deer, caribou, black bear, grizzly bear,

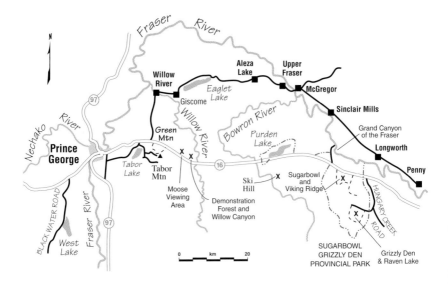

lynx, cougar, fox, coyote, and wolves. And if you are really fortunate, you may see the elusive mountain caribou in late fall as they migrate and cross the highway in small groups (of up to about nine animals) in Sugarbowl-Grizzly Den Provincial Park. All highway distances from Prince George that are given in this section are measured from the east end of First Avenue, at the west end of the Yellowhead Bridge.

Green Mountain

We begin our eastward journey just 20 minutes from Prince George, where, directly north of the highway across from the Tabor Mountain ski resort is a wooded hill known locally as Green Mountain. Its south-facing slopes are home to some of the northernmost stands of Douglas fir, where one can sometimes hear the howls of wolves. Green Mountain has been given the highest visual quality objectives with regard to forest harvesting, which means that after logging, it must appear from a distance to be essentially undisturbed. A few years ago, downhill skiers were treated to the spectacle of helicopter logging as individual bark beetle-killed Douglas fir were removed. Green Mountain can be admired from the road as you drive past. Or, if you are adventuresome and enjoy bushwhacking, it can be fun to scramble up and enjoy a quite different view of Tabor Mountain than you may be used to. Don't try this without a compass or without letting someone know where you've gone.

Tabor Mountain

On the south side of the highway, east of the ski resort, are several access points to hike, snowshoe, or cross-country ski part or all the way up Tabor Mountain. These are some of the old Sons of Norway Ski Club and Caledonia Nordic ski trails, and although the surrounding forest is starting to grow up, they still offer tantalizing views of the McGregor and Rocky Mountains to the northeast. Tabor Mountain can also be approached via Groveburn Road, west of Tabor Lake, which gives access to many side trails higher on the mountain, some of which connect with the Highway 16 trails. Following is an account of one of my numerous forays on Tabor Mountain, on the trail that starts across from the first paved highway pull-off, a couple of kilometres east of the ski hill.

Walking with wolves

Mid-November in the year 2000, and the ground is still bare of snow as we leave our vehicle and start up the trail. Evidence of a wet autumn is everywhere. Instep crampons would be nice as we negotiate the thick inclined sheets of frozen water on the north side of Tabor Mountain. The day is pleasant enough, but overcast. The woods are quiet. An ermine darts across our path and a rabbit hastens through the leafless trees; both are unaware that their stark white coats are a liability to them just yet.

Troll Lake on Tabor Mountain in winter. A popular cross-country ski destination.

Summer flowers on Tabor Mountain.

An hour has passed and we are nearing the halfway mark. A sound somewhere in the distance catches my attention. It had been there for awhile before penetrating my consciousness. Another long drawn-out cry, sounding like a factory steam whistle summoning its workers back to the job. Perhaps it's some kind of equipment working on the highway. We hear a more distant sound, responsive to the first. "I think they're wolves!" I said. We listen. The cry of the individual and the response of the pack slowly become evident. We continue on, and within a few short minutes the sounds are nearer. Recognizable now as wolves, the individual calling seems to be directly below on the track we have just traversed. The pack is close behind, a noisy scrabble of beasts.

I take cold comfort in the statistics. There is no record of a human killed by wolves in North America. Yet, as you will see later in the account of the Shelford family of Burns Lake, I have met one man who was convinced that it nearly happened to him. There may be no recorded human fatalities by wolves, but many people have disappeared in the bush. A few years ago, I came right up on two wolves feeding on a highway-killed moose less than a kilometre from the start of this afternoon's walk. They were large animals, upward of 175 pounds each and dressed in thick winter coats; one was brown and the other black, and I had taken them for bears as I approached. Our local wolves belong to the Columbia sub-species, *Canis lupus columbianus*, and are among the largest in the world.

I sat in my car with the side window rolled down—I should have felt secure there. The wolves stared me down, a few metres away. Not once did they break eye contact as they slowly backed away into the trees. I knew then that I did not want to meet these impressive animals face to face while alone in the bush. The pack coalesced and seemed awfully close as the snarls and angry yells of a dozen or more animals rose in crescendo. It's easy to understand why all other predators in North America, including grizzly bears and even polar bears, will give way before a pack of wolves. When local woodsman, Fred Van der Post undertook his solo 700-kilometre snowshoe trek through Northern B.C. in the early 1980s, he told of being surrounded by wolves at night. Fred had no tent; instead he slept on a snow bench or under a tree beside his fire. Although he scarcely caught a glimpse of the wolves, in the morning he'd see that their tracks had encircled his camp, the radius of their closest approach perhaps dependent on their degree of curiosity or hunger.

Damn the statistics, I'd much rather meet a bear than a pack of wolves or even dogs for that matter. Actually, a pack of dogs can be more dangerous than wolves since they lack fear of man. A wolf-dog cross is perhaps the worst, and there have been a number of attacks and a fatality caused by such crosses on Vancouver Island. Dan Hunter of Strider Adventures lives not far away from this side of Tabor Mountain, behind Green Mountain, across from the ski hill. A year earlier, he and his wife Dorothy had the rare experience of watching wolves bring down and kill a moose in their backyard. These could be the same animals I had just seen. We thought the wolves might have found a weakened animal below us, perhaps a moose injured last night on the highway. I had encountered such a moose there once with a broken hip, not far from where we started our trip. It had managed to get a few hundred metres above the road and was living on borrowed time when it obstructed the ski trail and forced me to turn around.

Nothing symbolizes the bone-chilling reality of wilderness more than listening to wolves blocking one's path home. Yet eerily on our return late in the afternoon, we could find no visible sign of their passing. Earlier that summer, high in the Southern Chilcotin Mountains, a pack had passed in sight of our camp as we ate supper one evening, appearing out of nowhere and disappearing just as mysteriously. They had made reassuringly different sounds than those did today, travelling noises I think, and we enjoyed their passage.

Now we are at a junction in the trail. We can turn left and continue for another hour to the top before returning the way we came, or we can follow the right fork to Tabor Mountain ski hill and walk back along the trail above the highway. "Well," we rationalize, "perhaps it's a bit late to go all the way to the top!"

Moose viewing area

Nine kilometres east of the Tabor Mountain ski resort is a pull-off on the north side of Highway 16, where a short trail leads to a wildlife viewing area that was originally built by Prince George's Spruce City Wildlife Association in the 1980s. Moose sightings are common along this stretch of Highway 16, as animals feed from the natural regeneration following the massive 1961 Grove Burn forest fire. From the viewing platform, swaths of trees have been cut, radiating out to the north and east to afford browse for moose and good sightlines for visitors. The platform was replaced and upgraded, and the viewing swaths renewed in 2002, and whether or not there are moose to be seen, this unique site with its interesting viewscape is worth visiting any time. Probably the best opportunity to see wildlife there is early or late in the day, especially in spring, when the new vegetation is at its peak.

Willow Canyon and demonstration forest

Two and a half kilometres east of the moose viewing area and almost 32 kilometres east of Prince George, is a rough access road to the Canadian Institute of Forestry's Willow Canyon woodlot and demonstration forest, with its trails and picnic shelters. And beyond that, the road leads to a viewpoint overlooking Willow Canyon.

Willow River in full spring flood in the Willow Canyon.

Like the moose viewing area, this was also built in the early eighties. Partly maintained through revenue earned from the woodlot, the demonstration forest includes a self-guided walk of about 45 minutes duration that is accessed from the Willow River highway rest area described below. The area contains many different tree types and successional dynamics typical of forests of the region. It is a popular destination for school tours, and they are typically guided by a professional forester from the institute. To reach the canyon viewpoint, continue on past the woodlot until the access road gains the canyon rim where a small parking area and fenced viewpoint is reached. The best time to see the canyon is during spring high water.

Back on the highway one and a half kilometres farther east, or 33 kilometres east of Prince George, is the connecting Willow River highway rest area and the main access to the demonstration forest trail. It was here in 1974 that one of Canada's worst canoeing accidents took place—it took the lives of all nine young men, aged 16 to 18, who were in the party. The teenagers are commemorated today through the plaque placed at the highway rest area. Their monument also serves as a reminder to others not to launch into the deceptively tranquil river just below the highway, as shortly downstream is the unnavigable Willow Canyon. The Willow River is popular with experienced canoeists, kayakers, and whitewater rafters UPSTREAM of the highway-bridge above the rest area. Such activities should only be undertaken in the company of people who are knowledgable of the sport and the river.

The clear waters of the Willow River make it a popular recreation and fishing destination. For those who care to bushwhack down into the lower canyon north of the viewpoint described earlier, there are many enticing fishing holes. Watch out, however, for black bears as they like to fish as well, and I have had several tense encounters with them there. On one memorable occasion, unbeknownst to us at the time, a sow black bear with cubs allowed my companion and I to pass late one summer evening. A few minutes later, without having reached the river, we turned around because of approaching nightfall and, patience clearly exhausted, the bear strongly objected to our return passage. Descending from a tree by the trail, where it had apparently taken refuge with its cubs, it now blocked our return path, its shadowy form making angry, huffing sounds. Glancing anxiously over our shoulders, we had no choice but to push on to the river, bushwhack half a kilometre up its banks in near darkness, and scramble up the steep embankment to escape.

Purden Lake

Continuing along Highway 16, Purden Lake Provincial Park, 57 kilometres east of Prince George, affords both day-use and summer camping. From the campsite, beach, and picnic areas, a rustic trail with views south toward Purden ski hill heads east along the lakeshore. Three and a half kilometres east of the park access road and 60 kilometres from Prince George, Purden Lake resort offers what may be the last chance for services for the next 140 kilometres until McBride, although meal services sometimes operate in the Slim Creek and Dome Creek areas.

The Bowron Valley

A few kilometres east of Purden, the highway passes the Bowron Valley. Here, in the 1980s, a total of 48,115 hectares were logged in a short-duration effort to salvage a forest that had been ravaged by the spruce bark beetle; a further 2,438 hectares were burned by wildfire. The infestation began in 1975 when strong winds caused scattered patches of blown-down trees. The large tracts of mature spruce, combined with the downed trees, provided ideal habitat for beetles, and a series of relatively mild winters contributed to the epidemic that followed. The forest service looked at their options and in a highly controversial decision, selected large-scale harvesting to salvage timber value, control the beetle infestation, and to facilitate replanting of the area. For awhile the valley enjoyed the dubious distinction of being one of the largest man-made disturbances visible from space. Over $30 million has been spent on reforesting the area with a mixture of 62 million white spruce, lodgepole pine, and Douglas fir trees planted. Some areas have had to be replanted several times after drying out and failing, and foresters have learned to use better seedlings. Wildlife populations, including grizzly bears, are now returning to the area, which is regenerating well.

Entering the Rocky Mountain Trench

Eight kilometres east of Purden Lake, or nearly 69 kilometres from Prince George, the Bowron Forest Service Road crosses the highway. Just past this on the north side of the highway is a nondescript-looking low, rocky ridge covered with young forest. Overgrown logging roads, but no trails, lead onto the ridge. The bush is quite dense in places, and this is definitely grizzly country, but if you are comfortable bushwhacking, the top gives one of the best perspectives of the entire Rocky Mountain Trench—a view right down the middle!

Sugarbowl-Grizzly Den Provincial Park

Sugarbowl-Grizzly Den Provincial Park, located on Highway 16 East less than 80 kilometres from the city, is the closest, most accessible, and popular alpine recreation area near Prince George. Well-used for decades, it was designated a protected area by the Prince George Land and Resource Management Plan in the late 1990s, and in 2000 it became a provincial park. The 24,765-hectare park includes three distinct areas, most of which are covered by the 1:50,000 topographical map, 93 H/13 Hutton.

1. The historic and scenic Grand Canyon of the Fraser, north of Highway 16, is situated in the middle of the Rocky Mountain Trench where the Fraser River has carved a passage through a central ridge of bedrock.

2. The Sugarbowl Ridge and Viking Ridge, immediately south of the highway, rise a vertical kilometre through old-growth interior cedar–hemlock and Engelmann spruce–subalpine fir forests, up into alpine tundra. This portion of the park provides excellent habitat for black and grizzly bear, marten, caribou, moose, wolves, and wolverines, and it provides important caribou range and movement corridors. Two trailheads, each with a small parking area, provide access to the ridge from the highway. The Sugarbowl trail is 78 kilometres from Prince George, and the Viking trail is located at the 84-kilometre mark. Each trail climbs to separate alpine meadows, ridges, and summits that can be hiked independently or connected via a crossover route. Once clear of the highway, this easily accessed front ridge system gives a remarkable sense of wilderness, as well as superb views along the Rocky Mountain Trench, the Northern Rocky Mountains, and the Cariboo Mountains.

3. The Grizzly Den and Raven Lake area is situated 10 kilometres south of the highway, and is accessed by the Hungary Creek Forest Service Road, the turnoff being 88 kilometres from Prince George. The Grizzly Den trailhead is located near the 12-kilometre mark on the Hungary Creek Road, and the Raven Lake trailhead is around the 15-kilometre point. The access road gains 300 metres elevation from the highway, leaving only another six hundred or so vertical metres to reach alpine. There are three public-use cabins in the area, one near the start of the Grizzly Den trail, and the other two in the alpine at Grizzly Den and Raven Lake respectively. Like the Viking and Sugarbowl front ridges, the Raven Lake and Grizzly Den trails can also be connected by a variety of routes, mostly unmarked. Winter travellers need to be cognizant of avalanche hazards, which have claimed two lives at Raven Lake.

Upper Grand Canyon.

Grand Canyon of the Fraser

There are presently no maintained recreational trails leading into the Grand Canyon of the Fraser, a fact that adds to its historical and scenic remoteness. The summer access is 71 kilometres from Prince George on the north side of the highway, just west of where it drops down to Kenneth Creek (all distances along Highway 16 are measured from the east side of the Yellowhead Bridge). The eight-kilometre trek to the canyon is twice as long as the more direct winter route, but by staying on the north side of Kenneth Creek, you avoid having to ford the creek. During the winter season (usually mid-January to early March) Kenneth Creek generally freezes over, and there is a more direct access to the canyon area from the highway, four kilometres east of its Kenneth Creek crossing. This route (an old winter logging road) skirts an open, black spruce bog to reach the Fraser River at its confluence with Sugarbowl Creek and Kenneth Creek, two kilometres above the Upper Canyon. Kenneth Creek was named after a Dr. Kenneth who apparently delivered a baby in the area during the railway construction era around 1915.

Grand Canyon in the spring

The time is noon on a Sunday in early May. The weather is clear and hot, the bush is dry, and there are no mosquitoes. Thirty people from the Caledonia Ramblers Hiking Club are exploring the rocks and sandy beach next to the rapids above the Grand Canyon of the Fraser. Just below the rapids, the river makes a 90-degree turn to the right. This is the upper canyon, where "Greens Rock" claimed many lives. We had started our trek two and a half hours earlier from Highway 16 just west of Kenneth Creek, less than one hour driving time from Prince George, and were surrounded by a wild grandeur.

Once a place of bustling activity, the Grand Canyon is rarely visited today. It is situated upstream of Sinclair Mills on the Fraser River, four kilometres north of Highway 16, and about 16 kilometres east of Purden Lake. There is, as yet, no developed access, and one must bushwhack using old winter logging roads and rough-cut trails. The Grand Canyon of the Fraser lies in the midst of the Rocky Mountain Trench, which stretches roughly sixteen hundred kilometres from the Yukon to the U.S. border. The Cariboo Mountains provide an impressive backdrop from winter to early summer, until the Sugarbowl Ridge loses its snowpack at the end of June. The Grand Canyon is visible from the Sugarbowl hiking trail after it gains the ridge nearly a vertical kilometre above the highway.

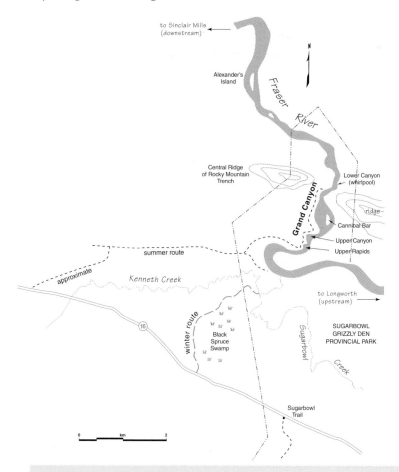

Grand Canyon of the Fraser

Activity Hiking

Rating 8 to 10 hours round trip

Distance 15 to 20 km round trip summer route, depending on how much of the canyon area is walked.

Principal Elevation Gain Minimal on the approach; lots of short up and down in the canyon area.

Map 93 H/13 Hutton

Details The summer route starts 700 metres west of the Highway 16 crossing of Kenneth Creek, on the north side of the highway. There are presently no official trails to this historic area, and good bush skills or a guide are essential. See the text for more details for the summer route, and for the shorter winter option.

Ray Mueller, who worked in the Canyon as early as 1925 takes the author and four other companions through the Grand Canyon of the Fraser in the summer of 1992 at the age of 87 in his specially designed riverboat.

As well as being a place of great scenic beauty, the canyon holds much historical interest. Father Morice was one of the first to document this in his *History of the Northern Interior* in the nineteenth century. Early in its recorded history, the canyon witnessed the passage of the Overlanders en route to the Cariboo gold fields, followed by (pre-railway) river freighting between the Yellowhead Pass and Fort George. In the fall of 1992, Ray Mueller of Sinclair Mills, then 87 years old, took me through the Grand Canyon in his specially designed riverboat. He talked about the canyon's history from his firsthand experience of having worked its dangerous waters since 1925. Later, in the same house that he had brought through the canyon on a raft and set up on the banks of the river at Sinclair Mills, Ray and his wife Louisa discussed their many years of living and raising a family in the area. They showed me the artifacts they had recovered in the canyon, including a stone pestle and a five-pound Mastodon tooth, both of which had been identified by the Royal British Columbia Museum.

Many of the travellers in the early years of the twentieth century were inexperienced on the river. Using roughly built scows, they plied the canyon on one-way trips to transport supplies to Fort George from Tête Jaune—many coming to grief on Greens Rock in the upper canyon, others being lost in the rapids or sucked into the whirlpools of the lower canyon. Many of the obstructions in the canyon were removed by blasting early in this century to allow passage of the sternwheelers travelling upriver to McBride. Loss estimates range from one or two hundred killed, and Ray told us of accounts that he had heard as a young man, of bodies caught in the endless whirlpools below the canyon. For every man killed, he said, there would be several more waiting to take his place.

There is much more in the way of canyon history: during the railway construction era, circa 1913, there was a large hospital camp located four miles downriver from Penny; in the 1930s, there were two Depression-era relief work camps located two and seven miles downriver from Penny, accommodating 60 and 40 men respectively; in the 1950s and 1960s industrial logging took place in the area, and an early forestry helicopter was lost when it hit a steel cable that crossed the canyon. The relatively tranquil appearance of the water in the canyon has always belied its true nature. Ray described an incident many years ago when he was taking his family through the Upper Canyon. Their boat was on the edge of a large eddy, or whirlpool, when suddenly, without warning, a large log that had been held down in the current, shot out of the centre of the eddy like a submarine-launched missile. With good fortune it fell clear of the boat on re-entry.

My first visit to the canyon was a solo ski trip in early 1991. Shortly after starting out, I lost what I would later discover to be the optimal "summer route" and spent many hours bushwhacking along Kenneth Creek, alternately skiing along the river ice where it was sound, and thrashing through a tangle of young forest where it was not. I reached the Fraser River and the canyon's upper rapids late in the day, and I decided, out of necessity, to bushwhack back out to the highway via the shortest route, using a compass. To my great relief, this took me through a black spruce swamp that was almost park-like under its winter snow and provided a quick, easy passage. A local man, Joe Plenk, had inspired my interest in the area after I had repeatedly seen his Volkswagen car parked on the highway near Kenneth Creek, where I had started my trek that day. Working alone on weekends, Joe developed many of the rough trails now found in the vicinity of the canyon.

The Grand Canyon has a special beauty in winter. One clear, minus 25-degree Celsius day in January, a short ski alongside the Fraser River from the mouth of Kenneth Creek brought me to the open water of the upper rapids. There, the mist rose off the boiling green waters to give me a photographic image that later became the 1993 Northwood Christmas Card.

There are healthy wolf populations in the area, and it is common to see fresh tracks on the river ice. As well, I have seen and heard wolves several times while hiking and skiing on the nearby Sugarbowl and Viking Ridges. Among the wolves' food sources are the mountain caribou that live on the surrounding ridges. Each spring and fall many of these animals migrate down from the mountains and cross the Fraser River. A radio collar study, ongoing since the late 1980s, has shown that the caribou travel farther than had previously been thought, crossing several ranges from the Cariboo Mountains to the Rockies.

In the early 1990s, I made a proposal to the Ministry of Forests for a forest recreation reserve at the Grand Canyon. It was turned down on grounds that there wasn't much there of interest—an assessment that staggered me at the time, but was probably influenced by the canyon's inaccessibility. Instead of dampening my interest, however, this rejection spurred me to send a report to B.C. Parks titled *Grand Canyon Provincial Park Proposal* in which I asked for full protection of the area. In his reply dated August 5th, 1992, the regional director for B.C. Parks' Northern B.C. Region replied: "Thank you for your proposal of June 1992 suggesting establishment of a provincial park on the "Grand Canyon" of the Fraser River. We will apply for a UREP (Use, Recreation and Enjoyment of the Public) reserve to cover this area. We will also add your proposal to our list of Parks and Wilderness for the 90's submissions for future consideration." This designation was essentially an expression of interest in the canyon area that would ensure that parks staff would have an opportunity to review any development proposals there. More importantly, a ball was set in motion at an opportune time, because a few years later, the province-wide strategy to double British Columbia's protected areas, locally became part of the mandate of the Prince George Land and Resource Management Plan. In that process, the Grand Canyon of the Fraser was included in the list of proposed protected areas. There's a message in this for anyone who believes passionately in something: First, get involved and initiate some action. If your first approach is rejected and you are not persuaded by the rationales for the rejection, try again by a different route; raise the stakes; take, rather than lose heart. With the Grand Canyon proposal, I was energized to take it further; just as in the 1980s I'd had similar experiences with flagging civic interest in Moores Meadow Park and the Heritage River Trails. In my experience, if the idea has merit, and support within the community, it will eventually take hold if you persevere, and the results will likely far exceed your first tentative expectations.

The Grand Canyon park proposal fell into a category designed to capture specific features; in this case, the scenic and historical aspects of the canyon, combined with B.C. Parks' desire to capture a representative sample of the Rocky Mountain Trench. The Grand Canyon was later approved as part of the larger Sugarbowl-Grizzly Den Provincial Park. The northern boundaries of the Sugarbowl-Grizzly Park were moved, first on my suggestion, from the alpine zone where they were initially proposed, north to the highway, and later, on the advice of the government team involved, all the way to the Fraser River. This new boundary captured better landscape connectivity with a movement corridor for the mountain caribou, as well as included the Grand Canyon in the larger park.

The summertime walk into the Grand Canyon starts at an old logging road on the north side of Highway 16, approximately seven hundred metres west of the highway crossing of Kenneth Creek. The trail is overgrown and almost indiscernible at first, but soon opens up into a more reasonable track. A map and compass are essential since the route is not marked in any way. After about two kilometres, the trail swings north, and after crossing a swampy creek it reaches a T-junction with another old forest road. This is a good place to stop and take a look around so as not to miss the side trail on your return. Continuing eastward, beaver ponds have flooded parts of the old track, requiring a detour around the wet spots. Lured on by freshly-green spring vegetation and distant snow-capped mountains, however, this seems like a small inconvenience. After six kilometres, and an hour and a half of brisk walking, the old road curves to the right and veers down toward the Fraser River near the confluence with Kenneth and Sugarbowl Creeks. Just before that overgrown descent, a rough trail leads to the left into mature forest and heads in a northeasterly direction down toward the Grand Canyon. Hazards here include rough terrain, thick bush, a poorly marked route, insects, bears, and fast water, but these are compensated by the rewards of the destination.

The best option is to first visit the scenic upper rapids, and then scramble downriver past the 90-degree right turn, climbing to reach a superior vantage point above the upper canyon. Descending to a large widening in the river, a beach near the remains of an old dock makes a nice lunch stop. One kilometre downstream, one can see the river pinching into the tight walls of the lower canyon, where it cuts through a seemingly misplaced 230-metre high ridge in the middle of the Rocky Mountain Trench.

The lower canyon – a historical journey

I returned to complete my Grand Canyon exploration a year later on a perfect day in May, accompanied by a pleasant breeze that matched the clear sky and 20-degree Celsius temperatures. Fresh leaves on the trees framed the sweep of the Fraser River. The snowy backdrop of Sugarbowl Ridge and Viking Ridge reminded me of snowshoeing up there a week earlier, and my encounter with a caribou on the descent. The long walk into the canyon from Highway 16 was mostly dry that year thanks to an unusual spring. Countless tracks of moose, wolf, and grizzly bear were frozen into the dry mud and spoke of earlier conditions, and there were hardly any mosquitoes yet.

Our objective on this occasion was to reach the lower canyon, and we therefore bypassed the upper rapids where the river makes the first of three 90-degree turns, so were soon on the rim of the upper canyon. From there, we looked down on the waters where many of the inexperienced river runners of the nineteenth and early twentieth centuries had died freighting from Tête Jaune to Fort George. The river today was high and brown. It was probably near this place that Father A.G. Morice in his *The History of the Northern Interior of British Columbia*, documented a bizarre case of cannibalism that occurred in 1862 after five men, the last of the Overlanders, were shipwrecked late in the season. A sandbar just downstream from the upper canyon became known locally as Cannibal Bar. It was presumed to be the "rock" where three of the men who were non-swimmers were

Surveyors taking loaded scow up through the upper rapids of the Grand Canyon of the Fraser in 1909. Photo provided by Olive Williams to Prince George author Jack Boudreau who has given permission for use in this book.

91

stranded for two days after the accident before a rope could be thrown to them. It may be argued that Morice's "rock" could not be a sandbar, and there are differing opinions among local historians as to where exactly the incident took place, but while we may never know for sure, this spot appears to be the best bet. Two of the three brothers named Rennie who had earlier made it to shore were fit enough to walk out to Fort George—a feat, according to Morice, that took them 28 days. Of the others, Morice wrote: "Helstone and Wright were still alive, but, maddened by hunger, had killed Rennie. When they were found they had eaten all but his legs, which they held in their hands at the time." According to Morice, the two men drove off their would-be rescuers with revolvers. When their remains were found the following spring, one of them had apparently killed and eaten the other, and in turn had been killed by a third party. There are slightly different versions of this grizzly piece of Grand Canyon history, but the essential facts aren't in dispute.

Immediately below the upper canyon, another stretch of rapids empties out into a curious lake-like widening in the river, where, on the far side, a hint of white water marks the point where the lake funnels into the lower canyon. On this occasion, high water forced us to bushwhack a few hundred metres before regaining the trail. Badly scratched legs and arms attested to what it must have been like for early pioneers, as well as to the limitations of modern shorts and T-shirts. The rustic trails eventually led us to a spectacular viewpoint overlooking the lower canyon. This was a perfect spot for lunch as we waited for the legendary whirlpool to appear. Sitting there, I recalled reading about the *B.C. Express* steamer losing steerage at this place 60 metres below us in June of 1913. The ship was fighting its way through the whirlpool when a large spruce tree appeared from the depths and jammed its rudders. In a scene reminiscent of the movie, *Titanic*, everyone was on deck watching the drama unfold, curious as to the outcome yet confident that the seasoned Captain Bucey would save the ship. All, that is, except a travelling salesman who had been selling diamond rings to the prostitutes in the railway construction camps along the river. As the ship swung around in the whirlpool and touched the canyon wall, he suddenly ran across the deck and leapt onto the rocky shore. As he clung to a ledge just six feet above the maelstrom, the ship broke free of the whirlpool and drifted downriver to safety. After tying up and starting repairs, a rescue party was organized and headed back upriver. To their amazement, they found the salesman still clinging to the ledge. They dropped a man with a rope down the 70-foot cliff and hauled them both to safety, where, after checking that his jewellry cases were still safely in his jacket pockets, the salesman collapsed. After he had partially recovered, they took him back to the ship, and following the standard first aid treatment of the day, put him in his berth and gave him a large shot of whisky. Our hike didn't end quite as dramatically—we explored a little farther downriver, and then after successfully locating everyone, happily began the long hike home.

Grand Canyon on skis

To hike into the Grand Canyon of the Fraser in the summer means committing to a 20-kilometre round trip from Highway 16 on the north side of Kenneth Creek, often a muddy and mosquito-infested slog on low quality, unmarked trails. While such access difficulties may have had something to do with the reluctance to consider the canyon for a forest recreation area, the provincial park designation didn't necessarily require immediate access. People undertake the walk because of the lush, wild country and its abundant wildlife, the snow-covered mountain backdrop, the rugged scenic trails through the upper and lower canyons, and because this is the only way to access the canyon by land in the summer.

An alternative way to see the Grand Canyon is on skis on a sunny and cold, late winter day when the creeks and rivers are still frozen, and one can take a shortcut to the canyon on a direct line from Highway 16. The route starts on an old winter logging road through a cutblock on the north side of the highway, 76 kilometres east of Prince George. It either skirts (by staying on the old road) or crosses, a striking black spruce bog to arrive at the confluence of Sugarbowl and Kenneth Creeks. It then follows Kenneth Creek down to its confluence with the Fraser River two kilometres above the upper rapids of the Grand Canyon. It is tempting to cut directly across to the Fraser River from Sugarbowl Creek, but the bush close to the Fraser riverbank is nearly impenetrable, and it's best to stay with Kenneth Creek. This route to the canyon should therefore only be undertaken when the ice on Kenneth Creek is safe to cross, a situation that is becoming increasingly uncertain with climatic warming. Once at the Fraser River, it is best to travel along the south shore and stay off the river ice as much as possible, especially near the canyon where there is always open water and very unsafe conditions. One of the really nice things about this winter route, apart from its wonderful setting and historic destination, is that it is almost entirely out in the open. This means getting a nearly uninterrupted view of the surrounding snowy mountains, and some much needed winter sun that is harder to find on more forested trails.

Upper Rapids of the Grand Canyon of the Fraser River on a minus 25 Celsius day – this photograph featured on the 1993 Company Christmas Card of Northwood Pulp and Timber distributed world-wide to customers and employees.

Mid-March would normally be late in the season for this shortcut route, but in 2002, the unseasonably cold approach of spring meant that conditions were still good. The Bearpaw Ridge shone brilliantly under its fresh cover of snow as we headed down from the highway into the cold northern breeze, breaking trail. Our path through soft powder snow was at first crisscrossed by the fresh tracks of many animals, including coyotes, wolves, moose, and weasels. Each track told a tale as the animal stopped to investigate something, or did a U-turn to hurry back to the cover of the forest. Leaving an old winter logging road and forcing our way through the thicket that surrounds the spruce bog, we entered a world that was serene and beautiful, but was completely devoid of tracks—an eerie wildlife no-mans land. The trip down to the Fraser was uneventful, and after travelling along its shore a ways, we heard the sound of the Grand Canyon's upper rapids, not even two hours after leaving the highway. As we ate lunch on the banks of the river under a blazing equinox sun (that was more than a match for the chill air), my partner observed aptly, "This is as good as sitting on the beach in Mexico!"

Landslide

In the early part of 2003, sometime in the middle of the night, residents of the isolated community of Longworth in the Rocky Mountain Trench east of Prince George, awoke to the rumble of what they thought was an earthquake. The "quake," was a very localized event. One kilometre downstream from the community, an enormous piece of forested shoreline extending hundreds of metres back into the bush had slid toward the Fraser River, partly filling the deep channel with debris that included still-standing trees. A few weeks later, as I drifted past the toe of the slide in a riverboat en route to the Grand Canyon, I couldn't help but be struck by the awesome power of nature, even though, as landslides go, this one would be considered small.

We often think of mountain landscapes as being immutable. Yet nothing could really be further from the truth, as that part of the earth's surface tends to be younger and more changeable than other features. And even if we can conceptualize mountains altering within a human lifespan, who among us would have anticipated, for instance, the two-kilometre long catastrophic slide that occurred on a mere three-degree slope in the Muskwa, in Northern B.C., in 1979? Such a landslide would be nearly impossible to predict.

There are many kinds of landslides that occur in Central and Northern B.C.and the overall incidence has increased owing to climate change. Some slides result from the normal weathering process; others from deep-seated tectonic activity (earthquakes), while debris

2003 landslide into the Fraser River below Longworth.

avalanches and debris flows detach from bedrock. Smaller movements can be reactive within older slides; rock falls result from freeze-thaw cycles; and rock avalanches are loosed by heavy rainfall. Sites that seem ideal for human recreational use, such as alluvial fans on shorelines, may be susceptible to collapse, and landslides can be triggered by bank erosion on rivers and streams. Rock avalanches release above glaciers when ice shrinkage (melt) causes loss of buttressing, and large slides can occur where pre-glacial lake sediments are later buried by glacial till. At higher latitudes, melting of permafrost can cause slides to travel extreme distances on shallow slopes of glacial till. Bedrock spreading causes tension fractures and is common in parts of Northern B.C. such as the Pink Mountain area near the Alaska Highway. And rock avalanches can result from mountaintop spreading as a result of tectonic activity in dip slopes. Forest fires, of which there was no shortage in 2003 in southern B.C., can also weaken soil structure and produce landslides, as can human forestry activities such as clearcutting and road building, although slides resulting from the latter are normally smaller than naturally occurring slides.

Although not all of the types of slides mentioned here can be attributed to climate change, projections call for continued increases in temperatures and precipitation, and we should therefore expect the trend for more catastrophic landslides to continue as well. It has even been suggested that we might think about staying out of questionable areas during high seasonal rainfall or runoff, as there is no way, according to one geomorphologist, to outrun "a two kilometre-long slide coming at you with the speed of a freight train." This brought to mind an enormous fissure that I and some friends had found early one summer, high on an innocuous-looking grassy slope while backpacking in the mountains. It changed our perception of the wide, easy valley stretched out below us from which we had just climbed, because it was chillingly obvious that the entire slope will someday separate and fill the valley below with rubble. Looking around with a new appreciation of where we were, we could see how the landscape had been similarly altered many times before. And looking at the shoreline as we approached the upper rapids of the Grand Canyon of the Fraser, it was clear that the recent slide at Longworth was one of an endless series of events as the Fraser River slowly reworks its way through the Rocky Mountain Trench.

Heather, with the summit of Erg Mountain in the mist in the background.

Setting sunlight reflected off the Bowron River.

Wokkpash Gorge's erosion pillars or hoodoos with their often precariously balanced capstones.

Waterfall near the start of the Viking Trail.

Alpine amphitheatre and lakes above Fang Cave in Evanoff Provincial Park – looking west towards unofficially named Pyramid Mountain, which can also be reached from 'The Farm'

Wokkpash River, just below Wokkpash Gorge.

Sunset over Highway 16 East.

Alpine lupines – Erg Mountain meadows. Summit of Erg Mtn on right.

Fall colours on the Salmon River.

Broad Leaf Willow Herb in rock garden below summit of Mt Terry Fox.

Sugarbowl and Viking Trails

The Sugarbowl and Viking trails are accessible year round from Highway 16 on foot, snowshoe, or if you don't mind the steeply wooded slopes, by backcountry ski. Combining these trails into one long crossover trip is one of the best mountain hikes in the Prince George area, especially in the fall season, but be prepared for a 1,400 vertical metre day and a poorly marked route on the crossover section. Conversely, the shortest option is the 670-vertical metre ascent of the Viking Trail to the meadows, where one has a striking view of the ridges above, and where, in the late fall, you may hear bull caribou bugling as part of their annual mating rut.

Sugarbowl to Viking crossover – walking with wildlife

Protected by interior cedar–hemlock and Engelmann spruce–subalpine fir forests, a wild mountain ridge that is home to woodland caribou, wolf, bear, moose, beaver, wolverine, and many others, rises a kilometre out of the Rocky Mountain Trench through the trees of the wet, cool, interior rainforest. Better yet, the area is served by two hiking trails, Sugarbowl and Viking Ridge, each with good access, and at 78 and 84 kilometres respectively, less than an hour from Prince George. Sugarbowl Ridge and Viking Ridge offer endless opportunities both on and off the trail, and after 25 years of exploring on foot, skis, and snowshoes, and coming to know the area well, there are still many spots that I haven't seen. This is part of the lure of a place that exists in a nearly untouched state next to a major highway.

The first kilometre of the Sugarbowl trail is easy, but soon afterward it begins a steep 900-vertical metre climb to the ridge. Three hundred metres below the top, it reaches a flat area near the base of a steep gully. The rock pile at the foot of this chute used to be home to an isolated colony of hoary marmots—the closest that I know of to Prince George, although I haven't seen them there for a few years. I once stood at this spot and watched two wolves emerge from the trees and cross the slope above the marmot colony. As I watched the first wolf, I thought, "How did my dog get all the way up there?" And then I saw the second wolf and realized that my wolf-like companion, a shepherd–collie cross, was actually standing right beside me.

The climb to the ridge is hard but rewarding, and most reasonably active people can do it in two to three hours. I met someone on the ridgetop who was training for competitive cross-country skiing and had made it in one hour, which is the fastest ascent that I know of. That individual jogged on the spot for a few moments as we chatted,

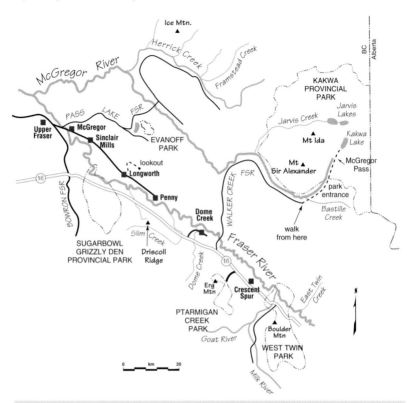

Sugarbowl and Viking Ridge

Activity Mountain Hiking

Rating To any of the main summits described in the text: 7 to 10 hours round trip

Distance Approximately 15 km round trip to either the summit of Sugarbowl or Viking Ridge; or 15 km one-way for the Sugarbowl-Viking crossover, not counting the possible 6 km walk back along the highway to complete the loop if you only have one vehicle.

Principal Elevation Gain 1,100 m round trip to the top of Sugarbowl

Map 93 H/13 Hutton

Details Well-marked trailheads on the south side of Highway 16, and mostly well-marked but steep mountain trails. The route becomes less distinct crossing the Viking Meadows and on the Sugarbowl Viking crossover trail. This is primarily a day-hiking area with excellent alpine ridge-walking and good views along the Rocky Mountain Trench. See text for more details.

Looking south across Viking Meadows towards the summit of Viking Ridge in the fall.

and then immediately started back down. On another occasion, I met a large family of varying ages who were clearly not used to mountain hiking and had taken more than five hours to gain the ridge. Of these widely different ascent times, the one that impressed me the most was the latter, because it showed the accessibility of mountain hiking to almost anyone who has the will to try it, and I could sense the joy experienced by this family who had achieved their own "Everest."

A short distance along the ridge, the trail crosses above the marmot gully, from where you can look down on the Grand Canyon of the Fraser, in the park's northwest extremity. This is a good place for a rest and a bite to eat. Continuing on, the trail soon emerges from the trees into alpine meadows, and climbs onto a knoll that gives good views of the surrounding valleys and the top of Sugarbowl Mountain. The mountain takes its name from the bowl situated on its northeast flank, which retains snow until June or July. From the knoll to the summit is two kilometres of pleasant alpine ridge-walking. The trail descends in a southeasterly direction before starting the final climb to the summit at 1,825-metres elevation. From the top, one can look north to the sweep of the Rocky Mountains, with such landmarks as Ice Mountain and Mount Sir Alexander. Swinging around to the southwest, there is a blue lake directly below the summit which is a good place to watch for caribou, as are the meadows all around. Farther to the southwest is the Bowron Valley, and to the south are the peaks of Raven Lake and Grizzly Den. One spring I was skiing over this summit, following

Hanging valley below the largest of the lakes on the east end of Viking Ridge.

the tracks of two wolves, when I slowed down to watch seven caribou enjoying the noontime sun in the bowl directly below me. The world all around was silent and still, when suddenly, a flock of ptarmigan erupted from the (apparently) undisturbed snowpack at my feet and took to the air. Recovering from the shock of this surprise event, I realized that they had followed their survival instinct during the previous night's storm by burying themselves in the snow.

From the top of Sugarbowl Mountain you can either return by the way you came, or instead descend down the east side of the pyramidal peak to start the crossover route to Caribou Meadows and the Viking Ridge trail. Hiking from the top of Sugarbowl to the high point of the Viking front ridge takes about an hour, and entails dropping down an average of 50 metres and climbing back up again four times in a distance of two kilometres. On one occasion, I had just completed this stretch to reach the second summit, when a young bull caribou walked quietly up the trail behind me. Circling around until he was downwind, he approached within six metres and stood there on the summit for several minutes sniffing the air. His heel tendons clicked as he shifted position, until at last his curiosity was satisfied and he slowly left. Appearing reluctant to go, he glanced back a few times before disappearing into the trees below. Experiences like this are rare, but by spending enough time in the mountains I have had many such moments, almost always when least expected.

Another kilometre of ridge-walking through gently sloping alpine meadows affords superb views over the Rocky Mountain Trench toward the northern Rockies. The trail then descends steeply for 360 vertical metres through trees to join the Viking Ridge trail in a wide expanse of wet, open meadows. It is an hour from here down to the highway and another six kilometres and an hour's walk along the road back to the starting point at the Sugarbowl trailhead. You can avoid walking this final stretch by leaving one vehicle at each end of the trail. But I have always enjoyed changing into lightweight walking shoes and stretching my legs at the end of the day to fully complete the loop and round out my experience of the park. This stretch of highway between the trails is the best place to watch for migrating caribou—sightings are most common in the spring and fall, and have typically ranged up to as many as 10 animals.

Approaching the route the other way around, the Viking trail starts climbing immediately from the highway, and maintains a steady grade for 640 vertical metres before reaching the Caribou Meadows. A branch of the trail forks to the right to start the crossover to Sugarbowl Mountain just described. The main trail continues on across the meadows. It was here, during the early snows of October, that I once had the thrill of watching two bull caribou lock antlers in their annual mating contest over a small group of cows standing nearby. On another occasion I listened to their bugling calls echo off the mountains. Bog orchids abound in the wet meadows, and, surprisingly at this elevation, there is an old beaver pond. It lies adjacent to the flooded remnants of a trapper's cabin. Crossing the meadows, the trail climbs steeply again for 240 vertical metres to treeline and a small alpine lake in a once-glaciated cirque. You can occasionally see moose on this high trail. A 200-metre scramble above the lake gains the main Viking Ridge, where another two kilometres of very fine ridge-walking and views await. Below, on the north side, are a series of small alpine lakes. One summer, while bushwhacking around one of these lakes, I came face to face with a wolverine. It sat quietly on the same game trail that I was on, less than four metres away, ears alert, watching, with none of the legendary ferocity that wolverines are known for. We looked at each other with mutual respect for awhile before it took off, running up the slope among vegetation and boulders, disappearing into the scrub alpine firs. For a brief minute in a lifetime our paths had crossed, and it had seemed like an eternity—perhaps it was.

Snowshoeing on Viking Ridge

The sky was dull as I left Prince George. It wasn't an inspiring start to the day, and yet as I drove east along Highway 16, the banks of fog and low cloud hinted at the prospect of clear weather at higher elevations. In winter and spring it's easy to be intimidated by the nearly vertical kilometre of steep forested slopes of the Viking and Sugarbowl Ridges, and most backcountry skiers prefer the longer drive to deep powder in the McGregor Mountains. But for others, the lure of Viking and Sugarbowl is the wildness of an area that is so accessible. In an early snow year it is possible to find ski routes that avoid the crusted ice below the old cedar forest by linking together small glades that get larger and more frequent with elevation. In an early season, wetter snow helps to lay down the slide alder and removes the obstacle of hard-to-penetrate thickets in the lower elevation glades. But there is another option to skis. The evolution of the recreational snowshoe has opened the backcountry to people who lack the costly equipment or the desire to use skis or snowboards. Today's snowshoes are pretty simple devices—there isn't much to go wrong, and they are easy to fix

Looking south across Viking Meadows towards the summit of Viking Ridge in the winter.

with a basic repair kit, or even with the materials at hand in the bush; they are light, easy to put on, work well on hills and for bushwhacking, are generally maintenance-free, and are relatively inexpensive. They don't require specialized boots or other equipment, nor do they need waxing, sharpening, or tuning up, and it is easy to outfit an out-of-town guest for an impromptu winter day in the mountains.

As I approached the trailhead, five young people accompanied by a dog were already starting up on snowshoes. "Great," I thought. "I'll have an easy walk following in their tracks." This idea quickly evaporated, however, as I caught up to the group who were moving quite slowly, and I found myself breaking trail ahead of them all the way to the meadows. Higher, in the subalpine zone, the trees were draped with pale, green curtains of arboreal lichen, backlit by the low sun. This tree-borne lichen is the main winter food of the mountain caribou, and a research study on Viking Ridge showed that while the caribou graze from lower branches, it is the old trees that fall down that provide the real winter feast. These old, undisturbed forests not only provide winter food for the caribou, they afford them a dispersal strategy to avoid wolves.

Leaving the trees, the Caribou Meadows stretched out in front of me beneath the snowy mountaintop, dazzling under the afternoon sun. A light crust made walking on snowshoes as easy as a summer stroll in a city park. Without them I would be floundering up to my knees or worse, a reminder of what could happen if my equipment should fail. This thought highlighted the need for quality gear, and for the ability to improvise if repairs were needed. Wandering in this temporary paradise, I checked out the tracks of a lone wolf and then looked for a good spot for lunch. The day was so warm that I didn't need to put on a sweater as I sat and ate, soaking up the light.

My route back took a meandering turn around the meadows. I didn't want to leave, but knew that as soon as the winter sun settled behind the mountain this would become a very different place. Avoiding my up-track, I opted for as much open powder as I could find to support a bounding "moon walk" type of gait down the mountain. I passed the party of five who had turned around just short of the meadows. They too were having fun, and we agreed that all of us would soon be back to renew the Viking "snowshoe track."

Looking north from the summit of Viking Ridge in the early spring (March) across the Rocky Mountain Trench and the meandering Fraser River towards Mount Baldy on the Bearpaw Ridge.

Spring in the mountains

We were in that pleasant seasonal interlude after the snow has left the trails, new vegetation is lush, and the bugs haven't hatched in force yet. With Victoria Day behind us, our gardens are in good enough shape so that we can take off for the hills to find that much needed fuel-for-the-soul that is so freely available there. The highways, especially Highway 16 east of Prince George, sometimes resemble game reserves in the spring as animals leave the stealth of the forest to graze on new growth along the right-of-way. Everything is fresh, signalling a time of rebirth in our accentuated seasons of the north. Even the awning of a downtown store is host to a scene of renewal as two small birds frenziedly mate under the canopy at Fourth and George, next to that other sign of spring, the Saturday morning farmers market.

Lower elevation trails, although still wet in many places, have been clear of snow for some time. And now, the mountain trails are opening up as the snowpack retreats quickly, and the rivers below turn chocolate-coloured from the snow's dissolution. Easier hill walks like Teapot Mountain at Summit Lake, Fraser Mountain at Fort Fraser, Mount Pope at Fort St. James, and Prince George's Tabor Mountain are all now clear of snow. And in Sugarbowl-Grizzly Den Provincial Park the snow has receded to the subalpine zone. This means that one can enjoy a 600-vertical metre climb through old-growth forest on either the

112

Sugarbowl or Viking trails, and take in tantalizing glimpses of the still snow-capped Bearpaw Ridge and Rocky Mountains to the northeast. The snow on the upper trail is generally too soft to walk on until mid to late June, but packing along a lightweight pair of snowshoes can win the rewards and views of the last few hundred metres.

A week earlier on Sugarbowl Mountain, I had discovered that I wasn't the only high-on-the-food-chain creature there. I came upon the tracks of a very large grizzly bear on the trail at snowline, only a few hours old. This was significant, because in more than two decades of frequent use of the area I had never seen a bear there, nor much sign of one on either of these trails. I knew that grizzlies occasionally travelled through the park, secretly climbing the rugged canyons and devils club jungle of Sugarbowl Creek, and crossing over a pass where I had seen their tracks on several occasions. But aside from that corridor, there hadn't seemed to be much to interest them there. One sighting wasn't a lot to go on, but I was inclined to take this as an indicator that the burgeoning grizzly population in the Rocky Mountain Trench that many of us have seen in the last few years, was spilling over into our new mountain park. This big bear was clearly at ease on a trail frequented by people, and it was a reminder both of the need to keep vigilant on all of our trails, and of the truly great wilderness that we can experience close to the unique place that is Prince George.

Dave King

This is an ideal place to introduce a man who, over the past 30 years, has probably had more influence on organized hiking in the Prince George area than anyone else. And, of all the trails that he either pioneered or helped to develop during that time, Dave King's work on the Viking and Sugarbowl Ridge stands as one of his best-known legacies.

Dave King spent his childhood years growing up on a fruit farm near Penticton, in the Okanagan Valley. As a kid, he had ample opportunity to hike, ski, snowshoe, fish, and hunt in the outdoors. Because of rattlesnakes and abundant other wildlife that surrounded him, and because of his father's strong interest in the outdoors (his dad was a founding member of what later became the B.C. Wildlife Federation), Dave decided to pursue a career in biology. He first obtained his undergraduate degree, and later his masters degree, both from the University of British Columbia, finding time in between to work for two years at the Mweka Wildlife College in East Africa. Most of his work there was in Kenya and Tanzania, and Dave described it as being an unbelievable opportunity to research, hunt, and observe large and

Dave King standing beneath ancient Western Red Cedar on Driscoll Ridge.

small wildlife with an international group of teachers who were part of a United Nations project. The students were from English-speaking African countries, learning to become park and game wardens, and spending fully half of their time in the field. Mweka Wildlife College is situated at the foot of Mount Kilimanjaro, Africa's highest peak at 5,895 metres, and part of the training for the students that Dave King came to relish was going out on the mountain. As a result, during his time there, Dave spent over 60 days above treeline (3,300 metres) and climbed Kilimanjaro an amazing seven times, including a solo ascent when he spent an uncomfortable night alone on the summit. While he was at Mweka College, Dave King helped to build two of the huts on the mountain, and later took on the task of rewriting the original guidebook for Mount Kilimanjaro. He also climbed Mount Kenya to within a few hundred metres of its technical summit on three occasions. In 1968, Dave climbed eight of the ten peaks over 4,876 metres (16,000 feet) of Africa's famed Rwenzoris Mountains, more commonly known as the Mountains of the Moon. This was during a year of unseasonably bad weather, and it turned out that he and his six companions were among the last people to do the climbs for several years owing to the political situation that was developing in Uganda. Dave's group reached the summits of the two highest Mountains of the Moon, Margherita (5109 m) and Alexandra (5091 m) in whiteout conditions on Christmas Day 1968, within hours of the Apollo 8 astronauts becoming the first humans to orbit the actual moon. Later, a friend of the family, working at NASA, sent Dave a commemorative shoulder patch of the Apollo 8 mission showing the earth and moon with the names of the astronauts inscribed on the flight path, plus a photograph of Africa taken from the final Apollo 17 flight.

Back in Vancouver, Dave worked and studied hard on weekdays and evenings, so that he could spend almost every weekend (even during exam times) hiking, skiing, and trail-clearing in the mountains of B.C.'s lower mainland. After completing his masters degree, which involved a blue grouse study on Vancouver Island, Dave spent two years working for an environmental consultant in the Skagit Valley on a U.S. related proposal to raise the Ross Dam. He then returned to Vancouver Island to do more fieldwork on blue grouse. He had intended at the end of that field season to travel to the Himalayas, and had already booked a flight when an opportunity arose that he couldn't turn down. Everything that Dave King had done up to this point in his life had prepared him for his arrival in Prince George in October 1973 as the newly appointed Regional Habitat Protection Biologist for Northern B.C., and for his pending involvement with the Prince George mountaineering community.

Dave's job in Prince George took him all over the backcountry of Northern B.C., from the Queen Charlotte Islands to the Alberta border, to the Yukon, where he was involved in anything related to human impacts on fish and wildlife. He spent his spare time during that first year in Prince George exploring the local mountains on his own, before joining the then newly formed Caledonia Ramblers Hiking Club in 1975. He immediately began to participate in designing, building, and maintaining recreational hiking trails. As well, he lead trips on many of the newer mountain trails around Prince George and in the Robson Valley. One of the first trails that he worked on was in the upper Ptarmigan Creek, 160 kilometres east of Prince George. It was here that he came face to face with his first grizzly bear, not far from where I would have my own first such encounter a few years later on Erg Mountain. Dave led the first three bushwhacking trips to Mount Terry Fox before the Forest Service built a trail. In 1979, Dave King became president of the club, a position he held for 15 consecutive years until 1994. During that time he also helped a founding member, Dr. Bob Nelson, edit and produce a trail guide. In 1995, Dave and Bob undertook a major revision of the guide, and thereafter Dave assumed the editorship of the popular, yellow-covered booklet. *The Prince George and District Trail Guide*, which in 2004 celebrated its thirtieth anniversary, is an inexpensive publication that is revised nearly every year with current access and trail information, making it an excellent adjunct to *Exploring Prince George*.

Dave King's professional life involved assessing many kinds of human activities that could impact fish and wildlife, such as forestry roads and logging plans, land leases, pesticide applications, subdivision plans, mineral exploration, and mine development. He was involved in doing wildlife counts, and in land use planning ranging from early forestry resource portfolios and Crown and Agricultural Land Use Plans in the 1970s, to the Land and Resource Management Plans and protected areas of the 1990s. Dave takes pride today in the working relationships that he helped to develop between different government agencies and industries, something that undoubtedly contributed to relatively few land-use confrontations occurring in this part of B.C. As well, he believes that the give-and-take on all sides helped to foster better forestry and road building practices that later meant an easier implementation of the Forest Practices Code in Northern B.C. Dave's approach was to look at what would work, and at how things could be made better; avoiding the head-butting that he saw taking place elsewhere. After he retired in 2000, Dave looked back on his involvement with the protected areas of the 1990s, and on the recently announced (in 2003) Ungulate Winter Range that he had worked on for nearly three decades. He described seeing these projects come to fruition as being the major highlights of his professional life—a cap to his career. Dave's considerable knowledge and expertise in the land use planning processes within government, complemented the public voice on the outside. His knowledge was unique in that it grew from a combination of time spent on the job, and innumerable hard-won, often exploratory, backcountry trips on his own.

In 2004, Dave King is very much active in Prince George, and his knowledge is still sought by government agencies and non-government groups alike. Apart from his near-legendary role with the Caledonia Ramblers Hiking Club, he has long been an advocate for the North, representing the area as a director of the Federation of Mountain Clubs of B.C., and as a founding director of the Backcountry Recreation Society of Prince George. Right in Prince George, Dave was one of the people who worked hard to persuade the city to establish Cottonwood Island Park, and he later served on the Forests for the World Commission that established that area and managed its development through its early years. Today, Dave is careful what he commits his time to, as he and his partner Judith Robertson are also inveterate world-travellers. They frequently undertake long, off-the-beaten-track journeys in faraway places—to the point where it would almost be easier to list places they have not been to.

Twenty-five years ago, Dave King saw the wildlife values and recreational potential of the Viking and Sugarbowl Ridge system better than anyone else did at the time. Although not the architect of the original Sugarbowl trail, he later undertook to re-route it to its present location, and was the main instigator of the Viking Ridge trail and its crossover connection with Sugarbowl. Other well-known backcountry trails that Dave King initiated are the Caledonia Mountain and Vineyards trails in the Everett Creek area east of Prince George. He has also been involved in many other trail developments and maintenance. In one instance he helped the late George Evanoff develop the Fang and Torpy trails in what is now Evanoff Provincial Park in the McGregor Range. The net effect of all this is that in the decades since 1973 when he arrived in Prince George, Dave King has played a lead role in helping residents and visitors alike to fully realize what is available to them here in the Prince George outdoors.

Grizzly Den and Raven Lake

Eighty-eight kilometres from Prince George and four kilometres east of the Viking trail is the Hungary Creek Forest Service Road that marks the eastern boundary of the park and leads 12 and 15 kilometres respectively south of the highway to the Grizzly Den and Raven Lake trailheads. They are both outstanding routes for either mountain hiking or ski touring, with the added security of three cabins. The road is usually unplowed in the winter but can be a pleasant ski trip as it climbs 300 metres to the trailheads. Be prepared to share the road with snowmobiles, as they use it to access other areas to the southeast.

Solo in the winter backcountry

It was 9 am as I parked my car at the start of the Grizzly Den trail and began the process of putting on boots and gaiters, and attaching climbing skins to my skis. The morning was cold, and by the time I had finished my fingers were beginning to freeze. The sun was shining low through the trees as I made the first steep climb to the forest edge. I skied through inch-long feathers of hoarfrost that refracted the sun like a fantasy of diamonds. The air was still and the day was absolutely quiet except for the gentle tinkling of crystals parted by my skis. My body unconsciously took in deep breaths of clear, cold morning air. This was what I had come for.

Working on the Grizzly Den cabin.

Grizzly Den and Raven Lake

Activity Mountain Hiking, Backpacking, and Backcountry Skiing
Rating 5 to 10 hours, or up to several days with overnight use campsites at Raven Lake and three public-use huts.
Distance 12 km round trip to either Raven Peak or to the Grizzly Den cabin; or 15 km for a one-way crossover route, plus a possible 3 km back along the road to complete the loop if you have only one vehicle.
Principal Elevation Gain 750 m to the summit of Raven Peak
Maps 93 H/13 Hutton; 93 H/12 Narrow Lake
Details This most popular of the alpine areas close to Prince George has three public-use overnight cabins and a lakeside alpine camping area. It is accessed via the Hungary Creek Forest Road south from Highway 16 to the trailheads at 12 and 15 kilometres respectively. All of the trails below treeline, with the exception of one of the crossover routes, are well-marked and well-used. The area is popular for both summer and fall hiking, and for winter and spring backcountry skiing, although the access road is usually not plowed during the winter.

I entered the forest, my fingers throbbing with the pain of returning circulation. This soon passed and I settled into the rhythm of the climb. I had this piece of the world to myself for the present and I relished every moment of it. Leaving the trail, I began to make my own tracks in the pristine snow that every year covers the detritus of the forest floor. Departing the usual route, I struck off for Leprechaun Ridge.

Solitary travel isn't recommended practice, but the absence of peer pressure and the knowledge of one's aloneness in the winter mountains reduces the likelihood of an accident, although it significantly increases its seriousness should one occur. Hiking with another person or with a group has its own rewards. Travelling alone allows the personal freedom to determine pace and route, to decide when and how long to stop and rest or eat, and to fully experience one's surroundings in the awakening of the senses. Inevitably you see more wildlife, and nearly always when not expected.

As I climbed, my path crossed many caribou tracks, some old and some obviously fresh. Possibly the faint squeaking of the skis had disturbed the animals as I approached. This was my third successive weekend in this place, taking advantage of the road that had been plowed to facilitate replacement of a bridge over Hungary Creek. I had come once on snowshoes and twice on skis; twice I was in the

Skiing at Raven Lake in May.

company of others and this time I was alone. I had yet to catch my first glimpse of the secretive deer of the mountains in this new millennium. It was early in the year 2000.

Climbing through the sparse clumps of subalpine fir nearly at treeline, the views in the clear morning air were spectacular. Mount Sir Alexander and Mount Ida, the two most northerly 10,000-footers in the Canadian Rockies, were dazzling on the northeast horizon. Looking west, I spied a track extending halfway across an avalanche chute on the east flank of Raven Peak that ended in a dark object. "Ah," I thought, "a caribou!" Stopping, I dug out my small spotting scope only to discover a tree and another faint track exiting the slide path.

Above treeline, the ridge narrowed and the snow became wind-packed. I thought I could hear the distant roar of a jet aircraft, but each time I stopped to listen there was only silence. Gradually I realized that it was the sound of my ski's propagating through the drum-like surface of the snowpack. Reaching the summit of Leprechaun peak, I looked down on Pat's Pass and Grizzly Den. Removing my skis, I sat down in the warm sun to eat lunch and sip hot tea. With the January temperature inversion, it was like being on a summer picnic. As I sat there, contented, not really looking at anything in particular, I spotted movement on the opposite ridge. My scope was still handy and soon I had a fine view of a caribou as it climbed. I lowered the glass and then became aware that 10 other caribou had started climbing below the first. It can be hard to distinguish a mountain caribou from a rock when it is not moving, and I had not noticed them before. Over the course of the next hour, I sat in perfect quiet and watched the 11 caribou climb onto the summit of Hagen Peak, close enough that I could hear the telltale clicking of their heel ligaments. The group was made up of antlered cows of varying sizes, accompanied by calves of last year. When moving, they walked carefully in their companions' tracks to conserve energy, occasionally splitting into two strings before merging again. When looking at tracks as I had done earlier in the day, it is easy to be fooled into thinking that there are only two or three animals in a group like this, walking as they do in each other's footsteps.

I finished lunch, stood up, and began to remove the climbing skins from my skis, and organize my gear. The caribou spotted me silhouetted against the skyline, became skittish and ran a short distance down the slope. After standing cautiously for 10 minutes, they became more comfortable with my presence and walked back to the summit to resume grazing on the grasses and lichens that had been exposed there by the wind. With some reluctance, but a great deal of satisfaction for what I had experienced, I tore myself away and began what proved to be a beautiful ski down to my car, and less than two hours later I was back in town, enjoying a mid-afternoon cappuccino.

Mountain park ready for use

Earlier in 2001, six local organizations reached an agreement with B.C. Parks to help maintain the trails and cabins in the new Sugarbowl-Grizzly Den Provincial Park. Together with B.C. Parks, the Caledonia Ramblers Hiking Club, Caledonia Nordics Ski Club, Prince George Section of the Alpine Club of Canada, Prince George Naturalists Club, Sons of Norway Ski Club, and the UNBC Outdoors Club made great progress during that summer.

The Grizzly Den A-frame cabin built nearly 30 years before with support from Northwood Pulp and Timber, and the Forest Service, had been fully insulated, with newly painted sheathing attached to the inside walls to brighten up the interior, and new screens put on the windows. The roof was repaired and patched, support posts reset, and the outhouse steps were rebuilt. In July 2002, a group of volunteers hiked in to begin three days of renovations on the twin cabin at Raven Lake. Although the weather was kind to them, I can attest from being in the mountains on one of those days that they had to contend with mosquitoes, black flies, and horseflies, all fighting for a piece of the action. It's one thing to hike among bugs like that when you can keep moving and seek windy ridges; it's quite another to be captive for three days in a windless subalpine work site. These volunteers deserve a big thank you, which is best expressed in how the sites are used. In particular, please leave the cabins as you find them, or preferably in better shape—there are always opportunities for friendly competition in cabin cleanup. If you are planning an overnight stay, bring your own sleeping pad, stove, fuel and pots, and please conserve the supply of firewood as it must be flown in by helicopter. This wood should only be burned in the energy efficient stoves inside the cabins, never used in open fires outside. The sign-in book, not the walls, should be used to record visits, and everything brought in should be packed out, especially food. There is no garbage service at the cabin and maintenance is almost entirely done through volunteer work. Leftover food is very unlikely to be needed by anyone else at a site as accessible as this, and it only serves to attract mice, which can be a nuisance as they run across sleeping bags during the night and chew through food bags. Their feces can pose a deadly health risk from hantavirus, which can be inhaled on airborne dust particles. People using the Raven Lake and Grizzly Den cabins are also asked to use the donation envelopes placed there to make contributions at the recommended rates. The money collected all goes into maintaining the cabins and replenishing the wood supply. At some point, reservation and host systems may be put in place, but until then the cabins are available on a first come, honour basis.

Interior rainforest

Between 18 to 24 kilometres east of Hungary Creek, roughly 106 to 112 kilometres from Prince George, lies the heart of the ancient interior cedar–hemlock rainforests below Driscoll Ridge. The ridge rises from the south side of the highway, between Driscoll and Slim Creeks, its unofficial name being taken from the first of these creeks. There are no trails, and serious bushwhacking is involved through the groves of up to thousand-year old cedars that are waiting to be explored. The easiest way to experience this area is on snowshoes from January onward, but the forest holds a different magic in each season.

Rainforest on our doorstep

In September 2000, UNBC was host to a unique event—"The Interior Cedar Hemlock Stewardship Conference: Managing a Unique Ecosystem." The ICH wet belt extends from the high mountains of southeast B.C. through the Rocky Mountain Trench to just east of

Prince George, with isolated areas in the Upper Skeena and Nass Valleys. The forests along Highway 16 east of Purden Lake were once thought by forest managers to consist of old trees of little value to society, and it was felt that they should be cleared as quickly as possible to make way for spruce and pine. Because of its combination of wet climate, high latitude, and continental location, the interior rainforest as it has lately become known, has been found to be an ecosystem that is unique on the planet.

The ICH has the greatest diversity of tree species anywhere in B.C.—comparable to, or greater than B.C.'s coastal rainforests, with individual trees over eight hundred and one thousand years old. And the soils contain one of the most diverse environments on earth, with astronomical numbers of protozoan species and individuals that, astonishingly, are thought to reach their population peak in the depths of January's cold. The diversity of lichen species increases with the age of the old-growth forest, and with more than 40 species of lichens, the ICH is again among the most diverse in B.C. Lichens are a combination of fungi and algae, and they provide an essential food source for the mountain caribou. Some lichens also play a key role in providing nitrogen to the soil. During the conference, a lichenologist explained the different ways in which lichens depend on old-growth forest. I wondered in turn how the forest is dependent on the lichens? "We just don't know," he replied, pointing out how much is not yet known of a region that is as diverse as it is unique. "But there probably are dependencies." Some species, such a pin lichens, are indicators of forest antiquity; while others, such as gold dust lichens, are indicators of lichen diversity, depending on the heights to which they grow up the stems of old trees. Some lichens, for instance *Lobaria pulmonaria* (Lungwort), fix nitrogen and add it to the ecosystem. Research suggests that lichen growth rates can be up to 25 per cent per year—much higher than had previously been thought.

The keynote speakers at the 2000 conference were asked what the ICH should look like in 30 years and 300 years, and what needs to be done now to make this happen. A difficult question to answer, particularly when one considers how fast things are changing. However, two messages came through for me. First, it doesn't matter what path we take if we don't know where we're going. This emphasized the importance of good research in the ICH and the need to explore alternative methods of forest management. Secondly, it may take a couple of harvest rotations to fundamentally change the nature of the zone, meaning that even where we have already logged, we may have one more chance to get it right.

The interior rainforest is of interest to the forest industry because of its high productivity, and is of increasing interest to the tourism industry because of its unrivalled scenery and old-growth dependent species. Most importantly, it has inherent values of its own that lie outside of human use. That was something that I knew intuitively when I first walked through stands of old cedars along the lower reaches of our mountain trails, reflecting on society's changing values. I rejoiced in the shafts of sunlight piercing the canopy, streaming through morning mist to light both the mosses on the ground and the lichens draped on tree branches.

Driscoll Ridge

Driving east along Highway 16 past the Penny Access Road 98 kilometres from Prince George, and a short time later past Driscoll Creek, you may notice a steep mountain ridge rising high over the south side of the highway. Its lower slopes loom sharply above the road and are still mostly clad in the old cedar forests characteristic of the Rocky Mountain Trench. Low clouds sometimes drape the prehistoric looking cliffs and give them a mysteriously forbidding appearance. On clear days, the wooded steepness presses down on motorists who mostly drive by without giving it a glance.

Group pauses to look for pin lichens on ancient Western Red Cedar tree while bushwhacking from Highway 16, below Driscoll Ridge.

Driscoll Ridge

Activity Mountain Bushwhacking
Rating up to 10 hours or more round trip to the ridge top
Distance up to 15 km round trip depending on amount of ridge-walking
Principal Elevation Gain 900 m to the ridge top
Maps 93 H/14 Penny; 93 H/11 Dome Creek
Details Bushwhacking, ranging up to steep and difficult; no trails.

Although isolated from other peaks, and presently devoid of trails, this ridge has some of the hallmarks of the popular Viking Ridge and Sugarbowl Ridge a few kilometres west. A glance at a topographical map shows a small lake just west of the summit. My thought was that this ridge might one day afford another highway-accessible mountain trail within easy reach of Prince George. So, a few years ago I began the first of many exploratory bushwhacks there. Alone, and with friends, I made forays there both in winter and summer. I found some of the wildest, most rugged, jungle-like country in the B.C. Interior—a place to experience land as it has been for thousands of years. On the lower slopes, just off the highway, there are cathedral groves of very old cedar trees—oases nestled on hidden (easterly aspect) benches and gentle slopes amid the steeply wooded gullies and cliff bands. Some of the cedars in this interior rainforest are over a thousand years old, with one that I found with a dbh (diameter of the tree measured at breast height) of 3.5 metres, or 11 metres around.

On the ridgetop there are several kilometres of easy game trails, occasionally opening into picturesque subalpine glades, and a small open summit that affords possibly the best mountain views in the area. Although disconnected from surrounding ridges, this same isolation gives Driscoll Ridge an unsurpassed 360-degree view over the broad sweep of the northern Rockies and the surrounding Cariboo Mountains. Because of this uncommon vantage, there is a radio repeater tower on the top there that you can see from the highway, and the idea had once come up of consolidating the old fire lookouts at Slim Creek and Longworth to this place. Across the valley, directly above Penny, is Red Mountain, where record numbers of grizzly bears congregate each year, and a little farther to the northeast are the high summits of the Kakwa.

In its present trail-less state, Driscoll Ridge is not for the faint of heart. The bushwhacking is fierce, and the notorious devils club rivals its coastal counterpart in its proportions. Approached with care,

Snowshoeing beneath the ancient Western Red Cedars on Driscoll Ridge.

though, there is a natural spur route that climbs easterly with less amount of fuss. I led a hiking trip up this route once—one of those memorable jungle walks on a day too hot for climbing that helps build character and leaves the leader with an undeserved (some would say deserved) reputation. We rode out that day in the luxury of one of the hiker's retail coffee chain customer service vans, plied with coffee and donut bits. Unfortunately, perhaps thinking that this was a typical club hike, our generous patron didn't come back.

The easy route (a relative term) gains the ridgetop east of the summit on the opposite side of the lake. Seeing the attractions of a trail winding around the lake, climbing gently through flowered glades up to the top, I put serious effort into finding a westerly route up the ridge. That's where it gets ugly, with steep terrain and sometimes only devils club for handrails. It takes about a week for the body to reject all the spines left in the skin by this amazingly adapted plant. On another attempt to find a route up via the lake, I solo-bushwhacked from the highway to a point two or three kilometres west where the ridgeline drops down to only a few hundred metres above the road. After a short, nasty climb, I theorized that I would wander easily along a caribou trail that was certain to grace the ridge even at its lower levels. Instead, I found myself battling for hours through some of the thickest jungle I have ever seen. At one point, despairingly, I found myself lifted and suspended off the ground in a tangle of resilient young cedar. The only thing absent from a feeling of being caught in a giant web was the spider, and I struggled frantically to get free lest this beast of my imagination should appear!

Cathedral Grove close to home

Words and images do not do justice to the Driscoll cedars—one has to walk beneath these giants to experience the deep sense of awe, and feeling of antiquity, that invades every pore of your being. Nobody knows how old many of these trees really are. Some are thought to be over a thousand years of age, perhaps even older. They can't be aged in the normal way, as most are hollow at the core, and an extrapolation has to be employed. One has to wonder if the decomposition of their centres has given these cedars an evolutionary advantage by reducing the mass that their root systems must support. Such is the case with old English oak trees. There are many more mysteries to be uncovered in these forests, providing long-lasting research opportunities for students and faculty at UNBC.

On one hike I led a group through the cedars for more than five hours, pausing to look at an individual colossus here and there, and cathedral-like clumps of slightly younger trees. The highlight of the field tour was when Darwyn Coxson of the Faculty of Natural Resources and Environmental Studies at UNBC called us back to look at something that he described as being very rare. "These are pin lichens," he said pointing to nearly microscopic growths on an old snag sheltering beneath a large cedar. Each lichen consisted of a tiny, black speck smaller than a pinhead, supported by a hair-like stem barely two or three millimetres long. As mentioned previously, pin lichens indicate great antiquity. They are found in forests that have remained undisturbed perhaps for fifteen hundred years. I marvelled at the size contrast between the forest trees and the indicator species, barely visible under Prince George Naturalist Club member Sandra Kinsey's magnifying glass. I wondered about the impossible niche that these organisms have found in the ecology of the forest and what it means to the whole ecosystem.

The timing of the trip was good as the Ministry of Forests and the Ministry of Sustainable Resource Management was delineating "Old-growth Management Areas" for the land around Driscoll and Slim Creeks, and they asked for input from tour participants. Some of that feedback spoke of the high scientific value of the forest's closely spaced benches with uniform old-growth characteristics. The forest is highly unusual in not having previous disturbance factors such as insect or fire outbreaks as it extends up the mountain slope. The easterly facing benches have good candidate stands of trees for elevational climatic studies. The forest is unusually valuable in terms of biodiversity, and it contains several of the lichen groups that would indicate a so-called ancient forest. The high elevation benches have attributes of lichen communities from both higher and lower elevation forest types. In summary, it was felt that this area could provide an important reference site for the region and a valuable complement to ongoing silvicultural studies. Given their relatively close proximity to Prince George and Highway 16, these stands also have high value for educational use and public viewing. On the more subjective side, a word that I heard frequently during the tour was "primordial." Naturalist Sandra Hepburn summed it up well with her final comment: "We owe it to our children and grandchildren to leave some parts of this world undamaged, and this area should be one of those parts."

Two weeks after the tour I went back to fill in some gaps of my knowledge of the mountain slope. Descending through an alder glade that would be impassable without its winter snow cover, I came across a tree specimen that stopped me in my tracks. It wasn't as tall as the other old cedars, but it had a dbh of nearly three metres and was heavily buttressed at the ground. Covered from crown to roots in gnarled burls, the tree was in an uncommon situation at the bottom of the forest opening, and spoke to me of antiquity in a way that none of the others had. I didn't have a camera with me, and I would be hard-pressed to find the tree again—perhaps that is as it should be. Unthinking, I took off my gloves, laid my palms on its trunk and imagined the millennia of history that had gone by as this living sentinel stood silent watch over its glade of alders and the cedars below.

Travelling back in time among the Driscoll Cedars

Leading the Prince George Naturalists Club on the second annual snowshoe trek to see the giant cedar trees of Driscoll Ridge, I reflected that these are the best examples of cedar groves that I have found in the Rocky Mountain Trench. And one of the pleasures of accompanying the naturalists club is the members' knowledge of the natural history of this area. It isn't uncommon to get out of a vehicle on a springtime trip and have someone identify 20 or 30 species of birds within the first couple of minutes, just by sound. On this occasion, birder Laird Law lived up to his august reputation by spotting three bald eagles over the Canadian National Railway yards in Prince George before we even got halfway down First Avenue!

It had snowed the night before and was sunny as we started breaking trail through 30 centimetres of beautiful new powder. A short climb took us past giant, isolated cedar trees, near to a northern pygmy-owl that was identified by call alone, and up onto a rocky promontory that gave us a spectacular view of Red Mountain above the village of Penny. It is possible under good viewing conditions to set up a 40-power spotting scope at this place in the fall and watch the bears of author Jack Boudreau's *Grizzly Bear Mountain* from a safe vantage point as they congregate to feed on avalanche lily tubers in the distant alpine meadows. We were still only a short distance above the highway, but could already see the sweep of the Rocky Mountains and the top of Mount Sir Alexander. This wonderful pyramidal peak and its surrounding icefields remain well hidden from view at highway level by the intervening ranges, and one must climb a little in order to see them.

During the course of the next five hours, we snowshoed through grove after grove of old cedars. When we reached an elevation of 425 metres above the highway, we had lunch in an open glade with a lovely view of Sir Alexander, now revealed in all its splendour. First explored by Mary Jobe and others in the early twentieth century, the peak was declared unclimbable in 1921 following an overflight, was summitted in 1929, and is now the centrepiece of the new Kakwa

Provincial Park. It was interesting to contemplate that with everything that has happened in the world during the last two millennia, the glades through which we walked that morning remain essentially unchanged and untouched by man. It was also sobering to reflect that the future is unlikely to be as kind to this forest, and that we may be among the last people to experience it in its original state.

Descending via a different route through the deep powder snow, it was time for everyone to rediscover their not so inner child as we carved winding luge runs down the steep terrain. The last members of the group sat or reclined on their snowshoes as they rocketed down the now slick, twisting half-pipes amid cries of laughter and the cascading snow.

The Longworth Lookout

Another opportunity to explore the old-growth forests of the interior wet belt is along the northern slopes of the Rocky Mountain Trench above the communities of Longworth, Penny, Dome Creek, and Crescent Spur. These south-facing slopes harbour larger trees than are typically found on the south side of the valley.

Primary access to the area is via the Giscome Road that branches north from Highway 16 just before Tabor Mountain, and winds through the rural communities of Willow River and Giscome. From Giscome, one has the first view of the McGregor Mountains across Eaglet Lake, and as the road twists around the shoreline it is worth watching for eagles, as the lake is well named. Continuing on, the Upper Fraser Road heads east through the communities of Aleza Lake, Upper Fraser, and McGregor as the hills appear to grow ever larger. Upper Fraser, until recently home to a large sawmill, offers one of the best views of the approaching mountains, while the once thriving company logging townsite of McGregor lies nearly empty close to their base. An alternate access, which is more convenient if

---

Longworth Lookout

Activity Mountain Hiking
Rating 7 to 9 hours round trip
Distance 10 km round trip
Principal Elevation Gain 1,035 m to the lookout
Maps 93 H/14 Penny
Details A good switchback trail leads from just north of the community of Longworth to the alpine ridge, and from there to the lookout building on the summit.

travelling from the east, is north on the Bowron Forest Service Road from Highway 16, almost 69 kilometres from Prince George, or eight kilometres east of Purden Lake.

An hour into the trip, the Hansard Bridge provides a crossing of the Fraser River at McGregor. This bridge is reputedly the only one of its kind in Canada where the highway shares the Canadian National Railway main line. Because of this interesting feature, safety measures require that the bridge be manned and periodically inspected 24 hours per day. The traffic light sequence is a long six minutes (more if a train comes through) which affords a wonderful leg stretch and bio break early in the morning. Once on the bridge, it is important to resist the sensation that you are driving a train when you reach the end of the bridge and the road swings away from the tracks! This unique arrangement may come to an end in 2004 or 2005 when a new Hansard bridge is scheduled to take highway traffic off the railway bridge.

In recent years, the unpaved road from McGregor along the north side of the Fraser River has been extended beyond Sinclair Mills. It is in good condition as far as Longworth, and a little rougher to Penny. After crossing the tracks in Longworth and driving straight ahead for a short distance, a track leads into the forest to a sizeable parking area at the Longworth Lookout trailhead. Until the last few years, the lookout trail was in poor shape, and not easily accessible. With the opening of the road to Longworth, work was done to clear the old trail. Originally built as a horse trail to service the fire lookout in the

Group shelters in lee of the old Longworth Lookout building on a blustery day. Fraser River below.

days before helicopters, it has many switchbacks that give it an easy grade. This makes it potentially one of the better mountain trails close to Prince George. Even if you don't climb the mountain, the trip is worthwhile for the historic drive and low elevation walk though the first few kilometres of old-growth cedar. If you go on, a climb of 1000 vertical metres leads to the first alpine meadow, beside the burned out remains of an old log cabin. A short distance past this, the trail climbs onto a pleasant alpine ridge, and from there to the lookout on the summit.

On a hike in mid-July, the weather was wet and misty as befits a rainforest. In the alpine meadows, the avalanche lilies were blooming amid remnant snow patches. I was inspired as I walked through this scene to compose a Haiku: a Japanese style of verse used to capture the simplicity of a moment in nature.

Avalanche Lily
Drooping down toward the moss
Yellow in the mist

A little farther on and slightly off the trail below the summit, there is an elaborate dog grave that reads:

In memory of
"MOJO"
A German Shepherd
Killed by Wolves
July 10/72
A good and
faithful dog

The lookout is well-placed, offering commanding views across the Rocky Mountain Trench toward the Cariboo Mountains. On an earlier climb to this place I was greeted by the resident fire lookout, Crescent Spur pioneer, Elisabeth Spaude Aubrey. Eager for company, she plied my companion and I with freshly made cake and coffee as we listened with fascination to her tales of the area. To be greeted at the top of a mountain with such hospitality is a rare experience that I don't expect to have repeated often.

Skiing on the Bearpaw Ridge on a four-day traverse via the Longworth Lookout.

A few years earlier, before the road was pushed through to Longworth, I was one of a group of six people who completed a four-day ski traverse of the Bearpaw Ridge in March. We were dropped off at the Pass Lake Forest Service Road 11 kilometres east of McGregor at 8 pm on a Thursday evening. From there we made an easy two-hour ski climb by headlamp up to the subalpine meadows where we spent the first night. After traversing many wonderful kilometres of ridge the next day in perfect weather, Friday night was spent in snow caves on the ridge top, looking across toward the Bowron Valley. Saturday was spent travelling in deteriorating weather and increasingly complex, avalanche prone terrain, to reach the Longworth Lookout. There we spent Saturday night, cozily ensconced in the mountaintop structure by pre-arrangement with the forest service. A full-scale blizzard raged outside and we wondered what the residents of the then isolated community below might have thought about the ghostly lights above. Descending into Longworth the next day, we were surprised to learn that the ice had gone out on the Fraser River a week ago, and we had no way to cross to our pre-arranged Sunday afternoon pickup. Faced with the prospect of a long wait and having to flag down a train early the following morning, we negotiated an exciting boat crossing over the ice shelves and open water of the Fraser River from some obliging Longworth residents.

More communities of the Trench

Back on Highway 16, the scenic Slim Creek Highway Rest Area offers picnic facilities and an opportunity to experience this beautiful mountain river in its wild-looking setting. In late summer, one can sometimes see the salmon running here. From this point on, the old Fraser River communities are mostly on the south side of the river, so detours by vehicle through the villages of Dome Creek, Bend, and Crescent Spur north of the highway offer interesting side-trips. With their sense of isolation and stepping back in time, these communities have the same feel as some of the smaller Gulf islands off B.C.'s coast. And like island communities, these places are situated in powerfully beautiful settings that have attracted a wide range of rugged individuals and back-to-the-land people over the past few decades.

Ptarmigan Creek

Since there are few other points of reference along Highway 16 East, I usually note my progress while driving between Prince George and McBride by the river and creek crossings. Travelling from west to east, they are the Willow River, Wansa and Vama Vama Creeks, Bowron River, Kenneth Creek, Sugarbowl Creek, Hungary Creek, Driscoll Creek, Slim Creek, Dome Creek, Ptarmigan Creek, Catfish Creek, Snowshoe Creek, Goat River, West Twin Creek, Clyde Creek, and nearing McBride, the Dore River. All of the mountain watersheds associated with these creeks on the south side of the Rocky Mountain Trench offer possibilities for off-trail exploration in wild and rugged surroundings. For example, I have bushwhacked both on foot and skis several times into the high country above Catfish Creek, and between Snowshoe and Ptarmigan Creeks—spectacular country, all of it, and prime grizzly bear habitat. On one occasion, I was sitting on a promontory overlooking Snowshoe Lake and I dislodged a large rock that went bouncing into the forest below. Since this was high, untrammelled country and I was sure there was no chance that anyone was below me, I didn't bother to shout, "Rock!" However, it turned out that a grizzly bear was taking an afternoon siesta in the scrub among the trees. Fortunately, the rock did not hit the bear, but I had a definite sense that the animal thought me impolite as rocks, dirt, vegetation, and the bear went flying in different directions. This was a lesson to be careful with loose rocks in the mountains even if there are no other people around, and a reminder that we share the outdoors with many other species.

Perhaps the most interesting of all the aforementioned creeks is Ptarmigan Creek. However, before venturing into its spectacular upper valley, two mountain trails, and new provincial park, let us first consider a place of uncommon beauty situated on the creek, just off the highway.

Ptarmigan Falls

West of where the highway descends to cross Ptarmigan Creek, a short side trip of 500 metres north on the Walker Creek Forest Service Road and northeast for another 600 metres along a narrow branch road, brings you to the top of the hill above Ptarmigan Falls. This is the site of one of the interior's most spectacular waterfalls and B.C.'s first independent power plant. The site is unmarked and gated, and the top of the falls, downstream from the hydro dam, can only be reached by bushwhacking above the creek. Considerable caution is absolutely essential because of fast currents, especially during high water, and there are extreme, unprotected drop-offs above the falls. Because of this exposure, ice climbers sometimes use the falls during winter months. This also means that visitors to Ptarmigan Falls could not be protected without changing the character of the site, and so it remains in a semi-wild state. The falls are composed of an upper and lower section, and a safer way to view them is to approach through the old limestone gravel pit below—it is accessed downhill and farther north along the Walker Creek Road. Here, the limestone is of such high quality that, as well as providing road and railway ballast, it was once used to supply the lime kilns in local pulpmills. I was one of the last people to see the area above the falls in its natural state, as my first foray into the area coincided with the site clearing for the power plant's intake channel.

Upper Ptarmigan Creek

A few kilometres east of the highway crossing of Ptarmigan Creek and roughly 160 kilometres from Prince George, is a side road that leads south to the Ptarmigan Creek and Erg Mountain trails. This is one of the new provincial parks recommended by the Prince George Land and Resource Management Plan in 1999. The access road winds in for about six kilometres to Ptarmigan Creek, where it now ends. Along the way it crosses three culverts that have all washed out at various times in the past, owing to spring flooding and beaver activity. Repair time generally depends on what access is currently needed for forestry purposes, so be prepared for an extra two or three kilometre

The lower of the three Hammell Lakes, looking towards Boxcar Mountain.

Upper Ptarmigan Creek

Activity Backpacking
Rating 3 or more days
Distance 22 km round trip to the first (lowest) of the three Hammell Lakes from the first crossing of Ptarmigan Creek.
Principal Elevation Gain 630 m to the first (lowest) of the three Hammell Lakes from the first crossing of Ptarmigan Creek, and another 400 m to the highest lake.
Maps 93 H/10 Loos; 93 H/7 Goat River
Details Ptarmigan Creek is accessed by a gravel road running south from Highway 16, a few hundred metres west of the highway crossing of Catfish Creek, or nearly 10 kilometres west of the Crescent Spur Road. The route involves several crossings of Ptarmigan Creek that are not possible during spring runoff without bridges that are presently (in 2004) mostly washed away. The route up the Ptarmigan Creek valley is highly avalanche prone during the winter (not a safe season to travel there) and as a result the trail is typically overgrown with lush, fast-growing vegetation during the summer, with grizzly bears being common. This is not a trip for the faint of heart, and is best done with a strong group, but the rewards at Hammell Lakes are worth the effort for those who persevere.

walk to Ptarmigan Creek. From there, the road used to continue for a further three kilometres, through a gravel pit used in 1960s highway construction, to the start of both trails. However, Ptarmigan Creek is a wild, glacier and mountain snowpack-fed creek that experiences periodic floods and continuously modifies its channel. The old road bridge that we used for many years has long since been carried away, as have various log crossings and a footbridge. A forest recreation site there was also washed out and is now abandoned.

If you are fortunate and are able to drive all the way to Ptarmigan Creek, you then have to find a way across on foot. As of writing, there is no bridge crossing, and the river must be forded. This is impossible to do safely during spring freshet and should only be attempted in summer or fall when water levels are low. If you find that water levels are too high, an alternate bushwhacking trip can be considered by following the left fork in the road just before Ptarmigan Creek, up into the Catfish and Snowshoe drainages described earlier. If you do cross the creek, choose a route where the water level is not much more than knee deep. Use a sturdy stick; carry spare shoes for the crossing; loosen pack straps so that the pack can be easily discarded

Outflow creek from the upper of the three Hammell Lakes – looking towards the small icefield west of the Goat River in the heart of the Cariboo Mountains.

if necessary; assist smaller and less experienced people; and be aware that the glacial melt cycle may mean higher water later in the day.

An amusing (in retrospect) incident occurred at this site a few years ago after the bridge had become unusable and before it had completely washed away. An individual, who had a reputation for getting his four-wheel drive SUV stuck in odd places, tried to drive across the remains of the bridge in order to facilitate a quick start to his hike. Halfway across the structure, his vehicle predictably became stuck and, with his wife opting to stay in the truck, the man started out on the six-kilometre walk to the highway, and a 60-kilometre hitchhike into McBride to fetch a tow truck. While he was gone on his mercy mission, a grizzly bear emerged from the bush and approached the vehicle that was stranded precariously in the middle of the remains of the bridge. The bear walked around the vehicle peering in at the woman inside for some time before eventually leaving. The story doesn't mention what words were exchanged between the couple when the man eventually returned to rescue his wife and retrieve their vehicle.

Walking from the creek crossing to the trailhead affords a good view of the upper Ptarmigan Valley. Always impressive, it is also one of the first places around Prince George to show fall colours because of cold air flowing down from the glaciers at the head of the valley. Shortly after entering the original old-growth forest, the two trailheads are reached. The Ptarmigan Creek trail descends to cross the west branch of the creek, while the Erg Mountain trail, described in the next section, contours to the right before starting its legendary steep ascent.

The Ptarmigan Creek trail is always problematic, as it has to make at least four crossings of the creek in order to ascend a valley that is wracked every year by avalanches and the spring freshet. Because of these avalanches, there are few trees in the upper reaches of the valley. Instead there is a two-metre high jungle of summer vegetation that defies most attempts to keep a trail open. Grizzly bears are common, the metabolites present in cow parsnip plants can cause serious blistering if bruised or broken plants contact the skin, and stinging nettles make their presence known immediately. Avalanches make the valley dangerous for winter and early spring travel, while in summer the trail doesn't yet get enough use to keep the vegetation down. Character-building travails aside, the summer or fall hiker or climber who perseveres is rewarded by a beautiful series of hanging valleys and three subalpine and alpine lakes at successively higher elevations below 2,404-metre Mount Hammell. This technical peak is only 20 kilometres from the northeast corner of Isaac Lake in the world-renowned Bowron Lake Provincial Park. For the serious adventurer, the rugged mountains and glaciers northwest of the Goat River also provide the backdrop to the Hammell Lakes, and at least one local individual has traversed this mini icefield to the Goat River in recent years.

Erg Mountain

The elevation gain is 1,500 vertical metres from Ptarmigan Creek to the summit of Erg Mountain, providing nearly a vertical mile of hiking and non-technical scrambling. Alternatively, the alpine meadows and lake can be a destination in their own right at only 1,000 metres elevation gain, and most of the mountain's outstanding views can be realized from the ridge at 1,200 metres. The trail is very steep, but is generally distinct until one reaches the subalpine meadows. From there it is marked by a combination of ribbons, blazes, and rock cairns. Dr. Bob Nelson, who taught physics and astronomy at CNC in Prince George, gave the unusual name to this mountain. Bob felt that this worthy peak and the nearby "Joule" Mountain deserved to be recognized as physical units of measurement. The word "Erg" (centimetre-gram-second unit of energy) is derived from the Greek "Ergon" meaning WORK, which is certainly what you need to do to get to the top! This is a serious, but non-technical mountain, and, as with many things, the rewards are worth the effort for someone who is in reasonable physical condition.

For a person just starting mountain hiking, it may be better to allow a few trips on easier trails to build up leg muscles before tackling this one. As well as its unsurpassed views of the Cariboo Mountains, Rocky Mountains, Mount Sir Alexander, and the Rocky Mountain Trench, this is an excellent place to see wildlife. I encountered my first two grizzly bears at the alpine lake while camped here with my children in 1983—the first of many such sightings both here and elsewhere in our local mountains. A few years later on the ridgetop, I was privileged to watch a rare scene when a boar grizzly bear mounted a sow in the meadows directly below me. In 1999, I surprised a large grizzly bear at a distance of 50 metres while descending through the meadows with one companion, an interaction that clearly annoyed the bear. Two years later, two groups of hikers collectively saw five caribou, one wolverine, three grizzly bears, and a mountain goat from the summit ridge all within the space of two hours.

Perhaps the finest day that I have ever spent in the mountains anywhere was in June in the mid-1990s when I went to Erg Mountain with the man who, 20 years before, had given it its name and had led the trail-clearing. Bob Nelson and I were alone, and the snow had melted from the alpine meadows four weeks earlier than usual. What we found was entirely unexpected. The alpine meadows were carpeted

Erg Mountain

Activity Mountain Hiking and Backpacking
Rating 9 to 12 hours round trip to the summit
Distance 16 km round trip to the summit from the crossing of Ptarmigan Creek
Principal Elevation Gain 1,500 m to the summit from the crossing of Ptarmigan Creek
Map 93 H/10 Loos
Details Erg Mountain is one of the most spectacular mountain trails in the Prince George area, and, like the Ptarmigan Creek trail, is accessed by a gravel road running south from Highway 16, a few hundred metres west of the highway crossing of Catfish Creek. The route involves first crossing Ptarmigan Creek, which is not possible during spring runoff without a bridge. As the book goes to press in 2004, the most recent bridge has been washed out for several years, and one should wait until later in the season when the water is more fordable. Watch out for grizzly bears both on the trail and in the alpine meadows above.

*Author's faithful dog on the Erg Mountain Summit Ridge. Starsky was rescued
from his early life on a short chain in an east Toronto backyard
to enjoy the very best that Canada's outdoors has to offer.*

with the best display of flowers that I have ever seen anywhere;
so alive and so fresh that we moved with exaggerated slowness to
try and avoid treading on a single plant. As we climbed the ridge
overlooking the spectacular Cariboo Range to the south, and Mount
Sir Alexander to the north, a hoary marmot (usually shy animals)
allowed us to approach within touching distance. The animal had
sensed our oneness with the world that day and perceived no threat
from us. Neither Bob nor I were in the slightest hurry, nor wanted the
day to end—we didn't summit until late afternoon, and it was 11 pm
when we ate supper back in Prince George. Relishing one of the peak
experiences of my life, on my favorite trail, I mentally thanked Bob for
having pioneered it.

Approaching Mount Robson from the north, looking across Adolphus Lake en route from Mount Holmes to Mount Robson.

Robson Valley

The Robson Valley is generally understood to be the stretch of the Rocky Mountain Trench around McBride, Dunster, Tête Jaune Cache, Mount Robson, and Valemount. For the purposes of this book, I will assume that it starts east of Ptarmigan Creek. The valley contains the Canadian National Railway; Highway 16, whose descriptive name, the Yellowhead Highway is taken from Tête Jaune; forest industries; valley farming; cottage industries; and increasingly, recreation and tourism. There are many mountain trails and other recreational opportunities in the Robson Valley (following are a few highlights). For more information, a Web search on any of the place names listed above, or a visit to one of the information centres in the valley communities will produce a bonanza of possibilities.

The National Hiking Trail

Still under development at the time of writing, Canada's *Sentier Pedestre* National Hiking Trail is being built under the auspices of Hike Canada *En Marche*. Part of writing about something in such a rapid state of change is that the details given cannot always keep up to the reality on the ground. But the following section will give you some starting points, and is thoroughly in line with the book's theme of self-exploration.

The National Hiking Trail will enter British Columbia north of the Robson Valley, after crossing the Rocky Mountains either through Alberta's Willmore Wilderness Provincial Park or more likely through Jasper National Park. The present leaning of Parks Canada is to *not* designate a specific route through the national parks, so as not to overload particular trails. Instead, hikers will likely be encouraged to decide their own route through Jasper and Banff National Parks after consulting maps and parks personnel. The preferred entry point into B.C. as this book goes to press is through Bess Pass at the head of the Holmes River, from where the trail will cross the Rocky Mountain Trench and the Fraser River at the community of Crescent Spur. The proposed alpine section of the route between Bess Pass and Chalco Creek, north of the Holmes River, crosses many kilometres of lovely open meadowland, and is further discussed in the section on the Holmes River. In 2003, a predominantly alpine route was completed between Chalco Creek, a tributary of the lower Holmes River, and East Twin Creek, a tributary of the Fraser River. From East Twin Creek to Crescent Spur, it follows a route along the north side of the Fraser River. South from Crescent Spur, the National Trail crosses Highway 16 to join the newly restored historic Goat River Trail that cuts through the Cariboo Mountains to Barkerville.

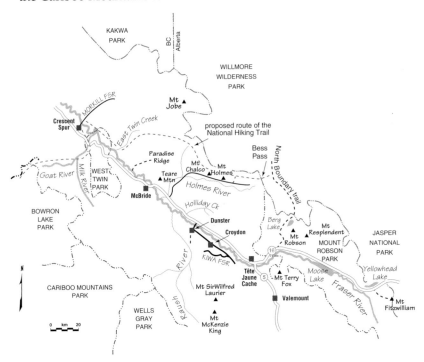

The section that is presently called the Lower Goat River Trail begins at the end of Prospect Road in Crescent Spur. From there, it is 11 kilometres to the Goat River Rest Area on Highway 16. The trail crosses the Goat River on the Highway 16 bridge, and immediately goes up a cutbank and into the bush. From there, it is another three kilometres to a logging block at the six-kilometre mark on the Goat River Forest Service Road. Another trailhead is proposed at this six-kilometre point on the Goat River Road, to be called "Kopas Camp" after Cliff and Ruth Kopas, authors of *Packhorses to the Pacific*. At the time of writing, however, one must follow the Goat River Forest Service Road between Kopas Camp and the Milk River trailhead, described below. About half of the 14-kilometre Lower Goat River Trail between Crescent Spur and Kopas Camp is in the new West Twin Provincial Park. The trail is cut out and marked, but it will be greatly improved in 2004, and better signage will be placed under an authorizing agreement with B.C. Parks. From the Prospect Road trailhead in Crescent Spur, back to the old road along the northeast side of the Fraser River, is also roadway, with no alternative currently in sight. The trailhead there will be the eastern side of the bridge carrying the Morkill Forest Service Road across the Fraser River. There is also quite a stretch of active roadway to walk along the Mountain View and the East Twin Forest Service Roads.

The National Hiking Trail includes several historic segments in B.C.'s Interior, thus providing opportunities both for an appreciation of Canada's and First Nations' heritage, and for recreation. Part of the 1861 Gold Rush Trail, for example, is followed from Barkerville to Quesnel. North of Quesnel, the Collins Telegraph Trail connects

Boulder Mountain / Goat River Trail

Activity Mountain Hiking / Hiking
Rating 8 to 10 hours round trip to the summit of Boulder Mountain
Distance 14 km round trip to the summit of Boulder Mountain
Principal Elevation Gain 1,200 m to the summit of Boulder Mountain
Map 93 H/7 Goat River
Details A mostly good trail, with superb views from the summit of Boulder Mountain over the Rocky Mountain Trench and the Goat River Valley. The trail is accessed south from about 1 km along the Goat River Forest Service Road, south from Highway 97, east of the Goat River highway crossing.

with the Nuxalk Carrier Grease Trail near the Blackwater River, as described in the section "South from Prince George." The Nuxalk Carrier Grease Trail, or Alexander Mackenzie Heritage Trail as it is otherwise known, actually starts 36 kilometres east of its intersection with the Telegraph Trail, at the confluence of the Blackwater and Fraser Rivers south of Prince George. From the Telegraph Trail crossing, it heads another 311 kilometres west to the Bella Coola Valley, where Highway 20 connects it to tidewater at Bella Coola. From there, the trail will pick up on northern Vancouver Island and run down the length of the Island to end in Victoria. The National Hiking Trail will provide a path for pedestrian traffic from Canada's East to West Coast, both complementing and contrasting the Trans-Canada Trail that crosses B.C. in the south. This latter portion is intended for multi-use, and in some places, for motorized recreational use. The National Hiking Trail will therefore afford a way of seeing Canada as its original peoples and many of its early explorers did, on foot. Best of all, it cuts through the area covered by this book, both east and south of the city of Prince George.

Goat River Trail

The Goat River Trail has been re-opened as a historic recreational trail that is part of the National Hiking Trail. According to Roy Howard of Dunster, who worked on both the Goat River Trail restoration and the National Hiking Trail, the original trail was established in 1886 between Barkerville and the Fraser River during the latter part of the Cariboo Gold Rush. It was first cut in 1886 by a crew answering to John Bowron, Gold Commissioner of the Cariboo, and it was very likely a First Nations route before that. Between 1886 and 1913, the trail was well-used by miners and packers to transport supplies between McBride and the Cariboo gold fields. Once the railroad was completed in 1914, the trail saw less frequent use, although miners were prospecting significant claims in the valley as late as the 1930s. Howard goes on to say that the upper Goat watershed with its stunning mountain vistas, provides an essential piece of wildlife connectivity that contains grizzly and black bears, wolves, wolverines, fishers, mountain caribou, moose, mountain goats, harlequin ducks, as well as spawning Chinook salmon and bull trout. The trailhead for the upper Goat is 13 kilometres south of Highway 16 on the Goat River Forest Service Road near its confluence with the Milk River. It is slightly over 25 kilometres from there to the Bowron Lake Provincial Park boundary on the eastern side of the new Wolverine addition that makes up the northern tip of the park. From there it is another 25 kilometres to the Littlefield Creek trailhead near Kruger Lake, a few kilometres north of the first leg of the world famous Bowron Lake Park canoe circuit.

West Twin Provincial Park

A kilometre south of Highway 16 on the south side of the Goat River Forest Service Road is the access to the Boulder Mountain trail in West Twin Provincial Park—one of the best mountain trails east of Prince George. In the meadows below the ridge lie the remains of a tiny mud-floored cabin where, roughly 25 years ago, a composer from Toronto is reputed to have spent several winter-long sojourns, working on his music in splendid isolation. From the summit of Boulder Mountain, there are good views of both the Rocky Mountain Trench and the Goat River Valley, through which run sections of the National Hiking Trail just described.

Rainbow falls, a short walk in McBride.

146

Rainbow Falls – McBride and Teare Mountains

There are a number of accessible peaks overlooking the town of McBride, some two hundred kilometres east of Prince George. Lucille Mountain and Bell Mountain on the south side of the valley, and McBride Peak and Teare Mountain on the north side, have rough road access almost up to alpine elevations. My favourite peaks are on the north side and are reached via the aptly named Mountainview Road. They are accessed just east of the town shortly after Highway 16 crosses to the north side of the Fraser River. A short distance along Mountainview Road is a narrow side road called Rainbow Road, which very soon makes a sharp turn to the left (west.) From this corner, one can access a short, steep walk up to Rainbow Falls. If you have time for just a quick stop in McBride, this walk affords a very nice half-hour exercise break, with a scenic waterfall and good views across the valley from above the falls.

From its first bend, Rainbow Road starts a long, narrow, often precarious zigzag up the mountain. You may be able to get part way up the hill with a two-wheel drive vehicle, but I almost lost a new car here a few years ago when its wheels caught the soft outside edge of the road; I would definitely recommend four-wheel drive only. The road terminates above treeline, just below an abandoned fire lookout on the slopes of McBride Peak. From this point, there is easy access to the alpine meadows (designated an ecological reserve) and the 2,270-

McBride and Teare Mountains

Activity Mountain Hiking and Backpacking

Rating 3 to 4 hours round trip to the summit of Teare mountain from the top of the road (summer, four-wheel drive recommended).

Distance From the top of the road 3 km round trip to the summit of McBride Peak and 9 km round trip to the summit of Teare Mountain.

Principal Elevation Gain From the top of the road 440 m to the summit of McBride Peak and 750 m round trip to the summit of Teare Mountain.

Map 93 H/8 McBride

Details There are no trails, but many route possibilities for a day or overnight hike exist in this alpine area, with superb views of McBride, the Rocky Mountain Trench, and the wild mountain country to the north. It is accessed via Mountainview and Rainbow Roads as described in the text.

Group hiking north along a ridge from Teare Mountain above McBride.

metre McBride Peak above. An alternate four-kilometre trail leads southeast down the ridge and climbs up to 2,438-metre Mount Teare. Other ridge walks head northeast from both peaks, providing lots to do for either a day trip or an overnight stay.

Paradise Ridge

Thirteen kilometres west along Mountainview Road from the Rainbow Road turnoff is the Paradise Ridge trailhead. This narrow, easy grade trail provides access to the west end of the same ridge that McBride and Teare Mountains occupy to the east. The difference is that the Paradise Trail climbs all the way from the valley bottom, offering rewards of more exercise and a greater sense of accomplishment. As it is a south-facing slope that loses its snowpack early in the season, Paradise Ridge is a good early summer mountain hike. Starting out at dawn is desirable on a hot sunny day, so it may be best to drive to McBride the night before. Early season mosquitoes on the lower part of the trail can be fierce, as the June hatchlings belong to that first hunger-crazed bunch of the year. By keeping on the move and flailing ones arms around however, it is possible to compensate for any lack of foresight in not bringing insect repellent.

The trail starts on an abandoned vehicle track in old-growth forest. The fresh smells of the forest are everywhere as the track works its way up the mountain between Coyote and Beaverdam Creeks. Walking through a small clearing in the early summer of 1996, I heard a slight rustle in the brush. Not more than 10 feet to my right was a yearling black bear cub. "Where's Mama?" I wondered. For the next kilometre, I kept a wary eye out as the old road skirted a large avalanche chute with lots of fresh bear sign. A mountain creek bubbled nearby, then as I left the area the trail climbed away from the gully, and the forest became drier and more open. There were now good views of the lush green valley below and the snow-capped Cariboo Mountains to the south. The Fraser River was high, and an old oxbow, or cut-off, lake was temporarily rejoined with its source.

About halfway up the mountain, a ribbon indicated a narrow trail taking off to the right. Years past, somebody had put a lot of work into grubbing out this trail, producing switchbacks with an easy grade to the ridge, over a vertical kilometre above the valley. The snow was almost gone except for the last 100 metres. It then alternated between a crampon-hard surface and exhausting waist-deep mush. Reaching the top, there were seemingly endless ridge-walking possibilities and superb views all around. The temperature was near freezing and the wind howled with alternating snow squalls and sunny breaks. Quite a change from the valley I had left behind. Once the trail gained the ridge, there were long walks available in several directions, including 2,301-metre Mount Monroe, two kilometres to the southeast. Although I haven't yet done it, one could presumably connect Mount Monroe with McBride Peak on either a very long day hike or an overnight trip. Mount Monroe was officially named on March 12, 1965 in memory of Canadian Army Lance Corporal Stanley James Monroe of McBride who died in a drowning accident on July 1st, 1942, age 24, while serving with the Canadian Forestry Corps in Val Cartier, Quebec.

Paradise Ridge

Activity Mountain Hiking
Rating 7 to 8 hours round trip to the ridge, plus time spent hiking the ridges and meadows on top, or visiting the summit of Mount Monroe.
Distance 12 km round trip to the ridge, and a further 4 km round trip to the summit of Mount Monroe.
Principal Elevation Gain 1,235 m to the ridge, and a further 380 m round trip to the summit of Mount Monroe.
Maps 93 H/8 McBride
Details The trailhead is accessed almost 14 km west along Mountainview Road from its intersection with Highway 16 just east of McBride. The trail grade makes this a moderately easy mountain hike with a big payoff.

The climb to the ridge takes about three hours, plus a few hours on top to hike around and enjoy lunch, then another two hours to descend—a good day, leaving ample time for supper in McBride and a two-hour drive back to Prince George. On one of my hikes to Paradise Ridge, I saw several hoary marmots and one mountain goat on the mountain, and on the trail down I nearly walked into a deer. On the drive out, I had to brake hard to avoid hitting two brand new tiny black bear cubs that mama, hidden in the bush, was presumably summoning across the road. Farther along, between the Bowron and Willow Rivers, a grizzly bear ran across the highway only a few metres in front of me. This was truly paradise.

Holliday Creek and Stone Arch

Twenty or so kilometres east of McBride is the very steep Holliday Creek Trail that leads to a natural stone arch where one also has a very good chance of seeing mountain goats. The trail is accessed via a short unpaved road that branches north off Highway 16 just west of Holliday Creek, which is alternately known as Baker Creek. Like the Paradise Ridge Trail, this is also a south-facing slope and warrants an early start on a sunny day.

The trail continues for about four kilometres gently climbing a beautiful mountain river valley. This part of the walk is worthwhile for its own sake if you just have a couple of hours to spare. Then, after crossing a side creek that flows under the natural arch higher up the mountain, the trail begins to climb rapidly. From this point on, the route is not for the weak of heart, as it is about as steep as you would want to attempt without a rope. Ski poles or trekking poles are definitely worthwhile to help spread some of the effort to your arms on the ascent, and to help you keep a good footing on the way down. The trick is to go as slow as necessary to keep your pulse at an appropriate level for your age, and to rest as often as leg muscles demand.

Eventually, the trail levels out on a sparsely treed open ridge where you can look across to the natural arch bridging the gully to your left. It is common, here, to see mountain goats on the surrounding slopes. On one occasion, we surprised a goat at very close range—it had been sleeping in a hollow and was alarmed to wake up and hear people talking nearby before disappearing at a high rate of speed into impossibly steep terrain. Freshly shed goat hair was everywhere on the nearby bushes. The route affords magnificent views back into the Rocky Mountain Trench, as well as of the surrounding mountains. One can continue on to the alpine, although there is a short exposed stretch where it is necessary to keep to the right of the spur ridge,

Holliday (Baker) Creek and Stone Arch

Activity Hiking and Mountain Hiking
Rating 6 to 8 hours round trip to the stone arch
Distance 12 km round trip to the stone arch
Principal Elevation Gain 950 m to the stone arch
Map 83 E/4 Croydon
Details Take the side road north of Highway 16, half a kilometre west of the highway crossing of Holliday Creek. After 600 metres, take the right fork to the Holliday (Baker) Creek trailhead. The first three or four kilometres of the trail stays in the lush valley bottom and is a worthwhile hike in its own right. After that it forks left and commences a very steep climb to the stone arch.

across and below a few steep scree slopes. Provided you pick your route carefully, it can be crossed safely. Higher up, there are goat trail "highways" snaking around the mountain as far as the eye can see. They are probably centuries old.

Holmes River – Beaver River

The Rockies begin to close in on the Cariboo Mountains east of McBride as the Rocky Mountain Trench starts to narrow. Just past McBride the road dips down to cross the Holmes River. Known locally as the Beaver River, its wide, clear, mountain waters are a major input to the Fraser at this early stage in its journey to the sea. On one side is a scenic trail that follows the riverbank to Beaver Falls. On the other, a forest service road starts its long journey up the Holmes River valley to Bess Pass on the border with Jasper National Park and Alberta. Two kilometres from Highway 16 a campground is situated on a scenic bend of the Holmes River. Forty kilometres farther on is a mountain trail known as "Blueberry" that leads to a beautiful alpine area close to the headwaters of the Jackpine River and Alberta's Willmore Wilderness. I was once dropped off by helicopter here, on the slopes of Mount Holmes, and with one companion whom I had met the evening before, did an eight-day backpack to Mount Robson. Our route took us through the historic Jackpine Pass, Bess Pass, then south on Jasper National Park's North Boundary Trail along the Smoky River, to approach Mount Robson from the north side. The logistics for a trip of this magnitude are really handy—you can leave one vehicle at the airport in McBride, and another vehicle only an hour down the road at the Berg Lake trailhead in Mount Robson Park.

Mount Holmes to Mount Robson

Activity Backpacking

Rating 2 to 4 days round trip on the Blueberry Trail; 7 to 10 days from Mount Holmes to Mount Robson

Distance 14 km round trip to the alpine lake above the Blueberry Trail

Principal Elevation Gain 930 m to the alpine lake above the Blueberry Trail

Maps 83 E/5 Chalco Mountain (only this map sheet is required for Mount Holmes and the Blueberry Trail); 83 E/6 Twintree Lake; 83 E/3 (East) Mount Robson.

Details The Blueberry trailhead is located 44 km along the Holmes (Beaver) River Forest Service Road, on the north side.

Dunster

Past the Holmes River, a side valley breaks away southeast from the Trench. The largely undeveloped Raush Valley was the subject of considerable debate in the Robson Valley Land Use Plan in the 1990s. The ridge that now separates the Fraser River from the Raush Valley widens as the community of Dunster comes into sight. Travelling that stretch of highway in early July, nearing the community hall, stuffed figures appear to be holding up some of the highway signs. I have now arrived for the annual Dunster Ice Cream Social.

Without question, the best time to undertake a hiking trip in this part of the Robson Valley is on the Saturday in late June or early July when the ice cream social is held. Facing a hard climb the next day, from a strictly calorific point of view, one need not hold back on the all-you-can-eat homemade pie and ice cream. Held at the Dunster Community Hall on Highway 16 across from the Dunster access road, it is one of the big social events of the year for the Robson Valley — people regularly travel from as far as Prince George to attend. It is both a fundraiser and a potluck, and anyone who is willing to contribute a homemade pie is welcome to do so. And, with the entire community in a friendly competition for the best country pie, need I say more? I'm not sure if it is the hike that is the excuse for the ice cream social or vice versa, but either way, the combination is splendid! At the social's turn-of-the-century event in 2000, there was an old-style village carnival atmosphere. Federal political hopefuls worked the crowd, and people lined up to sign the *B.C. Millennium Book,* and to buy raffle tickets for the millennium quilt on display. Freshly cut grass surrounds an ample-

Start of 100-km trek to Mount Robson from Mount Holmes. On gaining the pass below Mount Holmes, our destination is visible to the east. The route follows closely the intended route of the National Hiking Trail.

sized building, bordered by lush cedar trees—all set against the still snowy backdrop of the Cariboo Mountains. The doors were not yet open and hundreds of people lined up on both sides of the hall. The cedar trees were decorated with children climbing as high as eight metres off the ground in the thick, resilient foliage. People wondered who would be the first to fall out this year—somebody usually does. Typically, about five hundred people attend the annual fundraiser for the Dunster Community Association. A few dollars (and whatever else you care to donate) buys you all the pie, cake, and ice cream you can eat in two hours. Many residents of Dunster bake and contribute up to eight pies each. It is a tall order to feed over five hundred people all they can eat, but the organizers never run short, and there is a lot of friendly competition and pride in what they produce. All the pies that I tried were wonderful, but my favorites were the raspberry crumble squares and the indescribable rhubarb meringue! I struggled with thoughts of what constitutes a healthy diet as I ate five pieces of pie with ice cream in two helpings. Is it more or less harmful, I wondered, to eat this amount of dessert in one sitting versus spreading it out over several weeks? Nobody seems to know—perhaps there is a dietary researcher looking for volunteers? One hopes that the mountain hiking exercise the following day will suck all the bad lipids out of the arteries. There are many trails to choose from for that purpose, as discussed above, and to these must be added the Dunster Trail.

153

Dunster Trail

Take the side road from Highway 16 across from the Dunster Community Hall that leads down (south) into the community of Dunster. Cross the one-lane bridge over the Fraser River and continue onto Pepper Road just before the Dunster Store. Turn right onto Pepper Road, cross the railway tracks, and continue on the narrow unpaved road as it climbs to a gravel pit where the trailhead is located. The first part of the trail is brushy and can be tricky to locate, but once in the forest it is in good shape with a generally moderate grade. There is an excellent rest stop about halfway up the mountainside where the trail goes over a knoll above a rocky gully, before losing some 30 metres elevation. This natural viewpoint usually attracts a sufficiently strong breeze to keep the mosquitoes down. Upon reaching treeline, the trail follows a lovely alpine gully before contouring left (east) across a rocky slope to reach an alpine lake slightly below a pass overlooking the spectacular Raush Valley. The origin of this name is not, as I had supposed for many years, that of a Germanic pioneer. Rather, according to Roy Howard of Dunster, it is an abbreviation of Rivière au Shuswap, named after the Shushap (Secwepemc) people. The Shushap, Howard said, had a village at Tête Jaune that was encountered by the Overlanders and by the English adventurers, Lord Milton and Dr. Cheadle when they travelled through the Yellowhead Pass in 1863. There was possibly a seasonal camp at the mouth of the

Day-1 crossing alpine meadows on the trek from Mount Holmes to Mount Robson.

Group looks down on the Raush River Valley from the top of the Dunster Trail. Photo: J. Lett.

Raush. The total elevation gain to the lake is 1,250 vertical metres, plus a short scenic climb to one of the peaks above the lake that is well worth the extra 150 metres—it can provide some nice glissading, or boot skiing, well into July. As well as the Raush, there are superb views of the Cariboo Mountains and Premier Range on the south side of the Rocky Mountain Trench. You can also see the forbidding peaks to the north of the Trench between the Holmes and Fraser Rivers, that are hidden from sight lower down.

Raush River

In the spring of 2000, the Dunster-based Fraser Headwaters Alliance, with the assistance of a grant from Mountain Equipment Co-op, re-established a hiking trail in the middle Raush Valley. The trail is accessed by travelling to the back of the Kiwa Forest Service Road, which starts from the old Dunster–Croydon Road, just east of Kiwa Creek and 10 kilometres southeast of Croydon. Marked with orange metal diamonds on trees, the trail down to the Raush River begins in a logging block at Kiwa Pass. Eventually, the Fraser Headwaters Alliance hopes to install canoe rests along the way to provide canoeists and other boaters with better access to the river. The hiking trail descends to the Raush River and continues eight kilometres upstream (south) through old spruce, Douglas fir, and cedar forests, as well as through wetlands and past rock bluffs to the confluence of Black Martin Creek

155

(this is near the midpoint of the watershed). Two notes of caution that hikers should keep in mind here: don't attempt to cross Black Martin Creek, which has a considerable grade and can be life-threatening, and if you use a beach campsite, be wary of the potential for changing water levels on the river.

For boaters, the lower Raush valley offers a spectacular 50-kilometre river adventure back to McBride. Access to the river is gained via the Raush River Hiking Trail described above. Although the initial portage is a little long, the ensuing trip down the Raush is mainly a gentle float between spectacular mountains, with good wildlife viewing opportunities along the way. The river follows a meandering course between the steep mountain walls for approximately 33 kilometres, with opportunities to explore back channels and oxbow lakes. Despite the quiet, twisting nature of the river, you should be vigilant for logjams, sweepers, and other hazards. You should also be experienced and equipped for wilderness river travel. The crux of the trip is a 300-metre stretch of class-2 water near the railway bridge, close to the confluence with the Fraser. Use extreme caution if you run this stretch, and portage or line your craft if you have any doubts. The last 20 kilometres of the trip down the Fraser River follows a meandering course between the Cariboo and Rocky Mountains into McBride. You should be aware that most of the surrounding land on the lower Raush and Fraser Rivers is privately owned, so avoid trespassing. The takeout for the trip is at Koeneman Park located at the highway bridge just east of McBride.

Dunster Trail

Activity Mountain Hiking and Backpacking

Rating 8 to 10 hours round trip

Distance 12 km round trip to the pass overlooking the Raush Valley

Principal Elevation Gain 1,200 m to the pass overlooking the Raush Valley

Map 83 E/4 Croydon

Details Take the Dunster Road south from Highway 16, and after crossing the Fraser River, take Pepper Road to the trailhead in a small gravel pit. This well-maintained trail offers very nice views of the Raush Valley, the Premier Range, the Rocky Mountains, and the Rocky Mountain Trench.

Mount Terry Fox

The man who inspired Canadians everywhere with his run across Canada is honoured with a mountain in his name, located a few kilometres southeast of Tête Jaune Cache. Mount Terry Fox was chosen because it was previously unnamed and was visible from both Highway 16 and from Highway 5. Commemorative viewpoints were built on both highways, and a monument was erected on an adjoining ridge, high on the mountain. Most people see Mount Terry Fox from these viewpoints, but the mountain itself, although high, is not technical and has a good trail as far as treeline. It is a whopping 1,800 vertical metres elevation gain to the summit, and another 600 vertical metres to visit the monument on the next ridge. Because of its elevation, the long summit ridge of Mount Terry Fox can be quite a serious undertaking at any time, but especially early or late in the season, such as on Terry Fox Day, September 14th. And of course, it is impossible to hike here without thinking of the man whose name graces the peak, and to wonder at his accomplishments. The following accounts took place at opposite ends of the short hiking season, and they indicate the narrow window of opportunity available each year, generally from mid-July to late August.

Mount Terry Fox in July

It had started out as a hike to Berg Lake on the July long weekend. "You're crazy," friends had told me, "the trail will be overrun with people." "No," I thought, "things will be slow because of the cool wet summer." I was partly right, in that staff at the Mount Robson visitor centre were still issuing permits for Berg Lake. But in other respects, the visitor centre was a bit like a zoo. I don't mean that in a disrespectful way. There were people from all over the world enjoying the view, many of whom were about to set off on an adventure that they would long remember. But, considering the crowds, we decided on a less busy alternative. After phoning Prince George to let someone know about our change of plans, I backtracked 20 kilometres down Highway 16 and took the south fork toward Valemount. Immediately past the Terry Fox viewpoint on Highway 5 (not to be confused with the Highway 16 viewpoint) I turned east on Stone Road and followed the signs a short distance to the Mount Terry Fox trailhead. The contrast to the crowds at nearby Mount Robson was startling, and for the next three days we would not see another person.

The mountain was named in the early 1980s to honour Terry Fox and his run for cancer. Shortly afterward, in July 1982, a group from

Looking west to the Premier Range from treeline on the Mount Terry Fox trail.

the Caledonia Ramblers Hiking Club of Prince George, led by Dave King, bushwhacked up Teepee Creek just south of the present trail. Dave had developed some knowledge of the area having already led two prior bushwhacking trips on the mountain. After setting up camp in the meadows below the peak, we reached the 2,650-metre summit, shrouded in cloud, in the late afternoon. Although the mountain is now a provincial park, the approach is on crown forestland. So a year or two after the dedication, it fell to the Ministry of Forests to build a trail up the dry ridge next to Teepee Creek. The total elevation gain from trailhead to summit and back, including the ups and downs on the ridgeline, is over 1,800 metres, but there are lesser options along the ridge that afford nearly the same views. Those views are superb, particularly Mount Robson and Whitehorn to the north and the ever spectacular Premier Range to the west. Even if you only go as far as treeline, the views of the Premier Range are well worth that effort.

The trail to the start of the summit ridge involves a five-kilometre easy climb through mature forest. There are some 17 switchbacks, all with easy grades, and a nice viewpoint near the top. This part of the hike takes about two hours, and is followed by another hour climbing a narrow treed ridge trail with views across Valemount and the glaciers of the Premier Range. Treeline is sharply defined on the ridge, after which the trail gets steeper and more rugged. The ridge is long and dry, and once the snow has gone, there is no reasonable place to camp that has water nearby—a day-hiker must carry at least two litres to drink.

On this occasion, we planned to backpack over the summit ridge and drop down to a series of small lakes and streams on the north side. Unfortunately, the 1,500-metre climb to the first high point took on bigger proportions carrying 20-kilogram packs and we didn't get that far before deciding to stop. It was just as well we didn't reach our intended campsite, as the landscape of alpine-flowered pools and rock gardens that I remembered from my last August visit, was still locked in its wind-swept winter garb of snow and avalanche debris. So we camped at treeline next to a remnant snow patch that supplied us with water for three days. We didn't see any wildlife on the trail, and most of it seemed to be down in the valley. But we did watch a golden eagle soar from a ledge above us, and at 3 am in the morning I awoke to hear wolves calling nearby on the mountainside.

The next morning, we explored a new route around the north side of the mountain with a view to finding a shortcut to the Terry Fox monument. However, we soon found ourselves boxed into a steep-sided cirque filled with lots of recent avalanche debris. Several large snow cornices, hanging precariously on the north facing ridges above, were threatening. As we crossed a gully partly overhung by one such cornice, I remembered thinking that I hadn't expected to be taking avalanche precautions on Canada Day. It was still early enough in the day to be stable, but on re-evaluating the hazard, we retreated and climbed to the first summit by a safer route. We were by now only 150 vertical metres below the top of Mount Terry Fox, but still two

Mount Terry Fox

Activity Hiking and Backpacking
Rating 10 to 12 hours
Distance 20 km round trip to the summit
Principal Elevation Gain 1,800 m to the summit
Map 83 D/14 Valemount
Details The Mount Terry Fox trail is accessed from a trailhead on Stone Road across from the Highway 5 Mount Terry Fox Viewpoint, 7 km north of Valemount. Mount Terry Fox is a long, but rewarding hike that is best done in the safety of a group if going all the way to the summit. The trail is in good shape and clearly marked to treeline, but after that it is largely a matter of finding your own way along the ridge. Spectacular views of Mounts Robson and Whitehorn to the north, and the Premier Range to the west are obtained without going all the way to the summit.

kilometres away along the snow and cornice-encrusted ridge, with several false summits in between. Our preferred destination was the monument, which for some reason had been placed by helicopter on a separate ridge to the north instead of on Mount Terry Fox. But this would have been a difficult walk given our location and the prevailing snow conditions, and with a change in the weather threatening, it was time to turn around. Returning via the normal path, we were unable to find any marker cairns and spent an hour or two searching over steep, exposed, loose rock before locating the route. This isn't much of a problem if you go up and down via the same route in good visibility, provided you pay attention to the back track. But it did emphasize that the upper part of Terry Fox can be dangerous in bad weather and was in need of additional route marking. From time to time as we descended to our ridge camp, we heard the roar of avalanches and rock fall as successive cornices collapsed— our earlier decision had been a wise one.

Terry Fox Day

It had been 15 years and four visits since I first hiked up Mount Terry Fox, and I was still trying to find a way to visit the elusive monument. Leaving Prince George early on Saturday morning, we breakfasted in McBride and reached the trailhead just north of Valemount at 11 am. The weather was kind to us as we climbed, and we reached our 2,500-metre high point by late afternoon. Descending from the summit ridge, we found ourselves surrounded by a winter landscape in the snowy bowl below the monument. Our objective was a small alpine lake, which, if the weather held, would afford a quick ascent to the monument early on Sunday morning, September 14th—Terry Fox Day. As we approached our campsite at 2,300-metres elevation, we were treated to the sight of two large mountain goats climbing the monument ridge. We watched their route carefully, thinking we might need to follow in their steps. There were three other people on this trip, and their experience, strength and good humour were key to our safe enjoyment of the weekend. Unfortunately, the weather didn't hold for us, and we were greeted the next morning to fresh snow, low clouds, and strong winds on the exposed ridges above. We knew we would be challenged just to hike out of there, so despite the tantalizing closeness of our objective, we again decided not to give in to summit fever and concentrated instead on a safe descent. Over breakfast, we sat in quiet contemplation of Terry Fox and his achievements as a golden eagle circled overhead. We were the closest human beings on

Author approaching the summit ridge to Mount Terry Fox on Terry Fox Day 1997.

the planet to the Terry Fox monument on this special morning, and we were content. As expected, the hike out was difficult, with strong winds, snow, and poor visibility, and one person showing early signs of hypothermia. Winter comes early at 3,500 metres above sea level in the Rocky Mountains, and it is not a place to treat lightly. But, we had proved the feasibility of reaching the monument on an overnight trip, and we'll be back to try again!

Mount Robson Park

From Tête Jaune Cache into Mount Robson Park there are short side trails along the now narrow headwaters of the Fraser River, including Rearguard Falls and Overlander Falls. The high point of the journey east from Prince George is Mount Robson, which is worth at least one visit a year by those living in the closest city to this world-class backcountry destination. My favourite time is in late September, when the crowds are gone and the deciduous trees on the lower mountain slopes are beginning to show colour. The return drive from Prince George, and the two-hour round trip hike from the visitor centre to Kinney Lake, are easily doable in a day. This includes taking time to view wildlife along the highway, and stopping for one or two side trips.

Berg Lake Trail

If you enjoy backpacking, the hike into Berg Lake, below the north side of Mount Robson, can be done in one stretch of five to eight hours, or it can be broken into two segments, with a halfway stop at the Whitehorn campground. An easier option if you have small children along is to camp at Whitehorn, and day-hike up to Berg Lake. In recent years, animal-proof steel storage containers have been installed at each campsite and they seem to have resolved the problem of food theft by the park's highly habituated squirrels and other rodents. These small mammals used to regularly raid the traditional food caches. Fires are no longer permitted on this trail except in an emergency, and taking a cookstove along is essential. At Berg Lake there are many side trip opportunities, ranging from the easy stroll to beautiful Adolphus

---

Berg Lake Trail

Activity Hiking and Backpacking
Rating 3 to 5 days are recommended in order to appreciate this area
Distance 40 km round trip to the main Berg Lake campsite and shelter
Principal Elevation Gain 785 m to Berg Lake
Map 83 E/3 (East) Mount Robson
Details World-class trail, with an easy grade for the most part. Reservation and quota system in place for overnight stays, with predetermined campsites allocated. Connects with Jasper National Park North Boundary Trail 2 km north of Berg Lake at Robson Pass.

Lake in Jasper National Park, to the 22-kilometre round trip hike up to the 2,400-metre Snowbird Pass. From here you can look down on the extensive Coleman Glacier and Reef Icefield. This is a truly stunning climax to the Mount Robson experience as you climb alongside and above the Robson Glacier, below the north face of the highest peak in the Canadian Rockies. The Snowbird Pass route is usually closed to hikers in early summer until the caribou calving season is past.

Mount Fitzwilliam Trail

Approaching the Alberta border and the end of our journey east from Prince George, there is another alternative to the Berg Lake Trail if the backcountry quotas there are full, or if you just want to get away from the crowds. Mount Fitzwilliam is situated just south of Highway 16 on the B.C.–Alberta border, straddling Mount Robson Provincial Park and Jasper National Park. This is a first-class, but lightly used trail that was developed in the early 1980s as an overflow to the Berg Lake trail. Wildlife sightings are assured, with lots of mountain goats, hoary marmots, and pikas to be seen in the lovely alpine bowl below Mount Fitzwilliam. The trip can be done as a long day hike, but to really appreciate the area, allow two or preferably three days. Information on this trail can be obtained at the Mount Robson Visitor Centre.

Beyond Robson

Here, we end our journey eastward along the Yellowhead Highway. Just ahead lie countless other outdoor opportunities in Jasper National Park, Banff National Park, and Alberta's mountain parks northwest and southeast of Hinton. And returning to the junction of Highway 16 and Highway 5 in B.C., a few kilometres southeast from Tête Jaune Cache, brings you to the Valemount area. Of the communities of the Trench we have visited above—all of which are surrounded by incredibly beautiful mountain backcountry—Valemount has best understood the need to look forward to new economic opportunities, and and as a result, has provided many additional trails and outdoor activities. All of this is still within half a day's drive of Prince George, making B.C.'s northern capital an extraordinary place for those who enjoy an affordable city life close to limitless outdoor opportunities.

Alpine meadows below Mount Fitzwilliam.

East to the McGregor and the Rocky Mountains

Aleza Lake Research Forest

One of the longest running research forests in British Columbia is located at Aleza Lake, east of Prince George. The winding drive out past Eaglet Lake is worth the trip for its own merits, offering wildlife viewing, picnic sites, and tantalizing views toward the McGregor Mountains. Inside the research forest, there are no interpretive signs, but one can drive and walk around to get a sense of the different forest types native to the Prince George area, and the harvesting options available to foresters.

Located off the paved road between Giscome and Upper Fraser, the 9,200-hectare Aleza Lake Research Forest is valued not only for its size, location, and forest types, but also for its 80 years of data. Originally founded in 1924 by the Department of Forests and Lands, the Aleza Lake Forest Experimental Station became known for its well-documented, long-term trials of partial cutting and single tree selection. Situated on the boundary between the drier Interior Plateau and the wetter mountain belt, the experimental site was chosen for its wide-range of northern interior forest types.

After it ceased operations in 1963, the area remained largely dormant for nearly 30 years. By the late 1980s clearcutting was approaching its boundaries, and in the early 1990s a new northern university with a fledgling forestry program opened its doors in Prince George. Recognizing the importance of the site and its historical data, a steering committee was formed to coordinate activities and to develop a management plan. The committee was made up of government agencies, forest licensees, and university and government researchers. A management and working plan was approved in 1992

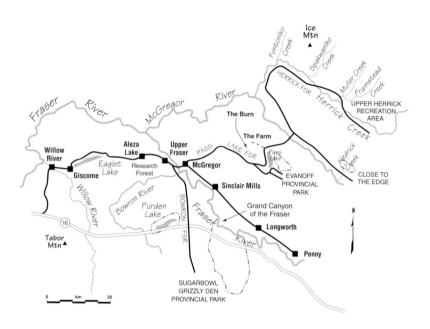

to frame research, harvesting, and forest management. Recognizing the uniqueness of the research forest, the Prince George Land and Resource Management Plan also established a separate resource management zone for it in 1999.

In 1998, the steering committee recommended that management of the Aleza Lake Research Forest should be assumed jointly by the University of Northern British Columbia and the University of British Columbia in cooperation with government and industry. In 2001, the Aleza Lake Research Forest Society was incorporated to provide co-management of the area, and in May 2002 the deal was consummated when 42 people from the Natural Resources and Environmental Studies Program at UNBC and the Faculty of Forestry at UBC jointly toured their new research forest. One of the highlights of the tour was a shelterwood block, where the benefits of leaving a sheltering canopy of trees vie with issues of blowdown and root rot. Other features included a birch forest with opportunities for non-traditional wood values, a pine plantation displaying the pitfalls of excess limbs on trees owing to too much spacing, and issues of "spiral root" and "bent tap root" relating to earlier seedling and planting techniques. The research forest also includes old-growth stands, where emphasis is on leaving some of the forest in its original condition for baseline research.

166

As the inaugural tour wound to a close, and the army of seasoned foresters moved noisily through the old forest toward the last tour stop in a recent clearcut, somebody called out, "Bear!" Stranded out in the open behind the only cover tree, was a large sow black bear with two good-sized yearling cubs. Faced with this mass of people crashing through the devils club toward her (somebody quipped later that a good portion of B.C.'s forestry expertise was in that crowd) the bear stayed put. Tree cover being important to her, she wasn't giving up the only one left, and she held her ground. The trek came to a confused halt and everyone milled around for 10 minutes while the sow alternately peered out first from one side of the tree and then the other, with a cub sometimes peeking out behind her. Someone suggested in jest that one of the professors be asked to give another talk, surmising that this would put the bear to sleep and allow us to sneak past. A few people unwisely started a flanking maneuver, until the sensible suggestion was made that we abandon the last stop and return the way we had come. The encounter with the three bears amply substituted for the last stop and reminded everyone about the respect owing to other forest users. And the next time I hear that groups of six or more people don't need to be concerned about bears, I'll just tell them about the 2002 Aleza Lake research forest tour when one black bear stood down 40 of B.C.'s finest.

Skiing the McGregor Mountains

The McGregor and Rocky Mountains, northeast of Prince George, are reached via the Giscome Road that branches north from Highway 16 just before Tabor Mountain, and winds through the rural communities of Willow River and Giscome. From Giscome, you can first glimpse the McGregor Mountains across Eaglet Lake, and from there the paved Upper Fraser Road heads east through the communities of Aleza Lake and Upper Fraser with ever closer views of the McGregor Range. The alternate access, if travelling from the east, is to use the Bowron Forest Service Road north from Highway 16, eight kilometres east of Purden Lake.

After crossing over the Hansard Bridge (the bridge that combines railway and highway on the same bed, described in the Longworth section), the Pass Lake Forest Service Road starts at what used to be the old townsite of McGregor. On the occasion related here, the high January snowbanks along Pass Lake Road reminded me that this is big snow country. Our destination was a slope known locally to skiers as The Burn, some 26 kilometres east along Pass Lake Road. Located at the southeast corner of the McGregor Model Forest, just before the road swings north to Pass Lake, the south-facing open spaces created by the 1981 fire were discovered shortly afterward by backcountry skiers looking for good telemark slopes. Now, over 20 years later, the standing, grey-coloured stems left by that long-ago fire are beginning to fall down, and travelling through them in a strong wind is probably not a good idea. Arriving at the usual starting point, there were already half a dozen vehicles parked at a widening in the road. One, still emitting clouds of exhaust gas, soon disgorged several skiers to join those already on the mountain.

The worst part of a winter backcountry ski trip is the act of getting out of a warm vehicle into an early-morning environment of minus 20 degrees Celsius with fresh snow falling. Struggling to adjust ski bindings with fast numbing fingers, not wanting to put on too many clothes so as not to overheat once I was underway, I went through the usual process of questioning my sanity, a state of mind that quickly vanished when I finally did start to move. Wearing breathable layers of clothing is essential to staying dry and warm in the winter outdoors. It's amazing how much body heat is generated and how little clothing is necessary while climbing—a thermal undershirt and a windproof shell are all that I usually need on the ascent. For me, the climb is the best part of the day—the poetry of gliding uphill on a well-broken track, my deep breathing supporting an instinctive meditation. This is a time for the head to clear and thoughts to crystallize. Everything fades except for the quiet motion and surrounding beauty of the winter mountain landscape—a kind of aboriginal "dreamtime," rare in today's fast-paced world, and it all washes over me.

Donning layers of warm clothing, we ate lunch amid trees deformed by snow and plastered by recent storms. The sun came out briefly between flurries, and a lone caribou, betrayed later by its fresh tracks, walked unseen through the meadow beside us. Peeling away the sticky climbing skins from our skis, we could at last run free, and we savoured the wide-open glades of deep untracked powder down to the vehicles. A few heavenly turns in pristine snow quickly took us to the top of The Burn. Spying a few people below me, I made a few more quick turns and stood among them. Barry Hagen, a Prince George outdoorsman of some repute, turned to me and said: "You guys are too late, we're getting ready for our third run—it's all skied out!" He wasn't kidding; but we enjoyed a great ski down anyway, picking our way through their tracks with only a few spills in a narrow band of crusty snow. Content with one ascent of the mountain, we started the mid-afternoon ski out as the serious group "skinned up" for their fourth ascent of the day. I left with the thought that this part of the backcountry is getting as busy as a ski hill.

Deep snow at The Farm

We might be excused for thinking that winter is over, with wonderful spring-like days in February. But March usually has a surprise or two. In Prince George, close to the spring equinox, any new white stuff usually melts by the end of the day. Not so in the mountains where the upper elevation snowpack usually accumulates until late April. This particular March, the deep powder snow had reached the point of being too much of a good thing.

My wife, Judy Lett, and I had joined four other people on an overnight ski trip to the part of the McGregor Mountains north of The Burn and west of Pass Lake, known as The Farm. The area had earned its name a few years earlier because of the number of mountain caribou known to utilize the high, flat, open subalpine meadows. We climbed on Saturday morning in a heavy snowfall that added to the nearly bottomless conditions already existing. It was a nice climb in beautiful surroundings, but we didn't get a chance to do much serious skiing owing to the amount of new snow. Except for the steepest grades, which we avoided because of avalanche risk, it was work even going downhill. A week earlier, two local skiers were caught in a snow slide just across the valley. Both men survived the experience, but one suffered serious injuries and had to be evacuated by helicopter late in the day after the other had skied out and raised the alarm just in time.

Spring Skiing (April) above 'The Farm'.

*Author's wife, Judy Lett approaches the snowed in cabin operated by
the McGregor Wilderness Society at the Farm.*

The McGregor Wilderness Society of Prince George manages the
treeline cabin where we stayed, and space there can be booked for
a nominal donation. The Farm, along with Fang Basin to the east
(western part of Evanoff Park), is designated a ski-use area. This is part
of an agreement worked out by backcountry ski and snowmobile user
groups, and subsequently given a stamp of approval by government,
for what is now called the McGregor–Torpy Winter Recreation Area.
It is a leading example, provincially, of what disparate user groups,
working together, can achieve when they put interests and mutual
respect above confrontation.

After organizing gear and eating lunch, we climbed above the
cabin and dug snow pits in two different locations to check the
condition of the snowpack. Identifying interfaces between successive
snowfalls and examining the crystal types at those boundaries helps
determine the likelihood of a layer sliding. Knowing the density of
snow in the different layers is also important, such as identifying
unconsolidated or metamorphosed snow that can collapse, or wind-
deposited slab that can fracture when a skier ventures onto it. In our
case, we found a moderately easy shear on a thin layer of buried
surface hoar down about 45 centimetres, and a harder shear on an old
ice crust at 95 centimetres. The main risk at our location seemed to be
the mass of new snow waiting to slough off the slope. Anyone who

The Farm

Activity Backcountry Skiing, Hiking, and Backpacking
Rating 4 to 6 hours return, although this frequently takes much longer in the winter after a McGregor snowstorm.
Distance 10 km round trip to the meadows (cabin site)
Principal Elevation Gain 655 m to the meadows (cabin site)
Map 93 I/3 Gleason Creek
Details The trailhead is located about 37 km along the Pass Lake Forest Service Road just past the north end of Pass Lake, on the west side of the road. The Farm can also be accessed in winter on skis via The Burn, 26 km along the Pass Lake Road.

goes into the mountain backcountry in winter should definitely take an avalanche course. A mix of science and art, it is an interesting study in its own right as well as for its safety value. The science comes from a detailed analysis of the snowpack and an understanding of its history and the physical processes involved. The art comes in applying that knowledge everywhere on the slope. The latter is key, because if you were to dig snow pits everywhere, not only would you would leave nasty traps all over the mountain, but more importantly you would never get any skiing done!

During the afternoon following our hike up the mountain, enough new snow fell to completely obliterate the deep tracks we'd made just a few hours earlier. Amazingly, this made the trip down the next day longer than the climb up. Judy, who was a strong downhill and cross-country skier, was new to backcountry skiing. After repeatedly getting off balance and disappearing into nearly bottomless powder snow, then facing the exhausting task of extricating buried skis still attached to her feet, her adrenaline would kick in and set the stage for another spill. If a person is not careful in this situation, panic and exhaustion can quickly take over. But, having the support of the group won the day, and she remarked at the end that while snow conditions were unlike anything she had ever seen before, the scenery was breathtaking!

Evanoff Provincial Park

My first introduction to what is now Evanoff Provincial Park occurred at Easter in 1981 when I was on a three-day ski trip with George Evanoff, in whose memory the park is now named. We had gone to the area later known as The Farm (described above) which was located west across the valley from the future park. This was in the days before the present cabin was built, and for our accommodation we constructed an elaborate and comfortable snow cave—George Evanoff never did things by half measure. During our stay, we enjoyed three days of powder skiing and blue skies, and George told me about what he called a big hole in the ground at the entrance of an alpine basin across the valley, just above Pass Lake. He called the area The Fangs because of the jagged peaks that guard the entrance to the alpine amphitheatre, now known as Fang Basin. From his description, it sounded to me like a limestone cave of substantial proportions and we agreed to hike in and see it as soon as the snow had receded from the lower elevations.

A few weeks later, George and I bushwhacked up to the start of the amphitheatre where the hole was, and I was astonished to see the entrance of a limestone cave that was large enough to drive a bus into. I had spent my first year in Prince George wandering the mountains with Claude Rouchon, a man who hailed from the Jura region of

Evanoff Provincial Park – Torpy Trail

Activity Backcountry Skiing, Hiking, and Backpacking
Rating 3 to 5 hours round trip to small alpine lake campsite
Distance 6 km round trip to alpine lake
Principle Elevation Gain 300 m to alpine lake
Map 93 I/3 Gleason Creek
Details This is one of the shortest trails to alpine in the Prince George area, but requires a high clearance vehicle and preferably a four-wheel drive to reach the trailhead. Or alternately, drive as far as you can and walk the last three kilometers of road. The trailhead is roughly 4 km east of the south end of Pass Lake as the crow flies. It can be reached by taking the upper Torpy Road, branching south at about the 29 km mark on the Pass Lake Forest Service Road and then taking left forks, climbing high on old cutblocks east of Pass Lake and northeast of the Torpy River. From the trailhead it is less than an hour to alpine, where many opportunities exist to explore the McGregor Range east of Pass Lake, and possibly see caribou and grizzly bear.

Alpine tarn at the east end of the McGregor Range. Picture taken below the highest peak known unofficially as Torpy Mountain. This beautiful alpine area is accessed via the Torpy Trail in Evanoff Park, and thence five kilometers east along the ridge..

France, an area famous for its caves., After learning a lot about caves from him, I felt that this find was very significant. We agreed to call Claude in Calgary as soon as we got home. Claude Rouchon had spent a good part of his time in Prince George trying to find out if there were any caves in the area, without much success, but walking in the mountains with him, I had seen his enthusiasm over even small cracks in the ground. My call to Calgary that evening caused a lot of excitement in the caving community there, but the snowmelt of an entire alpine basin was draining into the cave, and it wasn't feasible to do much until late summer. In fact, it was in September 1981, after a very dry summer and many wildfires on nearby mountainsides, including the one that created the aforementioned Burn, that we finally put a joint trip together. Claude Rouchon travelled to Prince George in the company of Tom Barton (who was then the president of the Alberta Speleological Society), and another Alberta caver, Randy Spahl. Together with George Evanoff, the five of us undertook the first serious exploration of what would soon be recognized as a world-class cave. It would turn out to contain many kilometres of passage and the second largest underground room in Canada. It wouldn't be an overstatement to say that on that weekend, the sport of caving in the Prince George area was born—an event that led to the discovery of many other significant finds in the area, some of which are discussed in the section on caving. A signal moment for me was when, a few years later, I received a phone call from a man newly arrived in Prince

George who introduced himself as Clive Keen. He had just been hired as the director of communications for the new University of Northern B.C. Clive had arrived from England, and was looking for a source of calcium carbide for his caving lamp. "How did you hear about Fang Cave?" I asked, curious and aware of the secrecy around such things. "Oh, I read about it in *Great Caves of the World!*" he replied to my astonishment. In 1982, I had written the first feature article to appear about Fang Cave for the spring 1983 issue of Canadian Caver magazine. More articles about Fang had followed, and collectively these were likely the source for *Great Caves of the World*.

To George Evanoff went the honour of naming the cave. George had broad interests in the area, and during the next decade he spent a good deal of his recreational time exploring the surrounding mountains. He constructed what became known as the Fang Trail and the Torpy Trail to provide access into the area from opposite sides. I had many hard, but rewarding, trips with George into the Fang and Torpy alpine areas on foot and on skis before the trails were established. Once, he and I were sitting alone on a mountain ridge on the Torpy side of Fang Mountain watching a group of six caribou in the meadows below us. "Mike," he said, "it would spoil this for me if I could see even one other person here." Yet his desire to share the area with others overcame this thought and led to his building of the trails below where we were sitting. George Evanoff died in a grizzly bear encounter in October 1998 on the nearby Bearpaw Ridge, and soon afterward the new park that he had proposed for the area was named

Young hoary marmot on an east ridge of Evanoff Park.

Spectacular flower meadows on a ridge in the Dezaiko Range.
Site of the golden eagle's aerobatic display. See back cover.

in his memory. Evanoff Park can be accessed from the Fang side, but the trail is steep and rough, and is prone to avalanche danger in the winter and spring. The more popular access today is via the Torpy Trail that can be reached from the Upper Torpy Forest Road that forks southeast from around the 28-kilometre mark on the Pass Lake Forest Service Road, a few kilometres before reaching Pass Lake.

Golden Eagle

Walking along a 2,000-metre alpine ridge in the Dezaiko Range of the Rocky Mountains, just north of Pass Lake on a warm summer day, I watched a golden eagle circling on fast rising thermals in the steep-sided valley below me. Reaching a good height, it suddenly folded its wings and dropped like a stone. Reaching terminal velocity, it spread its wings again to pull out of the dive and rise vertically until gravity overcame its momentum. At the moment of stall, it flipped over on its side in a perfectly executed manoeuver known to air show buffs as a hammerhead turn. As it went over, it folded its wings, fell and repeated the exact sequence two or three times, each time losing a few hundred metres of altitude. Then it sought out a thermal, climbed to its original starting point and began the entire sequence over again. I watched this bird engage in what can only be described as play for more than half an hour.

175

Upper Herrick Valley

On August 1, 1993, I was one of three members of the Herrick Creek Local Resource Use Planning team (LRUP) who, with three other companions, volunteered our time to fly into an alpine area in the upper reaches of the Herrick Valley. The Herrick is located in the Hart Ranges of the Rocky Mountains northeast of Prince George, and is one of the main watersheds of the upper Fraser River Basin. The river took its name from the surveyor Captain James Herrick McGregor, whose name in various forms adorns nearby features: Captain Creek, James Creek, and the McGregor River and Mountains. The objectives of our field trip were to check out the recreational potential of the upper Herrick Valley; to inventory alpine animal and plant species; evaluate visual quality objectives in proposed harvesting areas; provide on-the-ground experience to members of the Herrick LRUP Planning Team; and to enjoy a working vacation. A key recommendation resulting from our field trip was to establish visual quality objectives in the Framstead Creek drainage as seen from above, in the alpine. This was the first time this had been done in the Prince George area from a higher elevation vantage point. Our recommendations were later adopted in the consensus agreement. A forest company operating in the valley at the time donated helicopter transportation into the area, and a local helicopter company interested in future heli-logging prospects in the valley picked us up at the end of the week. Two flights

Herrick Falls – limit of navigation for jet-powered river boats on Herrick Creek. Accessible just below the Herrick Forest Service Road.

Upper Herrick Valley

Activity Backpacking
Rating 3 to 7 days
Distance 4 or 5 km from the Herrick Road to the alpine ridge above
Principal Elevation Gain 1,050 m from the Herrick Road to the alpine ridge above
Maps 93 I/2 Ovington Creek; 93 I/7 Wapiti Pass
Details The area can be accessed by relatively open bushwhack climbing north from the Herrick Creek Forest Service Road approximately 10 to 12 km east of Framstead Creek. The Herrick Road is accessed via the Pass Lake Road and turning northwest after crossing the McGregor River suspension bridge to follow the McGregor and then the Herrick Rivers. Road conditions in the Herrick Valley may be uncertain as logging activity is now being concentrated westward to harvest trees that are affected by mountain pine beetle. Another option is to do what I did on two occasions, and that is to fly into this area by helicopter. Either way, the Upper Herrick Valley is remote, and backpackers must be experienced and self-sufficient.

were required to transport six people plus gear to our alpine lake base camp east of Framstead Creek. We enjoyed clear skies all week except for the periodic buildup of localized afternoon thundershowers. This followed nearly two months of generally wet weather, so we were fortunate in our timing.

As we set up camp around noon on the day of arrival, we observed two mountain caribou on the skyline directly above the lake. We watched them for about 15 minutes as they climbed to the top of the mountain, while a golden eagle soared overhead and crossed the wide valley in seconds. In the mid-afternoon, we set off on an exploratory walk toward the pass north of camp where we soon spied a grizzly bear a few hundred metres below us. With mixed opinions about how close we were to it, we watched and filmed the bear for 10 minutes as it made its way along the draw below us and took a bath in a large hot tub-sized mud pond. The animal eventually started moving toward our camp, and, concerned about a member of our group who had remained there (and our food supply), we returned as quickly as we could. Meanwhile, back in camp, our sixth member, Sandra, watched the bear emerge from nearby tree cover and quickly leave the area when it caught our scent. Later, we observed that the hillside directly above camp had been extensively rooted over by bears. But this was to

Base camp for weeklong fly-in exploration of the alpine area between Framstead Creek and the Upper Herrick Valley.

be the last big game we saw all week, a fact that brought home to us the impact that even a small group of people can have on the wilderness. After the bear episode, we set off to explore the ridge around the lake. We observed fish rising and later identified these as Dolly Varden. The species seems well adapted to reach high mountain lakes, and this was not the first time we had observed this phenomenon.

We had selected our base camp with care after months of staring at topographical maps during late night Herrick LRUP meetings. As a result, we found that we had picked an optimum place for our camp and were not surprised to find traces of past human presence. Several spots around the lakeshore seemed to have been tent sites, although we estimated they had not been used for at least 20 years. Interestingly, the sites were located toward the other end of the lake, well away from the bear's "larder" where we had incautiously chosen to camp. Since we had put considerable effort into setting up our new home, however, and had already made our presence known to the local wildlife, nobody felt like moving.

We hiked to the pass and the peak north of camp where we observed a male American kestrel, as well as two more golden eagles. The peak afforded us our first views of the Framstead Creek drainage below, to the northwest. The very scenic alpine basin and lake below Mount Knudsen was six kilometres to the northeast. We were struck by the unlogged viewscape of the Framstead Valley; an impression that was reinforced several times during the week and which later became the basis for our visual quality proposal to the planning team. We were pleased to hear that the company foresters at the planning table did not see this as an issue as long as the visual objectives were established early enough in the planning process.

All around us we saw good mountain goat habitat, but the only actual goat sign we observed during the entire trip was a single old track near one summit. Mountain goats are territorial, and our guess was that the goat population had been hunted out 20 years earlier, or when the old tent sites had last been used, and they had not yet re-established a significant presence in the area. Descending toward camp, we followed the path of the bear from the previous day. It soon became apparent that we were travelling on an old horse trail of the same vintage as the tent sites, the trail having since been adopted by wildlife. The horses had probably come through McCullagh Pass, 20 kilometres to the south, since there were no obvious horse trails in the main stem of the Herrick valley from where we had come. We walked the ridges and peaks northwest and west of camp, and made our first planned radio check with the outside world. Again we were impressed with the Framstead viewscape. Descending, we discovered a good-sized hole in limestone karst, indicating the possibility of caves. As mentioned earlier, in 1981 two members of our party, George Evanoff and myself, had undertook the first exploration of Fang Cave in the McGregor

Knudsen Lake – in the upper Framstead Creek valley in the Upper Herrick.
This beautiful lake was once on a wish list for a future provincial park.

179

*Herrick River east of Fontoniko Creek. The picture was taken in 1986
just before the first logging took place in the valley.*

mountains 35 kilometres west-southwest of our present location. As a result, there had been a lot of caving interest in the general area. In 1985, the deepest pothole in either Canada or the continental U.S.A. was discovered in the Dezaiko Range just 16 kilometres southwest of where we were now standing, by Ian McKenzie, one of the early Fang Cave explorers. That cave, appropriately named Close to the Edge, has a classic entrance high on a mountainside above Hedrick Creek, another tributary of the McGregor River. Inside the entrance there is a huge shaft that varies in width from 25 to 50 metres, with a staggering vertical freefall of 251 metres! I knelt on a small overhanging ledge to look down this shaft, and it was one of the most impressive sights I have seen anywhere. A few years later the ledge disappeared down the shaft, fortunately without anyone on it, and whenever I look at a picture of myself or others kneeling on that ledge, I shiver at what might have happened. Our newest cave discovery was plugged with snow, and it was impossible to see if it went very far. At the time of writing, no cavers have yet relocated this Upper Herrick cave, despite two attempts. Apart from this karst anomaly, most of the geology of the surrounding area appears to be shale, with ridgetops carved flat by glacial action, leaving occasional erratic boulders perched in unlikely positions.

After ascending the ridge above our lakeside camp, we dropped into the drainage of a proposed special management area south of camp. Three people descended in the heat of the day to 1,372 metres, the proposed elevational limit to harvesting in the valley. Their objective was to sample the ages of trees by means of increment cores, and they were successful in aging four of the largest trees. Two spruce trees were found to be 214 and 175 years respectively, and two alpine fir trees were found to be 137 and 123 years old. Contrary to expectations, no old-growth trees over 250 years were found. The trees were evenly distributed between spruce and alpine fir. Several spruce bark beetle-infested trees were observed, typical of the entire valley, and entomologists at the time were unsure if this was a normal localized phenomenon or whether the entire valley was threatened with a major outbreak. Later, there were significant outbreaks in the Herrick, Framstead, and Mueller Creek valleys. While climbing back to rejoin the other members of the party, a grizzly bear den was located on a northeast-facing slope at 1,676 metres elevation.

The next day, in good weather, we explored the high ridges east and south of camp, and the final day was spent lazily packing up and restoring the site so that there would be no sign of our stay by the next season. Our magic carpet arrived mid-afternoon, and sitting in the jet helicopter amid the alpine flowers, listening to the distant airport

Visual quality mapping of the Framstead valley prior to logging. This mapping was a recommendation of the field trip that was organized by the author, and was among the first to be done from higher elevation vantagepoints, recognizing the mountain recreation potential of the area.

chatter on the radio, our slow, primitive existence was suddenly transformed into the fast-paced, high tech world of the late twentieth century. Back at the since dismantled Herrick forestry camp, we were treated to tea and cakes in the bunkhouse before collecting our vehicles for the ride back to Prince George.

The area we visited in 1993 offers excellent mountain hiking and wildlife viewing opportunities up to 2,134 metres in the Hart Ranges of the Northern Rockies. It is a fragile place better suited to small groups of perhaps two to eight people, rather than large groups. During our 1993 foray, the area was only accessible by helicopter or by a long horse-packing trek. Since then, the mainline Herrick Forest Service Road has been pushed east and there is relatively easy bushwhacking access from that road. There are excellent viewscapes formed by the surrounding mountains and valleys, with the larger, heavily glaciated peaks to the east of Mount Pearson, Mount Ovington, Mount Plaskett, and Mount Nechamus reaching to over 2,896 metres. There are also spectacular vistas of rainbow-coloured mountains with extreme S-shaped folds in them.

Visually, the area is fairly well-protected on all sides except the Framstead, where we made our main visual quality recommendations. On the south side is a forest ecosystem network, or wildlife corridor, and east are the protected old-growth areas of Upper Herrick Creek and Ovington Creek as well as the special management area referred to earlier. There are several natural burns on some of the slopes to the east, and there are large paths of avalanche disturbance along the north facing slopes of the Dezaiko Range. In the final document prepared for the planning team entitled, "Report on a Field Trip to the Upper Herrick Valley— August 1 - 6, 1993," a participant, Judy Leykauf, who was not a member of the Herrick LRUP, gave a hiker's perspective of the area: "Never had I seen such sweeping colors and folds in the rock. The campsite lay at the foot of a ridge next to a clear blue lake. The wildflowers were everywhere. But the overpowering mountains to the east and the south still dominated the view. In today's world, a wilderness experience is becoming increasingly difficult to find. Very seldom do I look down on a mountain valley and see nothing but the trees and avalanche paths. Our six days in the Herrick gave me such an experience. I could reach the mountain summits, look across to far ridges, and almost feel that no one had stood where I was standing. I could experience a true sense of solitude."

In the fall of 1994, the Herrick LRUP Consensus Agreement was signed, and later in the decade it formed part of the larger Prince George Land and Resource Management Plan. In October 1995 I returned to the area by helicopter with the regional landscape forester, Luc Roberge, as he did the photography and mapping for the visual analysis that we had recommended. On a clear day in the late fall, we landed on several different promontories above Framstead Creek, from the Herrick River to beautiful Knudsen Lake, and at each stop I climbed the ridge for up to an hour as Luc did his work. The helicopter was recently back from United Nations duty in the Far East and was still in its white UN livery, creating a stark contrast to the golden brown alpine vegetation. On one of my ascents that day, I was approached on the summit of a ridge by a young bull caribou that circled me for 10 minutes with apparent curiosity—the third time I had had such an experience with a lone caribou on a mountaintop.

Kakwa

Early in 1999, after a five-year public process, the British Columbia government approved the Prince George Land and Resource Management Plan or LRMP. The 34,000 square kilometres making up the planning area included a large section of the Northern Rockies. In total, 2,500 square kilometres of new protected areas were created, of which nearly 1,400 square kilometres were allocated to a single new Rocky Mountain Park called Kakwa. At the same time a northern addition to Kakwa Park, taking in the Narraway River drainage proposed by the Dawson Creek LRMP, was approved. In June 2000, the "Protected Areas of British Columbia Act" received royal assent and the 1,700 square kilometre Kakwa Provincial Park officially came into being.

Kakwa Park joins on its northeast boundary with Alberta's Wild Kakwa Provincial Park and on its southeast boundary with Alberta's Willmore Wilderness Provincial Park. It is a large, almost undisturbed ecosystem that is home to a wide range of wildlife, including the northernmost population of Rocky Mountain big horn sheep, as well as grizzly bear, black bear, moose, caribou, mountain goat, and many others. It contains the only occurrence of the Front Ranges in British Columbia, and has many other outstanding features, such as rare Triassic fish fossils. In addition, it offers a wide range of backcountry recreation opportunities that have to be balanced with each other and

Beaver float plane access to Jarvis Lakes – pilot paddles aircraft away from shore.

Kakwa

Activity Backpacking, Backcountry Skiing, and other wilderness backcountry activities
Rating 7 to 14 days to experience even part of the area
Distance 29 km from Bastille Creek to Kakwa Lake
Principal Elevation Gain Varies according to the many choices of routes and destinations in the park—refer to topographical maps.
Maps 93 I/1 Jarvis Lakes; 93 H/16 Mount Sir Alexander
Details Check with B.C. Parks as to the state of the Walker Creek Forest Service Road, and/or consider alternate access by air subject to park use permits and limits. Apart from the track from Bastille Creek to Kakwa Lake, this large area is untouched, remote wilderness, and backpackers must be experienced and self-sufficient. From Kakwa or Jarvis Lakes, there are many possible day or multi-day routes that can be explored.

with the ecology of the park. Kakwa is the terminus of more than a million hectares of unroaded parkland that stretches northward from Highway 16 and makes up the largest block of protected wilderness in the central and southern parts of the combined Rockies of B.C. and Alberta. This chain of parkland continues south of Highway 16 for a total of 600 kilometres from Kakwa to the Kootenays. Owing to Kakwa's outstanding features and interconnectedness with these other protected areas, Kakwa Provincial Park is a likely candidate for inclusion in the Canadian Rocky Mountains World Heritage Site.

Historically, the Beaver and Carrier First Nations were among the first people to use Kakwa; followed in the eighteenth century by Cree, Iroquois, and Metis who began to enter the area during the westward expansion of the fur trade. The name, Kakwa, is derived from the Cree word for "porcupine." In the winter of 1875, Canadian Pacific Railway surveyor Edward W. Jarvis led a mixed party of native and non-native men along the river that now bears his name, crossing the continental divide at Jarvis Lakes on February 25 of that year. Fortunately for the wilderness character of the future park, the grade was too steep for a railway. Indeed, the valley west of Jarvis Lakes with Mount Ida and the Three Sisters towering above on its south side, is one of the most spectacularly rugged scenes I have ever seen. By the early 1900s, Kakwa had begun attracting international parties bent on big game hunting, exploring, climbing, and surveying. The unavailability of the European Alps during the First World War heightened interest in the Canadian Rockies at about the same time

Hiking northwest from Jarvis Lakes – Mount Ida (most northerly peak over 10,000 feet elevation in the Canadian Rockies) in the background.

that Kakwa became accessible to long horse-packing trips staged from the new transcontinental railway.

This is a special place that receives a wide range of enthusiastic visitors from B.C., Alberta, and around the world. It rivals the beauty and grandeur of the national parks to the south, with the added aspect of being almost entirely undeveloped. One can still experience what it must have been like in Jasper and Banff around the year 1900, including (and because of) the difficulty of getting there. Recreational uses include mountaineering, backpacking, hiking, horse-packing, hunting, fishing, snowmobiling, backcountry skiing, wilderness camping, caving, photography, and natural history interpretation. Commercial recreation operations include lllama-assisted hiking, guided hunting, horse-packing, and guided mountaineering.

At the heart of Kakwa Park are the two most northerly peaks of the Rocky Mountains higher than 10,000 feet. Mount Sir Alexander is named after the explorer, Alexander Mackenzie who, in 1793, became the first person to cross the North American continent north of Mexico. Pre-empting Lewis and Clark by 10 years, Mackenzie crossed the divide only 50 miles west of the mountain that bears his name. The heavily glaciated Mount Sir Alexander is the taller of the two peaks at 3,270 metres (10,728 feet), while Mount Ida is just under a hundred metres lower, but holds the distinction of being the most northerly 10,000 footer. Before the twentieth century, areas of Kakwa Park such as Sheep Pass in the southeast corner were used extensively by native people for hunting. Then, in the late nineteenth and early twentieth centuries, railway surveyors and horse-packers began to explore and travel through the area. One of these was the famous packer, Donald "Curly" Phillips, who accompanied Reverend George Kinney on his controversial near-first ascent of Mount Robson in 1909. These early travellers knew the peak that would later become Sir Alexander by the unimaginative, if descriptive name "Big Mountain." Then, in 1914, a hunter from Boston, S. Prescott Fay, travelled to within a few miles of the mountain and named it "Mount Alexander" in memory of the explorer, the "Sir" being added later. Also in 1914, a New York schoolteacher named Mary Jobe, who had been at the Alpine Club camp at Mount Robson the previous summer, hired Curly Phillips to take her to this mountain, which she named "Mount Kitchi," taken from the Cree word meaning "mighty." Although the name didn't stick on the big mountain, "Kitchi" is still on the map for a lesser peak five kilometres north of Sir Alexander, as well as for Kitchi Creek that flows north and west of the mountain into the McGregor River.

Mary Jobe attempted to climb Mount Sir Alexander in 1914 and again in 1915. On the latter attempt, Curly Phillips and two other members of the party made it to within 30 metres of the summit, where, lacking the technical skills and equipment to safely pass the remaining cornices, they sensibly turned around. (See section, "Mountain named for woman adventurer.") Partly because of its inaccessibility,

Looking south across Jarvis valley, immediately below and west of Jarvis Lakes and Mount Netim – one of the most powerful (certainly spectacular) places the author has visited.

and partly because it was declared unclimbable in 1922 following an overflight, Mount Sir Alexander was left alone for 14 years. Then, in 1929, a party led by a 58-year-old American doctor, Andrew Gilmour, made the first successful ascent aided by photographs taken in 1915 by an amateur surveyor, Frederick Vreeland of New Jersey. Another 61 years were to pass before the first winter ascent was made in 1990 by Craig Evanoff, Bonnie Hooge, and George Evanoff, all from Prince George. Mount Sir Alexander, with a classic pyramid rising out of its own icefield, is a landmark visible throughout the adjoining Rocky and Cariboo Mountains, yet it remains rarely climbed today despite the proximity of an access road into the area.

For most people, the centre of the new park is at the south end of Kakwa Lake where the park headquarters and main campgrounds are located. Despite the existence of basic facilities, this is still wild country where visitors often share Kakwa Lake only with the moose that parade in the shallows each day. Mountain goats from the surrounding ridges sometimes traverse the valley, and a dozen or so grizzly bears wander secretively on and off the brushy trails. Grizzly bear biologist, Wayne McCrory, set up infrared triggered cameras in the late 1990s on trails next to bear rubbing trees. The resulting pictures and DNA analysis of hair follicles collected at the camera sites are helping to identify and track the movement of the bears, and helping to determine their potential interaction with people. Popular hiking destinations from Kakwa Lake are mostly toward the southeast. They include Mount Ruth, Kakwa Pass, Broadview Mountain, and Mount Cross. The latter connects with the Wishaw Glacier and towers over the flower meadows and deep blue waters of La Glace Lake. This is an area that I explored in the fall of 2000 as a writer–guest of Strider Adventures of Prince George who offered guided llama packing trips in the Kakwa.

The Walker Creek Forest Service Road leaves Highway 16 just west of Ptarmigan Creek, about 70 kilometres northwest of McBride. After crossing the Fraser River, it continues to the park boundary at Buchanan Creek, 85 kilometres from the highway. The last 12 kilometres from Bastille Creek to the Buchanan are presently in very rough shape, with 50-metre long mud holes and sections washed out by the McGregor River. Only industrial mine site vehicles and others that are authorized by B.C. Parks are permitted beyond Buchanan Creek. The walk from Buchanan Creek is a 12-kilometre gentle climb along the mining road to McGregor Pass, where a quartzite mine is located close to Wishaw Lake. Along the way, Mount Sir Alexander and Wishaw Mountain are glimpsed through the upper McGregor rainforest. Just past Wishaw Lake there is an excellent campsite on

Mariel Lake to break the trip, or one can complete the remaining six kilometres down to Kakwa Lake in one stretch.

The year 2000 wasn't my first excursion into the Kakwa. Nearly two decades earlier in 1982, I was part of a group that helicoptered into the alpine basin northwest of Kakwa Lake. We explored the fossil beds around Mount Jarvis and Mount St. Andrews, walked among the hoodoos above tropical-looking Jarvis Lakes, watched goats and caribou, and prospected for caves in the expectation that a group from the Alberta Speleological Society would join us partway through our trip. We located many cave entrances along the contact line between the roughly one billion year old quartzite and half-billion year old limestone. Two of these, Moon Valley Cave and Moon River Cave, were later the subject of much serious work by caving groups, and are still largely unexplored because of the extreme hazards to be found in them. We returned in 1983 by floatplane to Jarvis Lakes, north of our previous year's camp. Climbing to the northwest through lush huckleberry patches, we spent a week wandering the peaks and ridges between Jarvis Creek and the Narraway River.

The alpine area east of Gray Pass and Dimsdale Lake in the northwest corner of the park, is perhaps the best feature of Kakwa for hiking, and the vista across Jarvis Pass from the west flank of Mount Netim is among the most powerful that I have experienced anywhere. Sitting on grassy ledges watching a group of 20 mountain goats nearby, the valley dropped precipitously below us. Just as quickly, it

Fossils are abundant in the limestone of the Rocky Mountains northeast of Prince George.

189

Enormous entrance pit of glacier-fed Moon River Cave, south of Jarvis Lakes.

rose vertically to the towering, glaciated north flanks of Mount Ida. It seemed that we could almost reach out and touch the cascading waterfalls and adjacent peaks that were once called the Three Sisters and are now known by more exotic names: Mount Koona, Mount Awasie, and Mount Walrus. It was through this pass that the first surveyors travelled in January 1875. Edward Jarvis and his assistant, C.F. Hanington, whose names now adorn many features along their route through the park, surveyed the area for the Canadian Pacific Railway. It is a sobering thought that this small party comprising three white men and three native men on snowshoes, and with dogs, accomplished the journey from Fort George to Fort Edmonton in temperatures as low as minus 47 degrees Celsius. Inspired by the view, as we were as well 108 years later, Jarvis wrote about his passage below where we rested: "The entrance to the pass is very grand, being guarded on either side by high pyramidal peaks towering two to three thousand feet above the valley and covered with perpetual snow. To the most prominent of these points we gave the name 'Mount Ida,' and it was here we saw one of the most magnificent of the many fine glaciers along the route; it could not have been less than a mile long, and five hundred feet thick at the face; while it was of such a transparent blue that we could almost imagine seeing the rocks underneath and through it." Mount Ida remained unclimbed until the early 1950s. In their account in the 1955 *Canadian Alpine Journal*, Alice and Fred Dunn related how their party from the Harvard Mountaineering Club flew from Prince George to Jarvis Lakes as we had done, and spent three weeks exploring the area and making their ascent. From the summit of Mount Ida they had a splendid view of Jarvis Lakes and the Three Sisters. Before beating a hasty retreat in the face of an approaching thunderstorm, they took turns, "...lying on our stomachs and placing our hands on the cornice crest which was the highest point."

As I walked through the newly designated Kakwa Park in September 2000, I experienced some of the same thoughts that I had in 1983: that I might have been standing in what we now know as Jasper and Banff National Parks, but a century earlier. I hope we can in some measure keep today's sense of wildness in the Kakwa a century from now, while still finding ways to make this Northern Rockies wilderness accessible to people. George Evanoff had inspired, organized, and led our 1982 and 1983 trips into the Kakwa. George was also the main public proponent for protecting the Kakwa throughout the Prince George LRMP process. He climbed both Mount Sir Alexander and Mount Ida in the last years of his life, and led a highly successful Alpine Club of Canada climbing camp to Mount Ida and surrounding areas in 1998. He is remembered in Evanoff Park a few kilometres west of Kakwa.

Llama trekking in Kakwa Park

I had known of Dan Hunter since he had started his llama trekking business, Strider Adventures, in 1992. I ran into him a couple of times at meetings but don't think we had ever really spoken. So what was the chance that he would phone me in February 2000 on my last day of work after more than 19 years in the forest industry? "Mike," he said after introducing himself, "Dorothy (his wife) and I think that the kind of stuff you write fits what we do, and we'd like you to join us on one of our llama treks this summer." What could I say? Portents like this are not taken lightly.

We met at Dan's place east of Prince George on September 1, 2000. It was an inauspicious start as the rain typical of that summer came down hard. Other guests started to arrive, and we all sat down to muffins and coffee while the gear was being organized. The house quickly filled with the excitement of meeting new people and the anticipation of the trip that lay ahead. Outdoor adventure with a group of strangers is always a fascinating experience as names are learned, bonds are struck, and idiosyncrasies begin to emerge. It is a little like the reality TV shows that suddenly became popular at the beginning of the new millenium, except that nobody gets voted off! This trip was doubly engaging, as there were names and personalities of six llamas to learn as well.

The weather improved as we drove to the trailhead and the llamas were loaded. Strider, who was Dan's first animal and namesake of the business, along with Sierra, Safari, Sundance, and Six Pack, each carried 45 kilograms. Starbuck pulled a cart loaded with the rest of the gear, while the rest of us (humans) carried light daypacks and walked alongside the animals. This was a nice change after a trip that I had just completed in August when I had carried a 25-kilogram pack—it was almost an afternoon stroll in the woods. Almost, but not quite, as we all learned to handle our strong-willed pack animals. Llamas are native to South America and are members of the camel family. They share all of the camels' intelligence with almost none of their belligerence. They are sharp, gentle, sensitive animals, who can easily live off the land without impacting it noticeably. They crop the vegetation without hurting the roots, and their feet leave very little impression in the soft ground while carrying nearly as much freight as a packhorse. They are at once herd animals and individuals. Some like to lead or to be touched, while others do not. They have their preferences for each other, yet are uncomfortable if they become separated. They like to eat, and while they are strong, willing workers, when one of them spots its favourite food beside the trail it may either stop to contemplate it from a distance, or just turn off the track and head straight for it. Again they are partial to certain foods, some choosing lupine leaves and others going straight for the seed pods.

It took about five hours to walk into Kakwa Lake where Dan set up his base camp for the week. Because of our late start, we stopped just over the McGregor Pass at an attractive random campsite on Mariel Lake. The next morning we awoke to thickly falling snow as the landscape transformed into an unseasonably early white wonderland that none of us were psychologically ready for. After spending most of the day moving our gear down to Kakwa Lake, we set up a snug, if somewhat snowy camp of tents and guide tarps. Dan provided all of the gear except for personal items, and guests could just relax and enjoy their holiday, or help with camp chores and animal tending. Most chose to be involved, and soon everyone had found a way to contribute according to their preferences. People who had never set up a tent before learned to do that, and there were lots of volunteers to help with firewood. During the next five days the weather slowly improved and the snow melted back, culminating in a clear day for our last hike up to the deep blue waters and flower meadows of La Glace Lake. The llamas accompanied us on most of our day hikes, with one of them carrying lunches in a small pack. Each morning and evening, one or two moose would come out and feed in the shallows of Kakwa Lake—a million-dollar experience!

Helicopter access – alpine area south of Jarvis Lakes.

Mount Ian Monroe was visible above our camp on Kakwa Lake, and was well situated to catch the alpen glow on clear mornings. Members of the Monroe family of McBride were involved with the area that later became known as Kakwa from the late 1950s when Everett Monroe discovered colourful quartzite deposits at Babette Lake, west of Kakwa Lake that led to a mine development there. Later, one of Everett Monroe's sons, Ian Monroe was one of a number of people who lobbied the provincial government to establish a park around Kakwa Lake. Ian Monroe died in a helicopter accident in 1987, and a year later, in August 1988, the mountain was named in his memory.

Predictably, the rain started falling heavily again as we finished packing up for the trek out. But everyone was motivated, especially the llamas, and we made it back to the vehicles in record time where lunch awaited us. Ever mindful of the well-being of his wet animals, Dan cancelled his plan to stop for dinner on the way home and made full haste to get his four-legged helpers back to their pasture. He phoned his wife from Dome Creek to ask her to pick up pizzas, forgetting that we had all of the vehicles and she had no way of getting into town. So with only an hour's notice, Dorothy somehow managed to whip up a dinner for 12, which we ate with relish as we reminisced over our adventures and prepared to say goodbye to new friends— human and woolly!

Automatic cameras snap grizzly bears in Kakwa Park

Wayne McCrory is a biologist who was doing research on grizzly bears in Kakwa Provincial Park in 2000. Working with B.C. Parks, he had set up automatic cameras and hair sampling devices in the bush surrounding Kakwa Lake. When I was there with Strider Adventures in September 2000, I ran across Wayne a few times near the beginning of our trip. I didn't have an opportunity to talk with him as he left soon afterward, but two people arrived from Montana to continue his work while he was away. One evening, I took my notebook and headlamp and walked along the trail around the south end of Kakwa Lake to the B.C. Parks cabin where Lance and April Craighead were working. We drank tea and talked for an hour as darkness enveloped the mountains outside. Lance's father, Frank, had worked for the U.S. Forest Service, while his uncle, John, worked for the University of Montana. Together, Frank and John Craighead became widely known for their work with the grizzly bears of Yellowstone National Park from the 1960s on. They were the first to use radio telemetry for tracking grizzly bears, and were involved in the controversial decision to close down the garbage dumps in Yellowstone. In his high school years, Lance spent summers working for his dad and uncle on the Yellowstone project, so it was natural that he would continue this work in his adult life. When I met him at Kakwa Lake, he was an adjunct professor at Montana State University and he ran a non-profit grizzly bear conservation organization from his home in Montana. Lance told me that Wayne McCrory had set up 17 cameras around Kakwa Lake. All the cameras were located at bear rubbing trees; places that the grizzlies use for territorial and mating purposes to announce, "Here I am!" At each camera site, Wayne had set up traps to collect hair samples. DNA is later taken from the follicles and is used to identify individual animals. From the ratio of isotopes of nitrogen and carbon, analysis can also show whether they have eaten saltwater fish, or in other words whether they have travelled over to the Fraser River to feed on salmon. Lance felt that camera surveillance and hair sample collection is a less invasive way of tracking bears than by using radio or satellite collars. He said that Wayne had so far identified at least 10 bears by their physical features and had given them names such as "Old Scar Neck." Wayne McCrory had contracted with parks' staff to identify areas used by bears in order to try to minimize conflicts with people. Earlier in the week, we had carefully walked around some of his infrared-triggered cameras to avoid wasting film. Lance showed me pictures taken by the cameras of a large grizzly rubbing his back against one of the same trees that we had passed. "It's a strange feeling," he said, "to arrive at a camera whose timer indicates that it has exposed a picture only a few minutes before." The cameras have also been triggered by other animals, including a family of mountain goats photographed walking down the middle of the road. An unexpected bonus was the identification of a vehicle that had entered the park illegally.

What I really wanted to ask Lance was his opinion on the increasing numbers of grizzlies that many of us had noticed in recent years around Prince George. Is the population increasing, or is this a localized effect and are conservationists right when they say there is an overall decline? Lance replied that the population goes up and down, and you really have to look at a 30-year span to get a good idea. The main concern is the loss of bear habitat, although hunting may exacerbate the problem. He said it's really important to get a good sense of the population dynamics. For example, if there are a lot of young males they tend to disperse, and bears on the move tend to get into trouble. Big males will help to stabilize a population. If you kill big males, you upset the social structure. There may be more bears in the short term, but there will be more fights over dominance and a higher overall mortality. One study, he said, showed that to kill a big male grizzly bear is equivalent in the long term to killing two other younger males and a female. If left undisturbed, Lance told me that grizzly bears live 20 to 30 years in the wild. The oldest sow on record was 38, and the oldest boar was over 42 years and still chasing females! Bears are smart in the sense that they spend their lives learning where the best food is at particular times of the year. Therefore, it is easy to spoil a bear by habituating it to human's garbage—they will remember it for the rest of their lives. Around Kakwa Lake I saw no garbage and the bears have not yet become habituated. There are more bears around the lake in the early summer feeding on avalanche lilies and cow parsnip. Later in the season, many of them move to lower elevations for berries, although I still saw fresh sign of three or four grizzlies during our walks.

As I walked tentatively back to my tent, alone in the dark, I wondered how well we would share our new park with these magnificent animals. Have we learned enough from the Craigheads' original work in Yellowstone and from all the work done since to ensure that Kakwa will continue to be home to a healthy number of grizzly bears a hundred years hence?

Prince George's largest provincial park isolated

The heavy rains of July 2001 wreaked havoc on the country east and north of Prince George, with many road washouts and disruptions. One of the most serious road failures occurred on the 12-kilometre stretch between the end of Walker Creek Forest Service Road at Bastille Creek and the boundary of Kakwa Provincial Park at Buchanan Creek. This short stretch of road existed for the purpose of accessing the privately operated quarry at Wishaw Lake near the centre of the park, and was not being maintained by government agencies.

A few years before, there was a lively debate in Prince George as to whether private vehicles should be allowed to use this road for recreational purposes beyond Bastille Creek. At issue were questions of establishing historic vehicle use, versus conserving the natural resources of the park, before the management plan was completed. At first, the closure was established at Bastille Creek but was later moved up to the park boundary at Buchanan Creek. Only B.C. Parks staff, contractors, and quarry personnel would be allowed to take their vehicles beyond Buchanan Creek. The situation with the stretch of road between the creeks, as well as the bridge crossings, is always open depending on flood events and ad hoc repairs. Anyone going into Kakwa from the B.C. side on foot, horseback, or mountain bike should be prepared for the 12 kilometres from Bastille to Buchanan Creek, in addition to the 17 kilometres from Buchanan Creek to Kakwa Lake. The 29 kilometres to Kakwa Lake may be a little too much for most people to undertake in one day, especially if carrying heavy packs and starting in the afternoon after the long drive from Prince George. Options are to spend the first night at either Buchanan Creek, or at Mariel Lake just over the McGregor Pass.

In 2003, access to the park became even more limited owing to washouts on the Walker Creek Forest Service road. Anyone planning a trip into Kakwa Park should watch the weather and be aware that creeks can run dangerously high after periods of heavy rain. And as we found out in 2000, snow is possible at any time of the year. A good idea is to check current access and park conditions with park staff at the Ministry of Water, Land and Air Protection before going in. Despite its length, the walk into Kakwa is a very beautiful part of the trip, on a mostly excellent track that has a steady, but easy grade. When kept in perspective, the full 29-kilometre walk from Bastille Creek is not a lot different from the popular hike into Berg Lake at Mount Robson. And it certainly adds to the sense of wilderness and accomplishment when you arrive at Kakwa Lake.

South

Blackwater Road

The Blackwater Road winds south through rural countryside, leaving Highway 16 a few kilometres before reaching the southwestern boundary of the city of Prince George. It passes close to the Prince George Astronomical Society's observatory on Tedford Road, situated clear of the city lights and next to open fields that afford good views of the night sky. Here, public viewing sessions are held from time to time, often coinciding with interesting events in the night sky. Farther south, the paved West Lake Road branches east from the Blackwater Road 11 kilometres south of Highway 16 and heads down a steep hill to West Lake Provincial Park. The wide beach and extensive picnic area are popular day-use features of a park that is only a few kilometres from the city.

Fort George Canyon Trail

The West Lake Road continues southward above the east shore of West Lake until, 11 kilometres from the Blackwater Road, signs on the left (east) side of the now unpaved road point to the start of the Fort George Canyon hiking trail. After driving along a narrow track to a small parking area in the young forest, a five-kilometre walk through mixed woods (with interpretive signs), leads down to the historic canyon site on the Fraser River—this area has recently been designated a provincial park. The first two or three kilometres of the trail are relatively flat, leading to a viewpoint overlooking the wide Fraser River valley to the southeast. For cross-country skiers, this may be a good turnaround point and place to catch any sun while you lunch. From here, the trail descends, at times steeply, to the river. Total hiking time is a little over one hour each way, well within

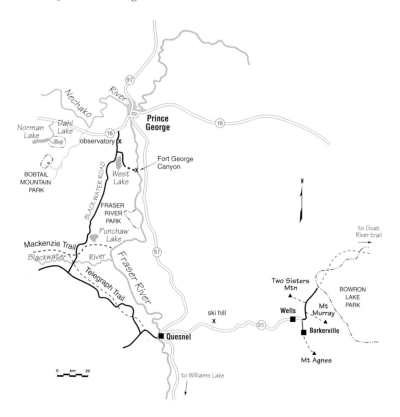

reach of almost anyone. At the river, one can picnic and watch the rapids, imagining the great sternwheelers such as the Charlotte, the B.C. Express, the B.X,. and the Conveyor plying through the canyon in the early years of the twentieth century. At first, the steamers needed the assistance of lines and winches to gain upstream passage through the Fort George Canyon and through the similarly hazardous Cottonwood Canyon downstream, closer to Quesnel. Today you can explore the riverbanks in Fort George Canyon for an old winch pin that was set in the rock where the trail meets the river, and for the remains of the historic portage trail downstream from there. In 1909, the experienced riverboat Captain O.F. Browne reported that, "...a modern sternwheeler of good power might be able to steam up both canyons at a fair stage of water in the river." On hearing this, the B.C. Express Company undertook to build a new sternwheeler to be ready in the spring of 1910. It would cost $40,000 and would be equipped with an electric light plant, searchlight, steam steering gear, and an engine that would develop 40 per cent more power than any other

Historic winch pin at the Fort George Canyon.

boat of comparable size on the river. It would have steam-heated, velvet-carpeted staterooms, crockery made especially in England, and a bridal chamber with a silk eiderdown.

We may be able to travel between Prince George and Quesnel much faster today, but certainly not in the style of those early years. More importantly, the B.C. Express Company signed Captain Browne to be master of the new steamer, which was named the *B.X.* Captain Browne took his time getting to know the *B.X.* and continued to line her through the canyons, until on June 24th, 1910, he made the first successful unaided navigation of Fort George Canyon heading upstream to South Fort George.

Baldy Hughes

Returning to the Blackwater Road and continuing south, the pavement ends at the old Baldy Hughes Canadian Forces Radar Base, now a resort. In 1980 I spent a weekend there, living in the barracks, eating the abundant meals available in the mess, and crawling around in the surrounding woods learning to track people under the direction of Joel Hardin, a member of the U.S. Border Patrol. Tracking was a tool that was then being adapted by search and rescue organizations in B.C. to significantly improve their effectiveness in finding lost people, or at least to help point the search in the right direction.

Punchaw Lake

The Blackwater Road continues south from Baldy Hughes to Punchaw Lake. This lake was described to me when I arrived in Prince George in 1978 as the first fishing lake in the area to open in the spring. And it was here in May 1979 that I saw my first wolves—a pack of seven animals silently crossing the road ahead of me as I drove around a bend at dusk. In those days, there was no sign that anything of great interest had ever happened here. I was soon to learn differently, however, as I read A.G. Morice's *The History of the Northern Interior of British Columbia*. Published in 1904, it includes an account of Alexander Mackenzie embarking on "Thursday 4th July 1793," on the last overland stretch of his historic journey to become the first recorded person to cross the North American continent north of Mexico. According to Morice, as Mackenzie left the Fraser River, "...he directed his steps in their company toward the village of the Naskhu'tins, which was then eleven miles distant from the mouth of the Blackwater River, on a lake called Poencho." Strangely, in the accompanying map, Morice labeled it "'Big Lake," but its name seems to have settled as "Punchaw." Mackenzie, in his journal, talked of his night at this place: "At sunset an elderly man and three other natives joined us from the Westward. The former bore a lance that very much resembled a sergeant's halberd. He had lately received it, by way of barter, from the natives of the Sea-Coast, who procured it from the white men." This was an indication that Mackenzie was within striking distance of his historic goal, the Pacific Ocean. Mackenzie and his men, carrying loads of 90 pounds each, and aided by native guides, walked to the Bella Coola River in only 12 days. Most present-day backpackers with the latest in high-tech gear take much longer.

Nuxalk Carrier Grease Trail

Surveying and re-clearing of the Nuxalk Carrier Grease Trail, or the Mackenzie Heritage Trail as it was otherwise known, began in 1975 and was essentially completed in the 1980s. It retraced both the historic Indian Grease Trail that was used in the trade of eulachon grease, and Mackenzie's journey to the Pacific. The Nuxalk Carrier Grease Trail historically connects the Fraser River across the Interior Plateau to the Bella Coola Valley at Burnt Bridge Creek, and has lately taken on additional significance as one of the westernmost sections of Canada's National Hiking Trail as it skirts Prince George. A pleasant day-hike can be had from the Blackwater Road parking area at the top of the hill leading down to the Blackwater River. There, the Grease Trail heads west along the top of the very scenic Blackwater Valley escarpment. Because of its southerly aspect, this escarpment has a climate more reminiscent of a few hundred kilometres south, and is always a good late or early season place to go hiking. On one early season walk, for example, the usually scenic valley was at first obscured in snowstorm, yet within half an hour, we were stripping off clothes and soaking up the spring sun while enjoying superb views across the Blackwater River Valley.

The Telegraph Trail

Intersecting the Nuxalk Carrier Grease Trail, a few kilometres west of the Blackwater Road hill, is another historic trail. The Collins Telegraph Trail climbs up from the Blackwater River and heads northwest toward the Bulkley Valley and Hazelton, before swinging north to the small community of Telegraph Creek on the Stikine River, and then on to the Yukon. The telegraph line was built in 1865 in a race to link North America and Europe via Alaska, across the Bering Strait, and through Russia. Unfortunately for the venture, a man named Cyrus Field successfully laid the first Atlantic cable, after several failed attempts, in 1866. The section of the telegraph line in B.C. was completed in 1899 to serve the gold fields in the Yukon, and remained in local use until 1935. One can see pieces of original copper wire and insulators lying on the ground both north of the Blackwater River and also in Raspberry Pass in Mount Edziza Provincial Park south of Telegraph Creek.

Blackwater River

The Blackwater River corridor was the subject of a Local Resource Use Plan in the early 1990s to integrate a range of overlapping interests that included recreation, scenery, wildlife, ranching, and forestry. The Blackwater LRUP was especially interesting in that it straddled parts of both the Prince George and Quesnel Forest Districts, where the Blackwater River marks their joint boundary. The river is sometimes used by canoeists and kayakers but can be dangerous, and there have been several accidents and missing person incidents, so extreme caution is advised. Where the road from Prince George and Baldy Hughes crosses the Blackwater River, there are also scenic walks along the riverbank.

Blackwater south to Quesnel

From the Blackwater River, rather than retracing ones steps to Prince George, another option is to continue south to Quesnel by the back roads, and return via Highway 97. The country south of the Blackwater opens up into more ranchland and takes on a gradual rural–urban feel, leading to a long descent down into Quesnel. On one such trip, I paused in the late afternoon for a snack next to a large open field of curious cows. As my car rolled to a stop, a sea of heads turned to stare at me in the light of the setting sun as if I was the highlight of their day.

In Quesnel, one can round out a day of historic walks by completing one or both of the riverside trail loops within the city. The main trail follows the east bank of the Fraser River to the hospital, where it crosses an old part of town to the Quesnel River, and follows it back to its confluence with the Fraser. There are many historic interpretive signs, old buildings, and artifacts on the paved five-kilometre route, and the hour that it takes to walk is a good way to build an appetite for dinner in Prince George's sister town before the drive north. If you have more time to spend in Quesnel, the decorated wooden pedestrian bridge across the Fraser leads to a small shopping centre and another loop trail between the Fraser River and Baker Creek. From this point, a seven kilometre drive north on the east side of Baker Creek brings you to Pinnacles Provincial Park, a stunning feature of Quesnel that is another must-see. A trail system there gives superb views back toward Quesnel, across a gorge filled with erosion pillars.

Wells and Barkerville

One of Interior B.C.'s main tourist and outdoor recreation destinations is Barkerville, 80 kilometres east of Quesnel. There is so much to be found here both historically and recreationally, that many books have been written about the area, including the recent publication from Rocky Mountain Books, *Hiking the Cariboo Goldfields*, by Garry Edwards, Dorothea Funk and Ken Stoker. I won't try to compete with these, and instead will point to just a few of the highlights. The centrepiece, of course, is the Cariboo gold rush town of Barkerville itself, preserved in its historic form with period-costumed staff and live re-enactments at the theatre, courthouse, schoolhouse, church, bakery, gold panning sites, and more during summer months.

Shortly after arriving in Prince George, I took a prospecting course at the College of New Caledonia. The instructor, a man who had worked as a geologist in prospecting and mining exploration all over the world, told us of his fantasy. He imagined an undiscovered

Isaac Lake – largest of the chain of lakes making up the world famous canoe circuit in Bowron Lake Provincial Park.

motherlode lying under the only piece of real estate that might not have been worked over near Barkerville. His secret reverie, he said, was to take a bulldozer in the middle of the night and dig up the main street of Barkerville to look for gold! Perhaps future archeologists will have a chance to do that, but in the meantime the site is much more valuable as one of British Columbia's principle historic tourist sites. Walking through Barkerville and past the Richfield Courthouse just outside of town, a first-class trail continues south for another seven kilometres to Groundhog Lake below Mount Agnes and Elk Mountain. In winter, the area is used for skiing, snowmobiling, and occasionally for dog sledding.

Another popular spot for hikers and backcountry skiers is located just northeast of Wells on the road to Bowron Lake Provincial Park. There are two trailheads to this area, located on the eastern side of the road as it heads north, at roughly four and six kilometres respectively. They mark the termini of a nine-kilometre loop hike that includes a cabin, the Waverly Hut, and the summit of Mount Murray. (Not to be confused with the Mount Murray in Pine Pass or the Mount Murray ski hill at Fort St. James!) There are many other trails in the Wells–Barkerville area that one can find by asking in Quesnel or Wells. Continuing north from Mount Murray, the entrance to Bowron Lake Park and its famous wilderness canoe circuit is soon reached. Check with B.C. Parks for conditions and access quotas. There are other stops of interest along Highway 26 from Quesnel to Barkerville, including the south-facing Troll ski hill that is great for spring sun, Cottonwood House historic site, and the historic town of Wells itself.

Cariboo getaway

A weekend destination that is within easy reach of Prince George but often overlooked is the Horsefly and Likely area, southeast of Quesnel and east of Williams Lake. From time to time we hear interesting tidbits about this historic part of the Cariboo, and it's definitely worth checking out. My wife, Judy Lett, and I chose the first Victoria Day weekend of the new millennium to head down there — a pleasant time of year, when one can reasonably expect to have good weather, few bugs, and not too many tourists. The lazy Saturday morning drive included a long stop in Quesnel to spend the afternoon walking the riverfront trails mentioned above, which the city has turned into a kind of giant outdoor heritage museum. The many artifacts, decorative trail signs, and interpretive signs are well maintained — a sure sign that Quesnel residents take pride in this feature of their community. Returning across the wooden pedestrian bridge over the Fraser River to our starting point, we enjoyed tea and dessert at a heritage-style restaurant that was housed in the 150-year old former Hudson Bay Company Trading Post, the oldest standing building in town. Quesnel and its riverfront trails are worth the drive from Prince George almost any time of year, and especially during the annual Billy Barker Days Festival in mid-July.

Heading on to Williams Lake, we stopped to check out the famous "Devils Fence Posts" located 56 kilometres south of Quesnel on the east side of the highway. These basaltic columns are similar to the

'Devils Fence Posts' — striking outcropping of basaltic columns on the east side of Highway 97 halfway between Quesnel and Williams Lake.

Giants Causeway in Ireland. Strangely, this formation has not been signed nor recognized in anyway and most people drive by without realizing its significance. Williams Lake is a good spot for supper before striking out eastward on the paved road to Horsefly. During my first drive on this road, I expected to see lots of bush, but was surprised to find that the entire 50-kilometre route has many rural property developments. Actually, it's really not surprising given its long history as part of the Cariboo Road to the gold fields. The road climbs for a few kilometres and then levels out through attractive rolling, wooded, and open countryside with many small lakes. In the distance are the snow-capped peaks of the Cariboo Range.

Like other communities off the beaten track, Horsefly has a pace of life that is just a little slower. During our visit in May 2000, we chose to stay in a provincial park campground a few kilometres east of town on the north shore of scenic Horsefly Lake. It was only lightly occupied that early in the season, and despite the lateness of the hour on a holiday weekend, ours was the only tent at a quiet spot near the waterline. We were greeted warmly by the park operator, and I inquired of her what time we could get coffee in town in the morning. The night was pleasant, with sounds of gently lapping water near the tent, accompanied by the calls of distant loons. We got up the next morning intending to take an early walk to a nearby viewpoint before heading into Horsefly in search of the coffee I had asked about. As I crawled out of the tent, I saw a bag on the picnic table that hadn't been there the night before. Curious, I went over to it and found a thermos full of fresh coffee, fixings, spoons, cups and a note, compliments of the park operator. When we returned the empty thermos to her house later in the morning, she said she had also meant to bring muffins, but had left them behind. We had stumbled upon the legendary Cariboo hospitality, and found a big reason to return to Horsefly on another occasion. The park operator had not expected anything in return, but I was able to repay her kindness by writing a newspaper column about our experience, and sending her a copy of the article. I was surprised, later, to discover that B.C. Parks had picked up the story for their internal newsletter as an example of a contractor providing service beyond the call of duty. There is justice in the world after all!

Fire lookout open to the public

There are not many opportunities left to visit an operational forest service fire lookout tower in the Interior of B.C. A few years ago, one could take a short walk up Pilot Mountain just north of Prince George during the fire season and visit the duty lookout person there. My kids and I were present one evening when the lookout spotted a fire west of Ness Lake. We ate our picnic supper and watched and listened to the radio chatter with interest as he directed the "bird dog," or guide aircraft, to lead the bombers to the fire. Most of the fire detection in the Prince George Forest District is now done by remote sensing, and the few lookouts that are left are located on mountaintops that are inaccessible to most people. But driving south to the Lower Mainland or to the Okanagan, there is an opportunity right next to Highway 97. The Mount Begbie Lookout Tower is located 20 kilometres south of 100 Mile House. Watch for the *Stop of Interest* sign then turn off at Lookout Road on the eastern side of the highway. There is a parking lot, washrooms, picnic tables, a large interpretive sign, and a short trail to the actual lookout. The site is perfectly situated for a brisk exercise break during a long drive. Begbie Mountain is part of the Interior Plateau and was formed during the Jurassic period more than one hundred and forty million years ago. The trail from the parking lot to the lookout is short and rugged, but it takes the average person only five minutes each way. A variety of trees and brush including juniper can be seen beside the path, along with crocuses and wild roses blooming in season. The summit is named after Judge Begbie, the infamous "hanging judge" during the peak gold rush years of 1858 to 1868. With an elevation of 1,276 metres, Begbie Lookout affords a stunning 360-degree view of nine million hectares of forestland and mountains; almost the entire Cariboo can be seen from that one vantage point. The first fire lookout was built on the site in 1923, and has been replaced at least once. At the time of writing this book, the lookout is staffed and operational during the summer fire season, and is open to visitors from 8 am to 5 pm, seven days a week.

As I approached the low structure, two dogs on the tower's catwalk announced my arrival. At this point on my first visit, I didn't know that the tower was officially open to the public as there was nothing on the parking lot signs to indicate this. But the duty lookout invited me to come up, gave me an interpretive pamphlet, and asked me to sign the guest book. She was welcoming, and explained that many people are hesitant to approach when they see that the tower is staffed, and hear the dogs. When I was there, the lookout was operational despite a wet summer, but all around were signs of showers that could easily develop into lightning as the day progressed. I looked around, not minding that the visibility was limited by weather. Softly overhanging clouds and showers added to the grandeur of the scene, giving it a sense of mystery—surface and atmosphere seemed to coalesce into one. And it gave me an excuse to stop again at this place of unusual beauty to experience it on a clearer day.

West

Otway – Miworth Roads

Otway Ski Centre

The Otway Road parallels the Nechako River as it winds west from the north end of Tabor and Ospika Boulevards within the City of Prince George. The river sometimes touches the road, and at other times meanders north. At the city boundary is the Otway cross-country ski centre, also serving as the northern terminus of the Cranbrook Hill Greenway trail. Directly across the road from the ski centre is a lesser-known tract of undeveloped land—the proposed Nechako River Park—bordered by a large meander in the Nechako River to the north and the Otway Road to the south. There are several rough trails in this area, making it a good place to practice both bushwhacking and compass use, as a straight-line compass walk in any direction will soon hit the river or the road.

Wilkins Regional Park – Miworth

Leaving the city, the Otway Road becomes the Miworth Road and soon enters the small community of Miworth where it makes a sharp turn to the left (south) above the Nechako River cutbanks. Although there is no parking at this corner, a foot trail leads downhill to the river and to Wilkins Regional Park. Continuing on the main road for a short distance, a side road heads west and descends into the park where there is ample parking by the river. Facilities include one of the best, yet lightly used, picnic sites close to Prince George, as well as a camping area for groups such as scouts or guides, an extensive riverside and forest trail network, and a boat launch area. During the summer months, the well-kept trail snakes along the river and through lush, seemingly tropical jungle,

Nechako River on a minus 25 Celsius day.

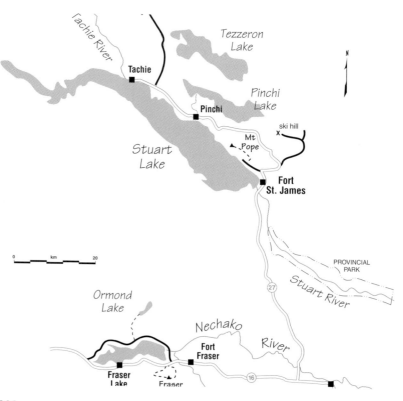

while bald eagles and ospreys can sometimes be seen overhead. In the spring, migrating geese and trumpeter swans can often be seen on the open water along the north side of the river.

By canoe from Miworth to Prince George

One of the most pleasing recreational opportunities in Prince George is to launch a canoe at Wilkins Park on a warm summer day, and paddle or float down the Nechako River to the city. Even without much effort, the five-kilometre per hour current, and the generally favourable prevailing winds, means the trip can be done in under three hours. The water is an easy grade all the way, although the Nechako is a fast-moving river that has claimed lives and must be respected. Shortly after putting in, the bleached remains of the old reaction ferry can be seen on the north bank of the river in the form of a wooden derrick and two skeleton hulls. Reaction ferries were once common in the interior of B.C. for crossing rivers like the Fraser and the Nechako. They were attached to derricks on both riverbanks by means of a cable system, and the energy of the river current was used to move the ferry across. The river sweeps north around two large meanders before straightening out for the long run into Prince George. Along the way there are forests, cutbanks, wildlife, rustic picnic and swimming possibilities, riverside residential areas, and a few riffles to add a little fast water excitement. Once, when sweeping around a bend in the river just above Miworth, I found my canoe heading directly toward a black bear sunning itself in the shallows. We both had only a few seconds to react and, with mutual consternation, to get out of each other's way.

Alexander Mackenzie bicentennial reenactment. Arrival at the confluence of the Nechako and Fraser Rivers in Prince George – July 1993.

Approaching Prince George, it's important to give a wide berth to all bridge abutments to avoid the danger of your boat becoming trapped and crushed by the strength of the current. Just past Foothills Bridge there is a takeout opportunity at Wilson Park on North Ospika Boulevard—a good choice if you live in that part of the city and wish to avoid the drive downtown. However, it is definitely worth continuing the ride downriver to the confluence with the Fraser, where there are two good takeout places, each with a parking lot. One is above, and the other is below Cottonwood Island Park. Just before entering the Fraser River, the Nechako widens and becomes flat and almost lake-like, making it a safe place to end the trip, or to just practice canoeing or kayaking on a summer evening. If you proceed into the Fraser, exercise particular caution around the bridge abutments there as well, as dangerous sheers and whirlpools can develop, especially during high water. If you choose this option, there are takeout opportunities below the Yellowhead Bridge at the Hudson Bay Slough in Fort George Park and at Paddlewheel Park.

The Hudson Bay Slough used to mark the end of the famous "Northern" canoe race from Isle Pierre, above Miworth to Prince George—an event that I hope will be revived someday. It has also been used as a takeout for historically significant events. One such event was the 1993 cross-Canada re-enactment of Alexander Mackenzie's first crossing of the North American continent north of Mexico, with a colourful flotilla of canoes arriving for ceremonies in Fort George Park. Amazingly, Mackenzie, who was looking for a river from the west and was making meticulous and detailed observations and journal entries, missed seeing the mouth of the Nechako!

Paddling or floating down the Nechako River is a leisurely way to spend a warm, sunny afternoon, and a chance to see the city from an entirely different vantage point. Logistics require having someone drop you off at Miworth, and either pick you up or leave a vehicle at your takeout point. Alternately, two vehicles can be used to ferry people and canoes. Another option that I have used on many occasions is to take a canoe and supplies out to Miworth early in the morning. After leaving them in a secure place, drive back to Wilson Park in Prince George and then walk back to Miworth! This is not as daunting as it may seem—using old rustic trails, plus more recent mountain bike trails, and by cutting directly across the top of Cranbrook Hill to pick up the old Takla Road into Miworth, it can be done in two to three hours at a brisk pace. The cool morning air is ideal for walking, with an arrival at the canoe in time for a refreshing swim and lunch before the float back to town in the warmth of the afternoon.

Eskers Provincial Park

It was in February 1988 that some 50 people met to help fast-track the planning process for what was to become Eskers Provincial Park. Located about 30 kilometres west of the Hart Highway along the Chief Lake Road, this unusual pocket of wilderness is more reminiscent of the Canadian Shield country in eastern Canada than central British Columbia. Uncomfortable at being asked to help plan an area that few of us knew anything about, I spent the next four weekends in February and March of 1988 on mountain touring skis with climbing skins, alone and with friends, exploring every nook and corner of the new park. There were no access roads or trails then, and my five treks into the area entailed bushwhacking from either Ness Lake to the south, or Murch Lake to the north. Later, I plotted my travels on the detailed 1:8,500 contour map that had been commissioned from air photos taken the year before and found that I had covered 72 kilometres, 1,682 vertical metres, and had visited 58 lakes and sloughs.

Eskers Provincial Park is part of the Stuart Eskers complex, running from the area of Fort St. James to the city of Prince George. The easternmost examples can be found west of Garvin Creek on the north side of the Nechako River just outside of the city, and Moores Meadow Park and other depression-like parks within the city bowl. Eskers Park is the best representation of this complex: it comprises a series of glacial kettle lakes formed after residual blocks of ice melted, interspersed with ridges of braided eskers built of debris left by rivers flowing underneath the ice sheet. As well as these impressive interpretive features from the last ice age, the park is a lovely wooded area suitable for walking, cross-country skiing, canoeing or fishing, and it is a wonderful place to visit any time of year.

The trail system covers only about half of the original park, leaving a lot of the area still in a wild state for those who like to explore off-trail. Looking back at my old map, I found notations that I made of places I had visited in 1988. Intriguing words and phrases such as pretty lake, rugged lake, very nice route, challenging route finding, avalanche slope, mature spruce, steep and thick bush, and nice open ridge, all entice me to explore some more. And since its initial inception, the park has been extended almost as far again to the northwest under the 1999 protected area recommendations of the Prince George Land and Resource Management Plan. Although they have quite a different geological origin, the lakes and hills of Eskers Park that give rise to its superficial resemblance to the Canadian Shield, have created a landscape that is unique around Prince George.

Fall in Eskers Provincial Park.

Eskers Provincial Park

Activity Walking, Canoeing, Cross-country Skiing and Fishing
Rating 3 to 5 hours round trip to Kathie Lake from the parking lot
Distance 11 km round trip to Kathie Lake
Principal Elevation Gain Many small ups and downs
Map 93 J/3 Saxton Lake
Details Follow the Chief Lake Road, Ness Lake Road, and Ness Lake Road North to the park entrance, west northwest of Prince George. Eskers Park is perhaps the nicest outdoor place to visit, year round, close to Prince George

Winter Solstice at Eskers

The parking lot is deserted, save for a pickup truck with, oddly, the driver's door left open. The day is clear, and the new snow that fell a few days before is perfect for cross-country skiing. Less than half an hour from the suburbs of Prince George, Eskers Provincial Park is one of my favourite places any time of the year. Ski tracks lead from the enclosed picnic shelter with its ample supply of winter firewood, past Pine Marsh to the beaver dams at the end of the special-needs trail, then skirt the swamp and lake to the north. Whoever left these tracks had not sufficient wax on their skis to avoid having to herringbone up the easy grades. The snows are late this year. Only days before, people in the area were enjoying nearly unprecedented ice-skating under a full December moon, on clear and deeply frozen lakes.

Climbing east from Ridgeview Lake then dropping north to intersect a chain of smaller lakes, there are few signs marking the newly covered landscape. The first snow of winter is at once both a finished masterpiece and an empty canvas—waiting for nature, the artist, to begin its work. Like a Tibetan sand mandala, each form has a destiny of impermanence as it merges with the next snowfall and ultimately into the melt of spring. The vegetation is dormant at minus 15 degrees Celsius, yet hidden from human sight the soil harbours a frenzy of protozoan life nearing its January peak. The trail climbs roller coaster over the braided eskers left behind by melting glaciers of the last ice age. Each climb is rewarded by a few minutes of serpentine descent through the mixed woods and lakes. I feel sufficiently confident with my skiing in the soft new snow to look around at the blur of trees and passing terrain. I am a passenger in my own body, looking out through the windows of my eyes.

At Camp Lake the tracks exit the trail and lead across the ice toward two figures standing hunched over a hole, fishing. I detour to tell them about the open truck in the parking lot; then, breaking trail for the first time, I strike northwest across Camp Lake. The rhythm of my old wooden skis breaks easily through the snow as I coast between long pinnacles of alternating sunlight and shadow. There is something pleasing, still, about skiing on wood. I climb a south-facing slope above an island where, before this place was developed, I had had to leave my dog for a few hours as I explored the northwest reaches of the proposed park—the snow was too deep for him that day. Thirteen years later, upon gaining the crest, I enjoy a short lunch in the sun at the picnic bench with its commanding view across Camp Lake. The trail is unbroken left and right. I continue on, making my own track and enjoying the varied colours of birch and aspen trees lit by the low winter sun hinting through the silent forest. I would return the next day with my camera to enjoy my tracks of today. But now, like the explorers of old, I have the pleasure of trail-blazing in the "New World" of winter. This is what life in the sub-boreal region is about for me, each unfolding season bringing its own magical renewal.

The summer trail ends on a peninsula near the south end of Kathie Lake, and I continue without pause onto its open expanse. Thoughts come to mind of early explorers who needed the frozen highways of winter to complete their surveys into uncharted areas. Men like Edward William Jarvis who, with five companions, journeyed in temperatures as low as minus 53 Fahrenheit (minus 47 Celsius) in the winter of 1875 from Prince George to Fort Edmonton seeking a northern railway crossing through the Rocky Mountains. Human tracks on Kathie Lake as well as Bow Lake mark where local people have walked in from the north to ice fish. I hadn't known there were fish in Bow Lake—most of these lakes are spring-fed from the surrounding water table and are not connected by streams. At the south end of Bow Lake I rejoin my in-track and start the hour-long ski back to the comfort of my car. The air is clear and cold as the winter solstice day fades into night. The three-hour trek through Eskers was just what I needed for a healthy dose of sunlight on the shortest day of the year, and to remind me why I live in the north.

Onto thin ice

November ended with cool temperatures and powdery snow that actually stays around instead of turning to "globally warmed" mush. Our local parks and trails quickly become accessible to cross-country skis and snowshoes, and in town, crystal-clad trees glint under blue skies, subtly changing light, and spectacular sunsets. The snow and cold were still around in early December 2001 when I made my first ski tour of the season into Eskers Provincial Park. A good trail led into Camp Lake, and from there the new snow lay clear and unblemished. For the second year in a row I had the pleasure of breaking the first track into Kathie Lake over an untouched and perfect path.

Arriving at the trail terminus on a peninsula of Kathie Lake, my plan was to ski down the lake and return via the Bow Lake trail. The ice should have been sound after several weeks of cold weather, and so it appeared for the most part. But there were open holes and dark patches visible in many spots. "Are they natural or ice fishing holes?" I wondered. This is a spring-fed lake, and last year, even in the depths of winter, I found a large open hole with water darkly welling upward. "Not a good place to be," I had thought, as I retreated to sound ice farther from shore. Travel over ice always carries some risk, but if you choose to do so, here are a few pointers. First, recognize that ice conditions differ from year to year owing to varying temperatures and snowfall. Heavy snow early in the season can insulate the ice before it has a chance to thicken. Springs are a common feature of many of our water table-fed lakes such as those in Eskers Park and around Bear Lake. Similarly, any moving water around inflows, outflows, and narrows can weaken the ice. Even if the ice is strong enough to support you, there may be surface or subsurface water that can freeze to skis or snowshoes and render travel difficult, possibly resulting in wet and frostbitten feet. Watch out for the sunny sides of lakes; note any darkness in the ice that may be caused by water seepage; and be wary of rocks or logs in the water that might absorb solar heat and weaken the surrounding ice. The tracks of animals can tell you whether the ice is likely to be safe or not depending on species and habits. You can distribute your weight by using skis or snowshoes, but make sure that your bindings can be released quickly under water. It is possible (perhaps counter intuitively) that a smaller person or child may exert more relative ground pressure because of their small feet, and could be at more risk than a larger person. A probe or a ski pole can be used to test the thickness of the ice ahead by the sound that the tip makes as it strikes the ice. And carrying something sharp may provide the means to grab the ice and pull yourself out should you fall through.

On that early December day, I paused to enjoy a soft palette of pre-solstice sun illuminating the frozen water and beckoning through snowclad deciduous trees on the far shore. After testing the ice, I resisted the temptation to cross the lake and returned via the now imperfect, but faster path of my outward journey.

Bobtail Mountain

Less than an hour southwest of Prince George is a moderately easy hill-walk over an unusual outcropping of serpentine rock, noted for harbouring special vegetation types. Bobtail Mountain is one of the new protected areas arising from the 1999 Prince George Land and Resource Management Plan. The new 1,300-hectare provincial park is located near the headwaters of Gregg Creek, and is situated to protect the ecological representation and unique rock formation found there, as well as the existing hiking trail. The trail and shelter were built by the now defunct Northwood Pulp and Timber Ltd. in 1993, and provide good views of the Interior Plateau. To locate the trail, proceed west on Highway 16 past the Mud (Chilako) River, and turn south on the Gregg Creek Forest Road about 28 kilometres from downtown Prince George. Continue south on this first-class forest road for 23 kilometres, before turning right onto a side road and heading west for another seven kilometres. The trail starts at a gravelled parking lot in the middle of a cutblock. The sign in the parking lot says that the trail is five kilometres long with an elevation gain of 470 metres. These statistics are misleading as the trail goes up and down and feels longer than the posted distance—perhaps it is. With stops and a couple of viewpoint side trips, it could take you as long as three hours to get up and two hours down.

Helicopter pilot, Don Buchanan and George Evanoff prepare to work on the new Bobtail Mountain hut – November 1993.

The initially rough trail leaves the parking lot and climbs to the top right-hand corner of the block, where it is blazed with plastic markers. Once in the forest, the trail is in reasonable shape and is well marked for most of the route, although some attention is needed from time to time, especially near the top, to avoid walking off the trail. A good tip whenever the route becomes a little indistinct is to check over your shoulder frequently to see what the back trail looks like. Wildlife viewing opportunities along the way include moose, bear, wolf, and cougar. In addition, there are many interesting glades, rocky outcroppings, and tantalizing glimpses of the surrounding plateau through the trees. At the top is a small hut that offers shelter from the elements, but little more, as it has no insulation, no stove and not much furniture. It is unsuited to overnight use, especially since there is no potable water on the route, and it is necessary for a visitor to carry whatever they need with them. When I was last there, it felt a little strange to see my name as the first entry in the book in 1994 when, with Don Buchanan and George Evanoff, I flew from Prince George to porcupine-proof the walls of the hut with sheet aluminum. One of the main ingredients in the glue that bonds the layers of veneer in plywood used in many modern buildings is animal blood. Whether it is the salt in the blood, or other ingredients in the plywood that attracts porcupines, leaving plywood unprotected in a mountain cabin is a sure invitation to porcupines to quickly eat it down to a 2x4 frame. On that trip, we also wind-proofed the roof by replacing the original nails with roofing screws, and while George and I worked on the cabin, our pilot, Don, made furniture and shelves from leftover building materials. Don Buchanan had arranged with his employer to donate the helicopter time to the project, and this was one of many times that I had the pleasure of flying with one of Prince George's best helicopter pilots.

On my most recent visit to Bobtail Mountain, we were late leaving town and didn't start hiking until 1:30 pm. It was tempting to sit longer in the sun at the top, but it was after 4 pm and we prudently kept our snack break short in order to get down by nightfall. The wind moaned through the predominantly pine forest for most of the trip, but died under a peaceful sky as we emerged from the forest below. A thin cloud layer overhead and clear sky to the west gave us a spectacular sunset as we drove home on the Gregg Creek Road.

Vanderhoof

One hour, and a hundred kilometres west of Prince George, Vanderhoof offers a wealth of outdoor opportunities that can be combined with a small-town evening out. This can simply be dinner at the end of a day of hiking, but another idea had been growing on me for a few years, and I finally tried it out in 2002. The result was unexpected. It wasn't the first time that Vanderhoof had surprised me. Ten years before, acting on a word of mouth tip, I drove out to Tachick Lake just southwest of Vanderhoof to enjoy the finest meal of my life prepared by a master chef from Germany.

First things first, though—let me briefly review some of the outdoor opportunities in the Vanderhoof area to properly set the scene. For an easy walk, there is the nature reserve and viewing platform on the Nechako River right in the town of Vanderhoof. A little farther afield, the Ormond Creek trails offer easy to moderate walks on the north side of Fraser Lake. On the south (Highway 16) side of the lake, Fraser Mountain provides a range of from one to four hours of walking with spectacular views. And, 54 kilometres northwest of Vanderhoof is the scenic Fort St. James, with its historic fort, south-facing ski hill (sun-drenched on a good day), and the spectacular Pope Mountain hiking trail. But the focus of my attention on this occasion was on the main street of downtown Vanderhoof. For nearly a quarter of a century I had been driving past the tiny movie house, with its ancient stucco walls and facade reminiscent of a small-town theatre of the 1930s. In fact, the building dates back to before the 1920s, and was probably a garage before it became a theatre. I was curious to see what it was like inside, and had been waiting for the right opportunity. The problem was, I never knew what was playing until one day, motivated after seeing a film set in a similar looking theatre in a small, mid-twentieth century U.S. town, I turned to the Internet and after searching "theatre," "movie," and "Vanderhoof" I quickly found the Grand Reo Web site. It was immediately clear that the Grand Reo might be something more than a leftover of another era. It was independently owned, and featured prominently as a historic building in a Canada-wide movie theatre directory. My interest was piqued, and I watched the site for a couple of weeks until a hiking opportunity coincided with a film that I wanted to see, and the die was cast.

Parking a few metres away from the old facade just before the early Sunday evening show, we felt that we had just travelled half a century back in time. Entering the lobby, the young man manning the ticket counter laughed as I knocked over a sign. "Don't worry, that happens to everyone," he said. Ticket counter was a misnomer as there weren't actually any tickets that night—we just paid the very reasonable admission price and walked in. Even the popcorn was affordable. Inside, we were in for the really big surprise. While the exterior of the theatre was kept in its historic form, the interior had been totally renovated. Comfortable new seats; a cozy, traditionally shaped theatre with excellent projection; and a state-of-the-art wraparound sound system played at a comfortable volume that is a rare find these days. And the finishing touch—wood laminate floors throughout. The theatre has one screen, but frequently offers a range of films staggered at different showtimes; and according to the Web site, even occasionally accepts film requests. We spent the next two hours enjoying both the theatre and a current-run film with its period flashbacks supplementing the ambience of the place. We left with the conviction that this was perhaps the nicest theatre we had ever been in, and drove back to Prince George in fading daylight, treated to a fine midsummer sunset in the rearview mirrors.

Fort St. James and Pope Mountain

The day was spectacular; the bugs kept us moving on the trail, but a light breeze held them away on the summit. For those who haven't tried Mount Pope at Fort St. James, it's a relatively easy hike as mountains go, and is often used as an early season warm-up before the snow has left the higher peaks. Trailhead parking is located in a gravel pit, reached by driving north through Fort St. James and turning west along Stone Bay Road for three and a half kilometres. Views across Stuart Lake are quickly earned as the good-quality trail climbs steeply past a series of viewpoints equipped with bench seats. For those who don't wish to go to the top, or don't have the time, this part of the trail alone is a worthwhile hike. After that, the trail heads inland for an hour before regaining views of the lake for a last gradual ascent to the summit, seven kilometres from the start. On the top is an unusual sight—a gazebo that was built by a Fort St. James forest company as a recreational project to replace the old fire lookout. The summit affords one of the best 360-degree views in the Northern Interior, encompassing Stuart, Pinchi, and Tezzeron Lakes in the foreground, with long-range views across the broad sweep of the Interior Plateau toward the mountain ranges to the west. On a recent hike on Pope Mountain, I passed a group of local hikers coming down after making their first ascent in 30 years of living in the area, an indicator of changing lifestyles perhaps. An hour and a half to two-hour descent brings you back to the parking lot northwest of Fort St. James in time, if one is inclined, for a refreshing dip in Stuart Lake and a visit to the historic fort.

Early winter snow.

North to the Nation Lakes

Driving through Fort St. James, there are large areas of low-elevation provincial forestland covering old lakebed soils. A strategy developed by the Fort St. James Land and Resource Management Plan in the late 1990s will gradually convert some thirty thousand hectares of these lacustrine soils to farmland, as they are suitable for growing hay, green feed, coarse grains, and for grazing cattle. The lengthy timeline, as well as the retention of wetlands and wildlife corridors, will mitigate impacts to forest harvesting and the effects of agriculture on wildlife and sustenance hunting.

The road on the north side of Stuart Lake heading west from Fort St. James to Tachie, was paved in 2000. At roughly the halfway point between the communities, it crosses Pinchi Creek, a popular fly-fishing stream that drains Pinchi Lake into Stuart Lake. Pinchi Lake was the site of a mercury mine that operated first during the Second World War, and again between 1969 and 1975. During the wartime, mine tailings were dumped directly into the lake, reputedly causing high levels of mercury in the water that then entered the food chain, especially concentrated in long-lived fish such as lake trout. On May 28, 2003, *The Province* newspaper in Vancouver reported that Tl'azt'en people living in the area of Pinchi Lake had begun documenting several decades of health problems that they attribute to mercury in the water. Pinchi Lake is located on the Pinchi Fault which contains a band of naturally occurring, mercury-laden ore called cinnabar that also affects other water bodies in the area such as Tezzeron Lake. Driving north on the Leo Creek Forest Service Road, the limestone escarpment that follows the fault is visible from the road. Running from Pope Mountain to Tchentlo Lake, Pinchi Fault is one of the longest in B.C. and provides an area of connectivity for many wildlife species.

Access management is an important part of road layout design in this area in order to minimize impacts to wildlife populations and habitats. Apart from human access needs, other considerations include travel convenience, avoiding excessive hunting pressure on wildlife, and routing roads around or away from sensitive meadows to reduce the impacts of four-wheel drive and off-road vehicles. After turning north from the Fort St. James to Tachie road onto the Leo Creek Forest Service Road, a 20-kilometre drive brings you to the Kuzkwa River crossing. Canoeing is considered good on the Kuzkwa River from Tezzeron Lake down to this road crossing, but increases in difficulty below the bridge to the Tachie River. Leaving the Leo Creek Forest Road at this point, the Driftwood Forest Service Road continues north for another 60 kilometres to Tchentlo Lake, the largest of the Nation

Lakes chain and a popular canoe route in B.C.'s Northern Interior. The canoe route begins with the 20-kilometre long Tsayta Lake, 180 kilometres northwest of Fort St. James, or another 40 kilometres along the Driftwood Forest Road past Tchentlo Lake. A six-kilometre river leads into the 11-kilometre long Indata Lake. From there, a five-kilometre river leads into the 45-kilometre Tchentlo Lake. A final five-kilometre stretch of river leads into 28-kilometre long Chuchi Lake to a takeout point that connects with the Germansen Indata Forest Service Road, and a 112-kilometre drive back to Fort St. James. In total, this trip adds up to 120 kilometres of lake and river canoeing, with many camping sites along the lakes to choose from. And, if you don't want to do a lot of ferrying of vehicles and canoes, several of the lodges and outfitters in the area can provide logistical support.

Approaching Tchentlo Lake on the Driftwood Forest Service Road, there are excellent views of Nation Mountain after passing from the Pacific into the Arctic watershed. At Tchentlo Lake, a reasonably priced lodge caters to a wide variety of clients, ranging from forestry workers, to snowmobilers in the winter, to fly-in or drive-in tourist parties in the summer. Just south of Tchentlo Lake the road passes a vantage point that offers good views of the Mitchell Range to the west and Nation Mountain to the east, where two caribou herds live by divergent means that require different forest management strategies. The Takla herd in the Mitchell Range numbers only around a hundred animals; it depends on arboreal or tree lichens since there are insufficient terrestrial or ground lichens accessible in its range. The Wolverine herd around Nation Mountain numbers some three hundred and fifty animals in scattered bands that tend to use more terrestrial lichens—the arboreal lichens aren't as critical to them.

Mountain caribou

Mountain caribou in British Columbia are considered threatened or endangered. They are subject to recovery planning under the new federal species at risk legislation that was enacted in the fall of 2002, and which comes into full force in June 2004. The problem is not so much the loss of their primary habitat, much of which is already protected; rather it is secondary predation by wolves, bears, cougars, and wolverines who move into the surrounding interface areas to prey on increasing populations of moose, deer and elk. Widespread human activity at lower elevations, especially logging, road building, and the cutting of seismic lines in potential oil and gas areas, creates more early seral forests and travel corridors that favour this ecological shift. And climate change is also a factor; for example, the large-scale disturbances resulting from insect infestations such as those of the mountain pine beetle.

Preserving mountain caribou populations may ultimately depend in part on society's willingness to engage in predator control, such as the killing of wolves or the capture and sterilizing of dominant pairs. But here, one has to be careful. Apart from the moral dilemma of controlling one species for the benefit of another, the indiscriminate killing of wolves is already driving down the size of wolf packs in B.C.'s interior, and paradoxically leading to an increase in wolf populations as more breeding pairs function in smaller packs. Every human intervention has a cascading effect throughout the environment that demands much research and careful balancing. In Germany in 2003, according to the Bavarian environment ministry, cormorants were feeding on rare species of fish such as grayling and pearl fish, creating the interesting situation of protected birds eating protected fish. Should the protected birds therefore be culled?

A study published in 2004 utilized a comprehensive data set of 20 years of mountain caribou radio and satellite telemetry that was collected throughout much of the animals' range in B.C. This study projects that all of the caribou in British Columbia north to the Hart Ranges are in steady decline. The study predicts that the mountain caribou from Prince George on south will be extirpated in the next few decades if present trends continue. And the reality is that the pace of human development is increasing and the decline in caribou populations can only intensify. Within living memory, mountain

Young mountain caribou approaching the author on a summit of the Upper Herrick Valley.

caribou used to travel through the city of Prince George and, as already related, across the Interior Plateau over such places as Coffeepot Mountain south of Bear Lake. The George Mountain herd, located just south of Prince George, in trouble for a few years, is believed to have finally disappeared in 2003 as I write. It may yet be possible to turn the situation around in the Interior, but this gets less certain the farther south one goes. Along with grizzly bears and a few other large animals, mountain caribou belong to what is euphemistically called "charismatic mega-fauna," that is to say, big furry critters that people most commonly associate with. In reality they are only part of the tip of a very big iceberg when it comes to species diversity, but their sensitivity to habitat disturbance makes them very interesting as an indicator species. Having had the privilege of meeting caribou many times in the mountains around Prince George, they have come to represent for me an essential wilderness value: that we must learn to co-exist with wildlife, and that we must not, through human action or inaction, deny them the future.

Fraser Lake

Fraser Mountain

One of the nice things about the Prince George area is still finding new places to hike after a quarter century of living here. I had driven by the Fraser Mountain trailhead many times en route between Prince George and points west of Vanderhoof, often thinking that one day I would take a quick walk up what appeared to be a short, wooded viewpoint trail. That opportunity came one September while driving home from Smithers. It was late afternoon, and I needed a short exercise break—was I ever in for a surprise. Once started I couldn't give it up, the trail and the views were that inviting, and it was three hours of hard hiking and nearly dark before I returned to my car.

The trail starts on the south side of Highway 16, just west of Fort Fraser. It is clearly marked with a hiking trail sign and a small parking area. The trail heads up an old skid road toward a rocky bluff that overlooks Fraser Lake. After a short, steep climb, the track starts to fade and a trail branches off to the right. It soon levels off and opens up into a well-built hiking trail that has been side-cut into the rocky ground. It contours through an old forest for about a kilometre before reaching a viewpoint overlooking the lake. Down on the highway, screened by trees, it isn't obvious how great the view is higher up. From here, the trail turns into the hill and climbs steeply. It gradually eases off at a higher viewpoint near the western end of the ridge. Leaving the second

Misty day over the east end of Fraser Lake from one of the early viewpoints on the Fraser Mountain Trail, just west of Fort Fraser.

viewpoint, the trail continues upward until it levels off to cross over to the south side of the ridge. A short side trail leads to an alpine-like knoll from where the hiker can look west across the Interior Plateau toward the Coast Mountains. The trail continues along the edge of the south side of the ridge for another two or three kilometres to the summit. The views throughout the hike are spectacular. On the summit there are several structures and microwave towers, and an access road from the other (east) side. If you are motivated by approaching nightfall, as I was, the hike can be done in a three-hour round trip. But, it's better to allow four or five hours for a more comfortable pace and a long picnic lunch on the ridge. Fraser Mountain is well worth the drive from Prince George, and one can stop for supper in Vanderhoof or Cluculz Lake on the way home.

Ormond Creek trails

Less than an hour and a half from Prince George, Fraser Lake affords a pleasant break when driving west, or it can be a destination in its own right for a day trip or an overnight camp. On the south side of the lake is Fraser Mountain, just described, with its trailhead on Highway 16, west of Fort Fraser. This first-class trail affords spectacular views across Fraser Lake as well as its other vistas to the west and to the south once the ridge is crested. At the eastern end of Fraser Lake, just off the highway, is Beaumont Provincial Park. On the north side of the lake just east of Ormond Creek, there is a campground at Peterson's Beach. To access this north side, turn off the highway just east of Fraser Lake and drive to the Nautley River before turning west on an excellent unpaved road. The Nautley has a good-size flow as it exits from the eastern end of Fraser Lake and shortly afterward flows into the Nechako River. Its approximately two-kilometre length makes the Nautley the shortest, full-fledged river in B.C. As we drove past this point one Easter, the sky was almost black with endless and continually reconnecting strings of migrating geese, a feature that the Vanderhoof area is famous for. Continuing west along the north side of Fraser Lake for about 12 kilometres brings one to the campsite at Peterson's Beach.

Across the road from the beach is the start of the Ormond Creek Hiking Trail. What makes this trail unusual for the Prince George area is that it is low elevation (which means that it is easy walking and the snow disappears early in the season) and it has two wilderness walk-in campsites 13-kilometres along the trail on Ormond Lake. Most of our other wilderness hiking/camping areas are in the mountains. If you are just looking for a break in a five-hour drive to or from Smithers, there is a shorter hike on this trail to Ormond Creek Canyon. The round trip hiking time is only an hour; the first-class trail is good for running shoes, and it has a scenic canyon at the end with views back toward Fraser Lake. Gaining less than a hundred metres elevation overall, the trail nevertheless provides a brisk exercise break. Signs near the canyon caution hikers with small children and pets about unguarded, steep drop-offs. A picnic lunch could be enjoyed either at the canyon or back at the trailhead on Peterson's Beach before continuing the drive west along the north side of Fraser Lake. The last few kilometres of this road are paved before rejoining Highway 16 near where the Stellako River flows into the western end of Fraser Lake.

An enterprising day-trip from Prince George would be to first stop at the Nechako River Bird Sanctuary at Vanderhoof for a leg stretch, remembering to take along binoculars and a bird identification book. Then continue on to Fraser Lake and warm up on the Ormond Creek Canyon trail. Complete the circumnavigation of Fraser Lake and hike up the Fraser Mountain trail at least as far as the viewpoint signed *Alpine Knoll* (one and a half to two hours round trip). You can reward yourself with a well-earned restaurant dinner on the drive home, perhaps enjoy a movie at the Grand Reo, and you can reflect on a day of varied exercise, wildlife encountered, new places and viewscapes seen, and the value you will have reaped from your high-priced gas mileage!

Watershed enhancement

The town of Fraser Lake is located on Highway 16 on the southwest side of the lake of the same name, close to the geographic centre of the Province of British Columbia. Both Vanderhoof and Burns Lake vie for this exalted geographic centre position, and the real honour must surely go to Fraser Lake which is situated midway between them. The town has depended in the past on forestry and the nearby molybdenum mine for its economic well-being, but longer-term uncertainty with these resource industries has caused residents to look at other attributes of the area. One group, a local watershed enhancement society, saw Fraser Lake as a community in transition. As well as the ups and downs of its mine, the town's second industry, forestry, is being significantly impacted by mountain pine beetle troubles. The society's aim, therefore, was to embrace the watershed as a valuable resource and to start the community on a transition from a resource-based economy to one of diversification. Their vision was rooted in watershed enhancement—they believed that the basis of good watershed management is public awareness through current and useful information, as well as through school programs and participation in community events. They wanted to assess the potential for job creation in the areas of watershed management, tourism, recreation, and education and research, while considering the values of the watershed that include quality of life, wildlife, and recreation. Some 20 other groups and organizations, including provincial, local, and native government agencies, and educational institutions, expressed interest in the program. In the meantime, the Canadian Nature Federation, in conjunction with the Federation of B.C. Naturalists and the Wild Bird Trust of B.C. had contracted a bird specialist to identify "Important Bird Areas" in the interior of the Province. The specialist's search quickly led him to Fraser Lake, where he found a receptive group of people with lots of energy and enthusiasm for the natural resources of their area, but lacking detailed knowledge about its birds. It was quickly established that Fraser Lake qualifies as an "Important Bird Area" and this could help to raise its profile with government and non-government agencies in a position to provide funding or help in kind.

There are large annual movements of waterfowl on Fraser Lake, particularly in the fall toward its western end near the town of Fraser Lake. Over twelve hundred trumpeter swans have been seen on the lake in the fall, with smaller numbers of trumpeters overwintering on open patches of water in the Nautley, along with other birds such as American dippers. The Prince George Naturalists Club, which regularly leads birding trips to Fraser Lake, has reported seeing thousands of Canada geese, and has estimated over ten thousand assorted ducks to be present during peak annual migration periods. Ducks Unlimited conducted aerial counts in the late 1980s and early 1990s and reported seeing as many as 28,000 waterfowl on the lake at one time! The watershed enhancement society hopes to enhance fish and bird habitat by mitigating the impacts of shoreline development and motorized use of the lake through public awareness. Despite its location on a major highway, Fraser Lake's shoreline is not really developed at the present time, and they would like to try to keep it that way. The society wants to enhance the overall enjoyment and viability of Fraser Lake and its watershed through the involvement of all its players. In short, their aim is to highlight the uniqueness of the area and to create an economic spinoff for the community from people who come to enjoy its magnificent trails and lakeshore. In return, Fraser Lake provides an opportunity for people in the Prince George area to benefit from the world's two most popular recreation activities—walking and bird watching—amid one of the largest migratory bird areas in British Columbia.

History in Prince George

The history of Prince George, although not extending back much more than two hundred years since the arrival of the first European explorers, is still a relatively untouched field, with much yet to be written. And First Nations history, before that, is largely oral. That being said, no book about exploring the Prince George area would be complete without at least a few anecdotes to tease the reader into digging further. Together with the historical notes that I have embedded throughout the book, the following stories will give you a sense of some of the richness of Prince George's history.

Mountain named for woman adventurer

A trip into the backcountry becomes more interesting if you learn about the history of the area being traversed. A few years ago, after browsing through some old maps in Jasper, and I decided on a weeklong backpacking trip from Mount Holmes just north of McBride, to Mount Robson—a wilderness walk of 100 kilometres. (See Holmes River section.) Travelling with one companion, part of our route followed historic horse trails over Jackpine Pass on the border of Alberta's Willmore Wilderness; through Bess Pass on the border of Jasper National Park; and down the Smoky River to approach Mount Robson from its north side. The route lay 60 kilometres southeast of Kakwa Provincial Park, where I have done three other hiking trips. (See Kakwa section.) These areas have something in common—they are all part of the country travelled in the early twentieth century by a young New York schoolteacher named Mary Jobe.

With the coming of the railway, the country northwest of Jasper began to attract American parties intent on hunting, exploring, and climbing. Mary Jobe, who had earned a masters degree in English and American history from Columbia University in 1909, attended the Alpine Club of Canada camp at Mount Robson in 1913 when Conrad Kain led the first ascent of the mountain. There she met guide and outfitter Donald "Curly" Phillips who had made the audacious attempt on the mountain with Reverend George Kinney in 1909 and had succeeded in reaching the summit ridge. While at the Mount Robson camp, Mary Jobe became interested in an unclimbed peak 125 kilometres to the northwest in what is now Kakwa Park. This heavily glaciated and spectacular mountain, known locally as Mount Kitchi or Big Mountain, later officially became Mount Sir Alexander. Mary hired Curly Phillips to guide her to Big Mountain the following summer, and then again in 1915. On both the 1914 and 1915 attempts, Mary Jobe made it onto the northeast glacier and reached an elevation of 2,375 metres, only 895 metres from the summit. On the 1915 attempt, Phillips, who despite his legendary Robson attempt wasn't really interested in climbing, went farther, reaching 30 metres from the summit of Sir Alexander before he was forced to turn back.

In 1916, Mary Jobe gave up teaching in New York to found a summer camp for girls in Mystic, Connecticut. She based the camp on the principles that she had learned in the Canadian Rockies, but this venture meant that she was no longer free to travel in the summer. In the fall of 1917, however, she made one more trip to Jasper, where Curly again guided her on an astonishing horse-packing trip from Jasper to the Wapiti River and back, extending well into November. According to Phillips' biography, *Tracks Across My Trail* by William Taylor, and *Off the beaten track—women adventurers and mountaineers in western Canada* by Cyndi Smith, a camp romance blossomed between Phillips and Jobe on this trip. Despite a later visit by Curly to see her in New York, Mary Jobe is thought to have declined his offer of marriage, and instead became the "other" woman in the failing marriage of Delia and Carl Akeley. Carl Akeley was renowned for having invented modern taxidermy, and for developing very lifelike museum displays. Carl and Delia (and later Mary) were inveterate Africa explorers and museum game collectors as well as advocates for reserves to protect Africa's soon to be endangered wildlife.

Mary Jobe wrote only short pieces about her northern Rockies adventures for magazines and journals, including those of the American Geographical Society and the Alpine Club of Canada. Yet as "Mary Jobe Akeley" (she married Carl in 1924 until his death in Africa only two years later) she wrote many full-length books about Africa and Carl Akeley, including *The Wilderness Lives Again - Carl Akeley and the Great Adventure* (1940.) Before their divorce, Delia was a formidable part of the Akeley "team," helping Carl to develop his wildlife displays, and saving his life on at least one occasion in

Africa. She later went on to become one of four top American women adventurers of the twentieth century recounted in Elizabeth Olds' book, *Women of the Four Winds*. Yet, despite the crucial role she played in Akeley's life, there doesn't seem to be any mention of Delia in *The Wilderness Lives Again*, not even in Mary's account of the elephant mauling, when, according to Elizabeth Olds, Delia had put her own life at great risk to save Carl's.

Mary Jobe wrote mainly under her married name Akeley, and as such is best known today. Yet when it came to recognizing her exploits in the Northern Rockies, an accident of timing meant that "Jobe" was the name chosen to honour this interesting woman. Mount Jobe, at 2,301metres, is located in the Morkill River Valley, partway between Kakwa and Mount Robson Provincial Parks, and was named by the Interprovincial Boundary Survey in 1923, the year before Mary's marriage to Carl. Mary (Jobe) Akeley died in a Mystic, Connecticut nursing home in July 1966, aged 88.

Pioneer packer

Cataline was a pioneer of repute in nineteenth century British Columbia, whose prowess was on a par with any of the legends from south of the border. Yet few, if asked, would have any idea who this man was. Jean Caux was born in the Province of Catalonia, Spain, in 1832, and was known throughout the Interior and Northwest of British Columbia as "Cataline" after his birthplace. Few could understand his broad mix of languages, but he was brilliant with horses and mules and understood them better than anyone in the country. Tall and straight into his seventies, he sported a magnificent head of shoulder-length curls that he attributed to saving portions of his Hudson's Bay rum to rub into his hair! From 1858 until he retired in 1912, Cataline ran a pack train in the Northern Interior of B.C., supplying goods that were essential to the survival of pioneers along B.C.'s Telegraph Trail and other local routes. With the advance of civilization, especially the rail, he gradually moved his base of operations north from Yale to Quesnel and finally to Hazelton where he died in 1922, aged 90.

Early in 2002, Prince George musicians Gordon Long, Gerda Wilson, and the Bel Canto Children's choir, wrote and performed a musical, *Cataline's Pack Train*, to showcase the choir as well as this little-known piece of local history. Among the 10 songs performed were "Pack Horse Blues", "Why do they treat me like this?", "Horse Power", and "Donkey See, Donkey Do." Anyone who has ever travelled in our local backcountry with a pack train of horses, mules, or even llamas would relate to the humorous scrapes they found themselves in. These included the horses' reluctance to carry their packs or walk through mud holes, as well as the encounters with mosquitoes, fire, snow, and a grizzly bear. Everyone attending the performance left feeling thoroughly entertained and a little more enlightened about Jean Caux "Cataline."

New Rivers of the North

Hulbert Footner was a Canadian-born writer from New York, who in 1911 journeyed from the headwaters of the Fraser River to Giscome Portage, and then north from Summit Lake to the Peace and Hay Rivers. From Fort Vermilion on the Peace River, he walked overland to the Hay River and canoed north to spectacular Alexandra Falls in the Northwest Territories before the lateness of the season forced him to turn around.

Hulbert Footner's journey took place at a time when the history of the area around Prince George as we know it today was just beginning. Although most of his route had been well travelled before him, this was the first time that it had been written about and photographed in the idiom of an adventure travel writer. His book, *New Rivers of the North*, was published in New York in 1912. It had 281 pages of fast-paced narrative and 76 historic black and white plates of places and people encountered along the way – some of it photographed for the first time. Parts of the journey took him through places that are little changed today. His enthusiastic description of the sudden view of Mount Robson, of the old growth forests and undergrowth in the Rocky Mountain Trench, and the Grand Canyon of the Fraser gave me confidence in the rest of his account.

Footner left Edmonton on the newly completed Grand Trunk Pacific Railway, which in 1911 had reached Edson, Alberta. From there, he rode a crew train on the roughly built working line as far as Hinton, whence he packed his outfit over trails and construction tote roads to cross the B.C. border and begin his long navigation down the Fraser River. Astonishingly, almost the entire river journey from this point on was accomplished in a tiny 12-foot canvass-covered folding boat that he christened the *Blunderbuss* when he assembled it seven miles above Moose Lake. One of the most remarkable parts of the trip was his passage through the Grand Canyon of the Fraser. Well appraised of the canyon's cruel death toll, Footner and his companion wisely portaged through the upper canyon on a trail that is still discernible today. Scouting the lower canyon and its deadly whirlpools from a spot where I have lunched on several occasions, they decided to run the river rather than brave the brutal portage and mosquitoes.

Taking careful aim at the entrance to the lower canyon, they guided the tiny Blunderbuss safely past the many whirlpools, at one point hanging precariously on the edge of a seemingly bottomless vortex before shooting clear. Terrified at the start of the run, they quickly lost all fear as they were caught up in the excitement of it. Some months later, near the end of their journey, they performed an even greater feat by sailing their impossibly fragile craft across Lesser Slave Lake in northern Alberta in the teeth of a gale that nearly destroyed them a hundred times over.

Downstream from the Grand Canyon, Footner arrived at the Giscome Portage around the time that the Huble Homestead was built. He gives an account of a night spent there, and of paying an inflated price to cross the portage in the company of a large church bell that had been purchased by the natives of Fort Macleod two years earlier. After spending the night at Summit Lake to enjoy local cooking, he headed north down the Crooked River. He described spending the entire first day in sight of the "little eminence known as Tea-pot Mountain"; of leaving it behind on the second day; and having it miraculously reappear on the third. The mystery was solved when a local freighter climbed another rise and discovered that there were actually two Tea-pot mountains, "...since when they have changed the name of the second one to Coffee-pot Mountain". The book goes on to describe and illustrate many features of the Crooked and Parsnip Rivers, as well as stretches of the Parsnip, Finlay and Peace Rivers that have long since disappeared under Williston Lake.

Footner was born in Hamilton, Ontario in 1879 and emigrated at the age of 19 to New York to become an actor. After a few unsuccessful small parts, he decided instead to become an author—a calling that he found more to his liking. At first he wrote about his outdoor experiences, including his grand quest through the Prince George area in 1911. Then, he began to write adventure stories drawing on his own experience, one of which became a successful Hollywood movie. Later, he turned his pen to detective novels that became a big hit on both sides of the Atlantic and allowed him to travel widely with his family in Europe in the 1920's and 1930's. He died in 1944.

The countryside and people of the Prince George area in 1911 come alive through Hulbert Footner's pen and camera. As well as its historic value, Footner's beautifully written and illustrated account fills the reader with the desire to get out and re-discover some of what he experienced here long ago.

1927 journey of Prentiss Nathaniel Gray from the Peace to the Fraser

Prentiss Nathaniel Gray was born in California in July 1884, and after graduating from Berkeley in 1906 went on to enjoy a successful career in shipping, real estate, government, railways, and banking. He was the sole American designated by President Hoover to remain behind and manage the food relief commission in Belgium during the First World War, an endeavour that earned him decorations from the King of Belgium and the President of France. Early on, Prentiss Gray developed a passion for hunting and the outdoors that remained with him throughout his life. This meant exploring and hunting in remoter parts of North America, foremost of which were two trips he made through the mountain country northeast of Prince George in 1927 and 1928.

An avid hunter, Prentiss Gray was interested in determining the northern range of Rocky Mountain bighorn sheep (now known to be in the northeast corner of Kakwa Park) and to learn to what extent they might overlap and interbreed with Stone's sheep. As an explorer, he was attracted by the prospect of filling in some of the white spaces on the official government maps of the 1920s. His interests also turned toward the difficult task of capturing wildlife and scenery through photography, a task that included making a motion picture of his 1927 expedition from the Peace to the Fraser. Unfortunately, the original film was lost owing to deterioration over time.

From 1900 to 1930, Prentiss Gray wrote a series called *North American Hunting and Exploration Journals* that he had beautifully typed and leather-bound in 20 large volumes, complete with unpublished photographs. He married Laura Sherman in Washington in May 1908; she was the niece of General William Tecumseh Sherman of American Civil War fame. Their son, born in New York in 1918, was given the first name Sherman. In 1994, Sherman Gray made his father's priceless unpublished manuscripts and photographs available to the Boone and Crockett Club's editorial and publications committee, and later that year 10 of the 13 journals were published in a beautiful volume titled *From the Peace to the Fraser*. The book takes its title from Chapter 8, which contains in its entirety the thickest of Prentiss Gray's *North American Journals*. This journal describes an expedition that he undertook in 1927 from Hudson Hope on the Peace River, through the Rocky Mountains to the Fraser River at Dome Creek just east of Prince George. During his 1927 and 1928 trips, he left behind several now familiar names on our landscape including Gray Pass, and features named after his daughter, Barbara, and his son Sherman. Prentiss N.

Gray died in the outdoors at the relatively young age of 50 in a 1935 motorboat fire and explosion in the Florida Everglades.

In July 2002, Sherman Gray at the age of 84 travelled from the eastern United States to Prince George to spend a day re-enacting his father's famous journey. Travelling by helicopter, he landed at many of the sites that Prentiss Gray had visited and photographed in 1927. Accompanying Sherman Gray on the daylong tour was Mike Murtha, a planner for B.C. Parks, and Sherman's grandson, Matthew. The re-enactment of Gray's historic journey arose from Murtha's research of this segment of Prince George history. After reading *From the Peace to the Fraser*, he telephoned the editor at the Boone and Crockett Club, who gave him Sherman Gray's telephone number in upstate New York. Gray was surprised at the local interest and generously offered photo albums of the expedition that have since been deposited in UNBC's Northern B.C. archive.

Mike Murtha was also intrigued by the reference in the book to the film that was made, but was told by Sherman Gray that the original had been lost. However, as it turned out, all was not lost. An artist named Morton Fadum, by chance had saved the film for posterity when a copy was about to be destroyed. Fadum, thinking that it might be of some interest, retrieved the film from a fiery end in a bonfire of unwanted household effects. When he later read a copy of Prentiss Gray's book, he realized that this was the same film he had saved. Mike Murtha later obtained a video copy from Fadum for use in Prince George.

The film appears early in the account of the 1927 expedition as Prentiss Gray relates the mid-afternoon arrival of two boats under the leadership of another member of the expedition, Harry Snyder. He describes shooting a moving picture of this occasion, and then of spending several minutes telling each other how glad they were to all be together. This is an interesting side story as Harry Snyder had apparently taken the long way around to meet his companions at Hudson Hope. Riding the train to Prince George, he had secretly secured what were considered to be essential liquid supplies for the intended journey, which, after dodging the local police, he freighted up the Crooked, Finlay, and Peace Rivers to join up with the main party. The old black and white film with its jerky action opens with the two boats doing a U-turn in the middle current of the Peace River and landing to joyful hugging and backslapping as the main party greets their friends and, perhaps more importantly, the liquid supplies. The film covers the first half of the journey through lowland forests, blowdown, shots of Kinuseo Falls in what is now Monkman Park southwest of present-day Tumbler Ridge, and Wapiti Lake. It ends in the high country with outstanding footage of bighorn sheep, after which, unfortunately, the remainder of the film actually is lost.

During the 2002 re-enactment, Sherman Gray was photographed looking down on Gray Pass, named for his father. On the south side of Gray Pass, which is in the northeast corner of Kakwa Park and in one of the finest hiking areas that I have seen, is Barbara Lake which Gray named for his daughter. On the north side of Gray Pass, he named Sherman Lake after his son. This lake is known today as Dimsdale, after H.G. Dimsdale, an Edmonton civil engineer accompanying Gray on his return trip in 1928. In another re-enactment photograph, staged close to the spot where Prentiss Gray's packhorses were pictured being watered 75 years before, Sherman Gray, looking very fit for his 84 years, stands in the meadows of Dimsdale (Sherman) Lake. The Prentiss Gray story emphasizes again Prince George's rich history, much of it dating back only 100 years. In Prince George today, we are only just beginning to write our history, and we are surrounded by landscapes that have hitherto only been lightly touched by humans. I am reminded that we are living on the doorstep of one of the great parts of North America that has been attracting people like Prentiss Gray for a century or more. As a child, I never fully appreciated the 2000-year old Roman ruins in my childhood town of Leicester, England—it was just part of the landscape, kind of like hanging out at the mall. In Prince George, it is just as easy to overlook the land that surrounds us, especially the wonderful backcountry from the Peace to the Fraser.

Passing of Pierre Trudeau

Moving to a piece of more contemporary history, this story concerns a man who only briefly trod the soil of Prince George, but who touched the lives of Canadians everywhere. Whatever the diverse feelings he generated in people, nobody was left unaffected by the man who came to epitomize what it meant to be a Canadian in the 1970s. As a relatively new Canadian then, I lived and worked in eastern Canada, mostly in Toronto, but with frequent trips to Montreal. And so it was in places such as Ontario's Bruce Trail and Algonquin Provincial Park that I discovered the Canadian outdoors for the first time. I would lie on a granite peninsula late in the evenings looking up at the Milky Way or the northern lights, and listen to the magical cries of loons drifting from lake to lake around me. Or I would paddle my canoe through endlessly linked waterways, thinking of the voyageurs who had gone before to open this great land. I worked for a week near the top of the Place Ville Marie tower in downtown Montreal, where I could look across at the grand display of fall colours on Mount Royal then walk there during my lunch hour. All of these thoughts came flooding back to me in October 2000 as I followed the events surrounding the passing of Pierre Elliott Trudeau.

This was a man who had inspired me during my first decade in North America, representing the only political Canada that I knew then. As I listened to all the familiar anecdotes expressed in the media that week, some common themes came through. This was a man of boldness, vision, conviction, intelligence, and passion. A man who took Canada onto the world stage as never before and who helped shape a national identity that had hitherto seemed less clear. A man who loved the outdoors and physical activity, a man who eschewed spectator sports in favour of getting out and actually doing things. Trudeau the cross-country skier, Trudeau the downhill skier, the canoeist, the swimmer, and I'm sure a lot more. Despite the political problems that dogged him in the West in his later years as Prime Minister, his love of British Columbia and the B.C. outdoors was always there. Ironically, his youngest son died in an avalanche in B.C. two years before his own death.

I thought of the times when I was unexpectedly near the man. A chance sighting in downtown Toronto once or twice. Once as the first car in line at an intersection, tired after working all night testing computer software, as the motorcade of visiting Soviet President Kosygin streamed past. I worked for Air Canada in the seventies, and one weekend the company threw a large morale-booster party for its Toronto area employees. They flew in a Caribbean band for the event and staged it in the cavernous space of the DC8 hanger at Malton Airport (as Pearson Airport was called then). It was around 9 pm in the evening and I had stepped back from the crowd when I noticed that two men in suits had entered the hangar and were wandering about the throng looking entirely out of place. Curious, I slipped through the giant hangar doors into the darkness outside. A company-owned DC9 aircraft pulled up close to where I stood in the shadows, and I watched quietly as Pierre Trudeau descended the stairs and was driven away in a limousine.

My move to Prince George in 1978 coincided with Trudeau's first retirement from politics. And then, suddenly, he was back for a final run that was to see the repatriation of the Canadian Constitution and a new Bill of Rights. During that campaign he stopped in Prince George, and I was one of many who waited at the old civic centre to hear him speak. Around that time, George Evanoff, representing the Canadian Ski Patrol, had asked permission to land a helicopter at the civic centre as part of their annual fundraising ski show. Approval had been reluctantly given by the Department of Transport and had taken months to obtain. It had even required that two officials fly to Prince George to inspect the site. On the occasion of Trudeau's visit, fog had delayed his arrival by an hour. So instead of riding downtown on the press bus, organizers hired a helicopter at the last minute to fly him to the civic centre. Once airborne, the pilot radioed the tower: "Permission to land in the bowl?" After an unusual silence, the controller asked tentatively "Who's on board?" "Pierre Trudeau," replied the pilot. "Well, land wherever you like!" was the reply. And so he arrived amid the roar of rotors, and to the delight of the local crowd he was well into his speech before the national TV media appeared.

Pierre Trudeau is a man whom I would like to have known, especially in an informal outdoors setting. There was something in him that resonated for me, as it did for many Canadians, although it was sometimes hard to define. Yet I feel that I do know him—then and now, and I am fortunate to live in a country that had this man as leader at an important time in its history.

Murder at Swift Current Creek

During a three-day backpacking trip in 1999 to Mount Fitzwilliam on the B.C.–Alberta border in Mount Robson Provincial Park, I took with me a recently-published book to read in the tent; a historical account of tragic events that took place in that locale exactly 100 years before. In her book, *The Colour of Gold*, Margaret McKirdy spent years researching the story of murder, injustice, deceit, and racism that took place in 1899 in what is now Mount Robson Provincial Park. It is a colourful description of living and travelling in what was then the backcountry of the Tête Jaune area and is a stark condemnation of inequalities in the treatment of Metis and Aboriginal people by many of the white people of the area at the turn of the century. It tells as well the story of the little known gold rush at Swift Current Creek, not far from the present day visitor centre at Mount Robson. It describes the efforts of local pioneers Jack Evans and Kid Price to help their native friends. Both of these men's names live on in our present day geography: Evans Creek in the Robson Valley and Kidprice Lake near Smithers. The book describes the hardships and wonder of travelling by horse down the Canoe River long before it was flooded for hydroelectric power generation. And it details the month-long journey of a Dr. Taylor, on the wilderness trip of his lifetime, with a grim autopsy that was the purpose of his trip.

Alex McCaulay, a Metis from what is now the Jasper area, was unarmed and tending his horse near Swift Current Creek with his young Cree wife and two young children, when he was shot in the face in front of his family by a man named Jim Hughes. With one eye and part of his jaw torn away and the bullet lodged in his chest, Alex took 12 days to die an agonizing death in the company of his family, his killer, and other trappers and prospectors who later arrived on the scene. Alex's wife, Adelaide, was persuaded to travel to Golden, to spend the summer and give testimony at the first Supreme Court trial to be held in that railway town. Despite clear evidence to convict, and a strong charge by the judge to that effect, the 12 white men of that jury acquitted Jim Hughes of murder, and even of manslaughter. After the trial, Adelaide was left to travel alone with her children over the mountains in the November snows to try and return to her people. She was never heard of again despite strenuous efforts to find her.

Margaret McKirdy's *The Colour of Gold* brought alive for me in a historical context much of the mountain country that I have hiked in east of Prince George. It left me with a sense of outrage over the senseless killing and later treatment of the victim's wife by the white community of the day. Certainly the Highway 16 crossing of Swift Current Creek just before Mount Robson will never be the same for me again.

John and Cyril Shelford - Burns Lake pioneers

Late in the year 2001, while en route to an appointment in Prince George, I caught a radio report about the death of pioneer Cyril Shelford of Burns Lake. In this broadcast, an interview that had been recorded with him a few years earlier was replayed. It was an empowering story of a man raised in the backcountry of Ootsa Lake who went to bat for his family's land that was about to be flooded by the original Kemano power project. Getting no satisfaction locally, Cyril Shelford led a deputation to Victoria where he found yet more disinterest on the part of the government, prompting him to threaten to run in the next provincial election. Although compensation was later raised to a fairer market value, he followed through with his promise and won a seat in the new W.A.C. Bennett government. Bennett was smart enough to realize that a man with a cause could upset a rural riding, and he went on to make Cyril Shelford B.C.'s Minister of Agriculture.

Cyril Shelford had a brother, John, whom I met in the early 1980s. I was a volunteer with the Prince George Search and Rescue (SAR) group at a time when the government was introducing new search management techniques and tracking skills into the province from the U.S. west coast. The impetus for this had much to do with a tragic search in Houston, B.C. in the fall of 1978, when two young boys were lost for several days and one died of exposure. As part of this program, the Provincial Emergency Program hired U.S. border patroller Joel Hardin to teach search and rescue volunteers how to track. Joel had learned his craft on the Mexican border trailing illegal migrants, where a chance encounter between border patrollers and the San Diego Search and Rescue team on a field exercise caused the SAR people to immediately see the potential of adding tracking to their trade. So it happened that an art passed down from western First Nations, to frontiersmen, to border patrollers, migrated to the west coast search and rescue community and north into British Columbia. A book called *Tracking—a Blueprint for Learning How,* was written by U.S. Border Patroller Jack Kearney. He and some of his colleagues found a second career passing on their skills to search and rescue people.

Joel Hardin came to Prince George on three occasions to teach basic, intermediate, and later advanced tracking skills to SAR volunteers who travelled from across Northern B.C. to participate. Each course was held in a weekend immersion setting, the first being at the then Canadian Forces Base at Baldy Hughes, on the Blackwater Road south of Prince George. Contrary to our early expectations, we spent the entire first morning crawling around on hands and knees—we covered a small patch of stony ground next to the officers' mess looking at grains of dirt, learning to see sign that we never knew existed. Joel claimed, after thousands of hours spent honing his skills, that he could follow a person through the woods up to a month after their passage. We certainly did not become as proficient as that, but we did become more observant and able to spot human sign that could aid in narrowing a search. Tracking is still taught by the Prince George Search and Rescue group, and one of the benefits of volunteering with them is the opportunity to learn this interesting and ancient craft.

It was on Joel Hardin's courses that I knew John Shelford. As we talked late one evening at one of the course camps, he told us of his experience as a teenager on a trapline near Ootsa Lake when he'd been treed for two whole days by a pack of hungry wolves. Although nobody has officially ever been killed by a wolf in Canada, there are lots of people who have disappeared in the bush. John left no doubt in my mind that the same fate would have happened to him had his dad not returned to drive the wolves off with rifle fire. After a lifetime spent in the bush, John had a good reputation as a tracker in the Burns Lake area. He told us of his experience on the Houston search and how he felt that better use of tracking skills might have produced a different outcome.

The U.S. Border Patrol approach uses a scientific method whereby the tracker finds sign of each footfall before moving on to the next. A tracking stick with marked graduations is used to aid in fixing the missing person's stride. John Shelford told us about his own method of tracking learned during many years of hunting where, in a sense, the hunter becomes the prey by walking in the prey's tracks. This, he told us, has the advantage of learning the feel of the animal or person you are following, thus enabling you to move faster by anticipating each step. The downside is that you have to be very good at it so as not to lose the sign, and in the process destroy the sign by walking on it. Each technique has its place, and John invited some of us to spend a weekend with him in Burns Lake learning the Shelford method of tracking as well. In the process, I came to know something of the Shelford family and the pioneering life they had led in the Lakes Country. I had often thought of this weekend during the 20 intervening years when driving through Burns Lake, past the site of John Shelford's landmark store. And it all came flooding back as I sat in my car outside an 8 am appointment listening to the engaging interview with Cyril Shelford.

Japanese Canadians in wartime Prince George

There is a part of Canada's history that ought not to be forgotten, especially in times of heightened global tension and conflict. Two books, *The Enemy That Never Was*, and *Years of Sorrow, Years of Shame*, speak to the injustices that took place in Canada during the Second World War and the effects on Japanese Canadians who were interned in their own country. British Columbia bore the brunt of Japanese Canadian internment because of its coastal location and fears of an attack by Japan. Fueled by political and public unease over where loyalties might lie, internment camps for Canadians of Japanese origin were set up in the Southern Interior at such places as New Denver, Kaslo, Greenwood, Sandon, Tashme, Lemon Creek, and Monte Lake. Families were often split up, with some men being sent to work camps as far away as Northern Ontario, and their property was often confiscated as well. What is not well-known locally, is that Prince George also saw a share of Japanese Canadian internees, and at least one man stayed on here to raise a family. Regardless of the wrongs done to them by their own government, relations between the internees and local people who worked with them were, for the most part, positive.

I first became aware of this fascinating piece of local history in the early 1990s when I was researching and exploring the Grand Canyon of the Fraser. As related earlier in this book, in 1992, I rode through the canyon with Ray Mueller of Sinclair Mills in his riverboat where I had a firsthand opportunity to discuss the history with him. And he spoke, then, of the arrival of Japanese internees during the Second World War. It was not until over a decade later, in 2003, that I pursued this story, and by then Ray Mueller had passed away. So, I telephoned Ray's widow, Louisa Mueller, who was spending part of her winter in Prince George. Louisa remembered me from my visit to her house over 10 years before, and we arranged to meet that afternoon and talk about the internees over coffee and cookies. Without initially remembering where I had first heard about this unusual piece of Prince George history, I had come full circle.

Louisa told me that in May 1943, her husband and another man from Upper Fraser travelled to the internment camp at Monte Lake near Kamloops and met with Japanese Canadian internees there. They discussed the possibility of some of the men working in two Northern Interior communities. At the time Ray was the superintendent of the main logging camp near Sinclair Mills, where he already had 60 or 70 men employed, part of the Sinclair Spruce Lumber Company. The Japanese Canadian men's initial reaction to the offer was negative because of the remote location and the lack of running water and baths in the camp. Undaunted, Ray struck an agreement that showers would be provided, and 28 men agreed to return with him. It isn't clear whether all 28 men came to Sinclair Mills and a similar number went to Upper Fraser, or whether the 28 were divided between the two communities. Unions were just getting established at the time, and the men already employed at the bush camp outside Sinclair Mills were also asking for showers. The new arrangement worked for both groups, and probably didn't hurt the relations that ensued.

In their first summer of 1943, the Japanese men stayed in a small camp five miles up the road from Sinclair Mills to the west of Bearpaw Ridge. It was probably a tent camp, and was known in the vernacular of the day as the "Jap Camp." In the fall of 1943, they moved two miles farther up the road to the "Big Camp" as it was known, where some of them had a cabin for themselves and the remainder dispersed among the men in the other cabins. The two groups worked both in the bush and the mill, and got along well together. At that time, logs were floated down the Fraser River and brought up a "jack ladder" to the mill, with the result that each year at freezeup, many of the jobs, except for winter logging and possibly the planer mill, shut down. Most of the workers returned to their homes as far away as Saskatchewan, while the Japanese men stayed on and worked at various jobs. They were free to come and go, and after the first year there were no restrictions on their local travel. By then they had money, and often went into Prince George in small groups of twos and threes, where the first stop after getting off the train was often at an establishment called Mason's Cafe. Most of their families moved to beet farm country in Alberta near Medicine Hat and Lethbridge, and one man received permission to visit his wife there when she was sick. For recreation, the men fished, but did not generally participate in the local pastimes of hunting and trapping. Some worked on Ray Mueller's cabin and fished part time while they were there.

After the war, some of the men stayed on in Sinclair Mills and other surrounding communities. One man, Mr. Kabuki, married a woman who came from Japan, and they had a daughter in Sinclair Mills. They stayed there until the mill closed in 1966, after which they relocated to Giscome for awhile, before moving to the coast. A few years ago, Mr. Kabuki's widow and daughter visited Louisa Mueller to talk about their years in Sinclair Mills. Another man, Mr. Takata, was a carpenter and spent two summers building Louisa Mueller's kitchen. After leaving Sinclair Mills, he moved to Vancouver where he worked at remodelling ships, before going to Japan. The five remaining buildings of the Big Camp west of Bearpaw Ridge where the men had stayed were burned on the orders of the Forest Service in 1963. A small part of this history wasn't erased however, as some cabins were moved, and Louisa told me that at least one still survives in Sinclair Mills today. If you are interested in learning more about the Japanese Canadian internment era, both the National Nikkei Heritage Centre and the Japanese Canadian National Museum are located in Burnaby, British Columbia.

Centre for Caving

The discovery of Fang Cave by George Evanoff (introduced previously in "East to the McGregor and Rocky Mountains"), and its subsequent exploration by our team of five, led to a burst of caving activity that continues to reap ever more significant finds today in the Prince George area.

Redemption is near

Redemption Cave was first spotted from the air in June of 2000 in the Cariboo Mountains east of Prince George. No attempts were made to reach the cave until the following winter, but then, fixed-wing aircraft and ground assaults both failed to locate it because of snow cover. It was not until June of 2001 that six people from the Northern B.C. Caving Club became probably the first humans to enter what was to be described as "easily the most important cave find in Canada in a decade." This was the latest and possibly the best of a string of spectacular finds that had begun 20 years earlier when our original team had ventured into what became known as Fang Cave, and which together have put Prince George on the map as a world-class centre for caving.

There were still two metres of snow around the entrance during the first foray into Redemption Cave. There had been a lot of debate in the previous 12 months as to whether the stream in the original aerial photograph was exiting or entering the pit. That mystery was now solved: a large stream fed by the melting snowpack clearly poured into the hole. The entrance was technical, requiring specialized climbing equipment designed for caves, and this, together with its remote location, will help to protect the cave from damage that inevitably results from casual access. From what the team could see beyond the first pit, the cavern looked immense. They rigged a rope to descend the nine vertical metre entrance drop, and from there they explored and

Author rappelling into 'The Coliseum' middle entrance of Fang Cave in October 1981 – on the occasion of the first entry into the cave via this entrance, and only the second caving trip to Fang. On this trip, the 'Corkscrew' and 'Queens Gallery' were entered for the first time by humans, a reasonably safe assumption since the route was technical, and there was no sign, nor is there any documentation of a prior visit.

surveyed a quarter of a kilometre of very large passages and grottos, including what they later named the "Hall of Biblical Proportions." From there, after passing through a short crawl, the team entered the "Common Room" that led them to an eight-metre descent dubbed "Prophet Drop." They had now left behind the "active" passageways, those with stream flows, and had entered a "fossil" or dry section of the cave. As they moved forward they were the first people ever to see Redemption's calcite decorations, estimated to be tens of thousands of years old. They were probably as excited as the first people to walk on the moon. I have some idea of how they felt—in 1982, along with George Evanoff, I was part of the small group who were the first to descend the "Corkscrew" and stroll alongside the meandering stream of the "Queens Gallery" in Fang Cave.

The absence of fast water in parts of Redemption Cave has facilitated growth of cave decorations from the action of more leisurely seeps and drips. These include big walls of flowstone; gour dams containing step pools of water in the flowstone, and other features including helictites growing out from the walls, plus "moonmilk," and "soda straws." The calcite structures are typically made when water dissolves limestone and re-deposits it over thousands of years.

The approach to the well-named cave known as 'Close to the Edge' is precarious indeed.

At the end of this spectacular passage, another drop named "Misty Mountain Drop" stopped further progress. At the end of an amazing first day in the cave, a member of the party stood on a raised mound beside camp, hair and beard unkempt, survey book in one hand and pencil waving around with the other. He appeared to the others like a biblical prophet of old, and so the name of the cave and some of its features arose from the camaraderie of this event. That individual, Kirk Safford, was one of several key people involved in the cave's discovery, and he later produced a very fine survey of Redemption.

Since the early 1980s, it has become known that the mountains north and east of Prince George harbour some of the best caves in North America. Caves such as "Fang" and "Close to the Edge" in the McGregor and Rocky Mountains are significant more for their size than decorations, because for the most part, the known caves in this area are relatively young and active. Redemption Cave breaks that trend, raising much excitement in the caving community both for its size and its decorations. When one looks at pictures of the beautiful and delicate structures found in solution caves, it is not hard to understand why people engage in what can be an arduous, and at times dangerous, sport. And why, no matter how tough a caving trip gets, they are always drawn back by the promise of finding something like Redemption.

Explorers from the Northern B.C. Caving Club went back to Redemption Cave in July 2001 on a four-day weekend that, after time spent hiking in and out, left two days for actual exploring and surveying underground. Cave ethics require that cavers survey new passageways as they explore. This entails the difficult work of measuring and recording bearings, distances, and features in a dark and hazardous, three-dimensional world. When I used the expression "three-dimensional world" in a submission to a well-known Canadian geographical magazine a few years ago, I got a testy reply back asking me, "What other kind of world is there?" Obviously the editor was neither well-versed in theoretical physics, nor had tried to survey a cave that entailed crawling into a hole in the roof and emerging from one in the floor. Cave ethics demand that great care be taken not to damage speleothems, or cave decorations, and if possible to leave no trace of being there at all. Any damage to the delicate and exquisite calcite features that have taken so long to form is essentially irreparable, and some of them are right there on the floor where a simple misstep can mean disaster. These factors, when added to the dangers of caving and the immense difficulty, cost, and uncertain outcome of trying to rescue an injured or trapped person, mean that caving should only be done with an organized and well-experienced group.

Armed with extra rope on their second exploratory trip to Redemption Cave, the team negotiated the 250-metre decorated passage they had surveyed the month before to the pit called "Misty Mountain Drop" that had previously stopped them then owing to insufficient rope. They negotiated three new drops there totalling 14 vertical metres to emerge into what caving enthusiast Bob Rutherford described as a "very big passage of clean rock descending downward." The sound of water was getting louder, and they were soon back in "a huge active underground room that looked like a big canyon, with clean water-washed rock." A 25-metre waterfall cascaded into the room, creating a feature at its base dubbed the "Perfect Storm" — waves of spray resembled scenes from the movie of the same name. They continued to survey downstream, descending rapidly without needing a rope until they came to another waterfall with a three-metre drop. Although they had more rope with them, there was nowhere to tie it off and they judged it unsafe to free-climb through the waterfall. Thus ended their second attempt at Redemption.

On the team's third visit in August 2001, 11 people arrived at the cave for a week-long stay. This time the snowmelt had pretty much ended, and the water flow in the cave was reduced. That fact enabled the party to free-climb the three-metre waterfall that had stopped them on the second trip. They surveyed another 50 metres there until, rounding a corner, the stream entered a room (an old passage, actually) that Bob Rutherford described as appearing "phenomenally ancient." He said it was 150 metres long, with a 50-metre high ceiling and was 15 metres wide. Depending on the criteria used, this easily makes it the largest underground room in a Canadian cave. "Everyone in the party," according to Rutherford, "was dumbstruck!" According to Clive Keen, who several years before had spearheaded the second wave of caving in Prince George, some of the accolades in camp that evening were: "It just keeps on going!" "It's incredible!" "It doesn't get any better!" "This is caving Valhalla!" The stream crossed the room and sank below a wall. The fossil passageway continued on and was decorated with forests of soda straws up to four feet long, and cascades of flowstone on the walls. A side passage bypassed breakdown (rubble) and re-entered the main passage christened "151 Overproof Hall" after its 151-degree compass bearing. It continued on for another 150 metres straight ahead, ending at last with a deep 25-metre pit and a sump comprising a small lake of still water. Possible leads continued, but were getting tight and wet.

During their week at the site, members of the team explored other features, including a large seven-metre wide shaft with a lot of air movement toward the surface 200 metres above. They found a half-metre long soda straw with a triangular-shaped flag growing from the end, indicating that a strong airflow had existed in the cave for a very long time. Several phreatic tubes (circular passages created by water dissolving limestone under pressure) were observed high in the walls, and other leads were partly explored near the cave entrance. Naturalists were interested to learn that a rare black swift nest was found by Kirk Safford at the entrance, one of only three ever heard of in this region. And a few bats were observed inside the cave. Much exploration work remains to be done in Redemption Cave, which should keep cavers busy for a few years. Bob Rutherford added: "There is huge potential for lots of vertical passage in the ridges above the cave." He was reluctant to put an age on the cave, but when pressed he guessed it had been forming for perhaps half a million years. Clive Keen reflected: "We've a great new cave, now 1.3 kilometres long, but surely with the potential for many kilometres more. We'll be back." I asked Bob Rutherford what it was that made this cave so special. After reflecting for a moment, he told me that there are 1.3 kilometres of passage surveyed so far, which is not a lot compared to other caves, but in all that length there are only 10 metres where you have to crawl. "That's unheard of," he said, "and makes it number one in Canada passage size-wise," adding, "it's also on a par with anything in Canada with its decorations."

One chance for young cave birds

High on the side of a mountain in the Dezaiko Range of the Rocky Mountains, 750 vertical metres above Hedrick Creek, hangs the cave known as "Close to the Edge." The principal feature of a new provincial park recommended in 1999 by the Prince George Land and Resource Management Plan, its classic entrance is tucked away into the side of a near vertical cliff that shelters the deepest pothole in North America. This enormous shaft is 30 metres wide and 10 metres across at the top, and has a continuous free-fall of a quarter of a kilometre straight down, the longest such shaft on the continent north of Mexico. It was Canada Day 1998, and a friend and I were eating lunch after a hard bushwhacking ascent to the cave. Suddenly a bird flew into the cave and executed several bat-like manoeuvres before landing on a small ledge on the far wall, a mere three metres above the shaft. Closer inspection with binoculars in the half-light revealed a nest that appeared to be constructed of grass, about 20 centimetres across. After a few minutes, the bird, an American pipit, identified by my companion, Lyle Daly, flew off the ledge and disappeared.

Three thoughts occurred to me, then. First, this has to be the most secure nest site possible. Second, what kind of worldview would the

Looking down into the 250-vertical meter freefall shaft of 'Close to the Edge'. The picture was taken from a small ledge that was everyone's favourite vantagepoint for the first few years following discovery, but which later gave pause for sober reflection after it fell away into the shaft.

chicks have growing up in a cave over this enormous hole? Finally, and definitely most interesting, I wondered how any American pipit chicks we presumed to be in the nest would make out with their first flight. This latter thought after watching a young robin survive its first flight and 45 degree crash landing into the lawn outside my office. Unless they cleared at least 20 metres of horizontal distance without losing more than a couple of metres of height, they would surely be swallowed up by the bottomless shaft. It would be interesting to know if there are any bird remains at the bottom. One thing seemed likely, the bird we saw fly onto the nest had been raised there herself and must have survived that first step into space. Why else would she have picked such a bizarre place? What kind of evolutionary factors would be at play with a totally secure nest and a do or die first flight? Perhaps the security of the nest and the partial darkness of the cave mean they don't fly until they are absolutely ready.

Caves of Prince George

I have not, in this short section, provided a comprehensive list of Prince George area caves, but I have made more references to caves in other sections of the book: "North to the Pine Pass", "Evanoff Provincial Park", "Upper Herrick Valley", and "Kakwa." The inventory and access is changing all the time with new cave discoveries and varying access logistics. I have avoided being too specific about cave locations, as this type of information is not generally publicized in order to protect both human life and irreplaceable cave speleothems.

It is thanks to the combined inspiration in the late 1970s of Claude Rouchon, native of Jura, France, and George Evanoff, discoverer of Fang Cave, that many explorations in the area have led to significant finds. These have included a number of international expeditions. There are many karst formations and caves, both discovered and awaiting discovery, especially throughout the McGregor, Rocky, and Cariboo Mountains east of Prince George. An important clue that there are more to find was the discovery, early in the twentieth century, of the deepest cave in North America, Arctomys Cave, on the east slope of Mount Resplendent, just east of Mount Robson.

Anyone wishing to get involved with caving and cave exploration should do so through an organized caving club that will provide training in safety and ethics essential to the protection of both caver and cave. For those who wish to experience a cave just once or twice, there are caving groups that will occasionally organize a guided trip. In the long run, there may be opportunities locally for commercially guided tours such as exist on Vancouver Island or in parts of the U.S. and Europe. However, as many of the caves are in high mountain areas, difficulty and cost of access will continue to be a limiting factor.

Crossing Hedrick Creek on a four-person tram at the start of the climb to Close to the Edge Cave.

Encountering Bears

First experience

As with any risk activity, one's first encounter with a bear, especially a grizzly bear, is always memorable; after all, it's the only one you will ever have with absolutely no prior firsthand experience to fall back on. For me, it happened on a fine day in July when I was camped at a mountain lake with my children in the meadows below Erg Mountain, 160 kilometres east of Prince George, above Ptarmigan Creek. I had been hiking in grizzly country for five years since arriving in Prince George in 1978, and had yet to see a specimen of *Ursos arctos horribilis* in its natural environment. On this particular morning, my kids (aged six and twelve) and I broke camp and crossed the lake's outflow creek, heading for the ridge above. We were about to move behind a screen of small trees that would have blocked our view when my son Jason announced in the matter of fact way of a kid who has too much faith in his parent, "Look Dad, there's a grizzly!" I looked up sharply from the fresh bear diggings I had been observing at my feet, and sure enough, there was a bear on the skyline just ahead—it was down on all fours, large head and prominent shoulder hump leaving no doubt as to what it was. It started moving toward us; no distant speck watched safely through binoculars. This wasn't how it was supposed to happen—this bear was close and closing. Taking my six-year old daughter, Sarah, by the hand I announced in a voice that intentionally carried more confidence than I felt, that we would walk calmly back to the camp we had just left. The reality was that I was scared for them—there were no large trees to climb, but our campsite offered some security as it was laden with the scent of people and the remains of our fire. Jason kept an eye on the bear and maintained a running commentary: "It's still coming, Dad. It's still coming." We stepped over the creek and walked into the camp. The bear followed us to the other side of the stream and stopped. I looked around, and immediately saw a second grizzly bear on the other side of the camp. This one, larger and a little farther away, was standing fully erect in a classic pose that can easily be misread as threatening, but that in reality is mostly inquisitive. We were between the two animals, probably a boar and a sow mating pair judging from their sizes. I surmised later that they had crossed the ridge and gone separate ways around the small lake just as we were breaking camp. If we had delayed our start by a few minutes, they would likely have gone by without our being aware of their presence, a situation more common than we might like to think.

After a long pause the second bear dropped to all fours and ran a short distance away, then stopped to look back. The first bear that I presumed to be a sow, joined him and they retreated in short runs, halting frequently and disturbingly to look in our direction until they passed over a low ridge and out of sight. The adrenaline rush was something that I would get to know well in the years ahead.

In my experience, grizzly bears generally avoid people. With one exception, all those that I have met quickly went the other way as soon as they knew what I was. Sub-adult males, newly on their own, sometimes push the limits and may need to be discouraged. Older, malnourished bears may be inclined to predatory behaviour if they are hungry enough. Barring surprise encounters though, most non-habituated bears usually shun contact with humans unless they feel it necessary to defend cubs, a mate, or a carcass that they are feeding on.

Whenever I have spied a distant grizzly bear, I have never mistaken it for something else, a characteristic that isn't true for other large animals. A caribou for example, can be indistinguishable from a rock when lying still, even when seen through a scope. Yet I have never once trained my glass on an object that I had not been able to immediately and positively identify as a bear, but that later turned out to be one. And conversely, I have never mistaken an actual bear for a rock or a tree. The difference is like snagging a fishing line versus having a good-sized, "fighting" fish take the lure—you know when it's the real thing. Grizzly bears never seem to stop moving when they are out in the open. When travelling they have an unmistakable gait, and when resting they fidget and roll around—always moving. Each of my surprise meetings with grizzly bears have occurred in open alpine country that, moments before, had seemed empty of wildlife. In situations like this, bears and people need space to feel comfortable.

Up close

While hiking alone on a hot August afternoon in the Dezaiko Range of the Rocky Mountains northeast of Prince George, I decided to take a dip in an inviting-looking alpine stream. I was about to strip off and take the plunge, when at the last moment something prompted me to check out better prospects farther downstream. Walking over a slight rise in the ground next to my first prospective bathing hole, I was shocked to find a grizzly bear grazing only 20 metres away! It was standing low in the tall, lush vegetation and I hadn't noticed it earlier. I quickly ducked back out of sight and, heart pounding, beat a hasty retreat up the opposite slope until I had reached a safe place from which to watch the bear. I hardly dared contemplate the comic tragedy that might have unfolded had I splashed unclad into that creek.

I have learned to be especially wary when approaching a mountain pass where wildlife and people are funneled into a tight corridor, with fickle winds and limited sightlines. On four separate occasions I have met a pair of grizzly bears at one favoured pass. The first I took to be a once in a lifetime experience, and was therefore quite surprised when the same thing happened a year later on the same mountain pass. On the third occasion I had become so wary of that place that instead of making a direct approach, I climbed off to one side and descended from above. With bear spray in hand and all my senses on "red alert", I scrutinized the area very carefully. There was nothing at all to be seen. Dropping down to the pass, I relaxed and eased the repellent back into its holster, feeling a little foolish at my excessive caution. Suddenly, from perhaps as close as five metres away, came a loud snorting and hissing. I was standing in hummocky terrain that had appeared flat and deserted from above. Amazingly, with limited visibility and a variable breeze neither the grizzly bear nor I could locate each other and I was once again extremely fortunate to have time to retreat off the pass. Only half an hour earlier I had approached a cow and calf caribou, a situation where I was perceived as the predator—now, in an ironic twist, I was the prey. Returning the next morning with my companion George Evanoff, we met a light-coloured sow grizzly bear with a single yearling cub near to the previous evening's encounter—almost certainly the same animal. This time we kept a respectful distance from each other and went our separate ways without incident. I was reassured by the presence of the older cub, as it seemed unlikely that the sow would try an opportunistic charge while it was safely at her side, although others have noted a different behaviour in such circumstances.

Demonstration of power

Trusting in one's experience and intuition is essential in bear country. Lingering once in a high mountain meadow, the socked-in ridge above effectively putting an end to thoughts of going higher, I felt the presence of a bear, subliminal perhaps, but real nonetheless. I took a few pictures, ate lunch and left early, all the time feeling that I was being watched. I returned a few days later with a friend, Lyle Daly, and on our descent at the end of the day we surprised a large, dark coloured grizzly investigating our up-trail. It whirled around and pounded the ground with such force and vibration that I felt about as significant as a ground squirrel. Every other bear that I have ever encountered moved quietly— this one left no doubt as to its power and its unhappiness at our meeting. This was probably the same bear I had sensed earlier—its message was clear, and I stayed away from that place for the rest of the season.

Territorial habits

Bears are territorial and inquisitive. In wooded country they sometimes announce their presence by leaving scent and hair on rubbing trees. This is more common among bears of the densely treed coastal areas, but can also be seen in the subalpine forests of the Rocky Mountains. A newly built structure in grizzly country will often be investigated, marked, and then left alone. If any changes are made to the structure, fresh claw marks and hair may be found on the next visit. Grizzly bears seem to be more comfortable with things that they have thus checked out and marked.

When food and cover are abundant, grizzlies may be more tolerant of other bears and people than at leaner times. There is a story that I heard from a bear biologist that highlights the amazing tolerance of one coastal grizzly bear, and the good fortune of its human pursuer. Two biologists were employing a technique of snaring and tranquilizing bears using a syringe fastened to a long stick. Finding that a snare attached to a log had been dragged off into the bush, they separated and commenced crawling through the underbrush looking for it. Soon one of the biologists came face to face with the bear, and jabbed it in the shoulder with the syringe. The grizzly was understandably annoyed, but the biologist lay facing it for the several minutes that it took for the drug to take effect, confident that the animal was securely attached to the jammed log. After the bear was fully sedated, he went looking for his partner who, in the meantime had found and tranquilized the grizzly that had actually been caught in their trap!

Of particular interest are the encounters that we know nothing about. This was vividly illustrated by something that happened to me during a group hike on the Torpy Trail in Evanoff Provincial Park in the McGregor Mountains. I was walking a hundred metres or so ahead of the others as we emerged from the forest into subalpine meadows. It was early July and the ground was wet from recent snowmelt. Walking past a tiny clump of trees and bushes, I veered away at the last moment to avoid boggy ground. Continuing on, I heard a shout behind me, "Mike, Bear!" I looked around but couldn't see the cause of the excitement. As the others caught up with me, I learned that a sow grizzly bear with three small cubs had been hiding in the clump of trees as I had walked past only three or four metres away. She took her cubs and ran away from me in full view of the rest of the group. This was my closest, and likely most dangerous encounter, and I had neither seen nor heard anything. If I had been alone I would have had no idea that this incredible event had taken place, and the obvious thought struck me, how often has this happened in the past?

Bear safety

Bear safety begins by learning about the habits of bears before venturing into the outdoors. The best Canadian text for this is Stephen Herrero's *Bear Attacks, Their Causes and Avoidance*. Herrero stresses the importance of learning about bears and their behaviour, and he emphasizes the importance of differentiating between defensive and aggressive (predatory) behaviour by a bear.

The probability of having a problem with a bear in the first place is very slight, but in the event that you do, you can significantly increase your chance of surviving the encounter through knowledge and action. First, it is helpful to understand how B.C.'s two species of bears have evolved. The grizzly bear's long claws, as well as the muscle mass that makes up the prominent shoulder hump, have developed mainly for digging in the open alpine and tundra of the western mountains and arctic regions for roots and small mammals. Its claws are poorly suited for climbing trees, yet some of them do climb well. Because it evolved in mainly open habitat, a grizzly is more likely than a black bear to defend its personal space, its cubs, or its food, as a black bear has more cover available to it. The black bear evolved in the forest, and as a result can climb trees very well and is more likely to retreat and seek shelter in the forest. A black bear may not flee if its intentions are something other than defensive: that is, predatory, curious, or habituated to human food. Early in the game it is important to learn how to distinguish a grizzly bear from a black bear. Size and colour don't necessarily help—there are large, brown coloured black bears and small dark coloured grizzly bears. The characteristic shoulder hump, dish shaped nose, and long claws distinguish the grizzly from the black bear.

Grizzly bear attacks are often defensive in nature, resulting from a surprise encounter when a person gets too close to the bear for its comfort. The most dangerous and perhaps the least predictable situation is getting close to a kill that is in the possession of a grizzly bear. Such an event took the life of my friend, George Evanoff, in 1998 on the Bearpaw Ridge above Sinclair Mills east of Prince George. Nearly as dangerous is getting between a sow and her cubs or between a boar and sow mating pair. Black bear aggression, when it occurs, is more likely to be predacious. It is essential to understand the difference between these types of aggression as the appropriate response depends on which it is, and your life may depend on making the right choice. Although each species of bear leans toward a certain behaviour, it is the behaviour, not the species, that is key. If you come across a bear and it does not appear to have noticed you, retreat quietly. Do not run unless you are sure of reaching safety as it may trigger an automatic chase response. Remember that a bear can run at least three times as fast as you can, and can probably climb trees much better than you are able to, even when you are motivated by the bear snapping at your heels. Being caught in a situation where the bear feels trapped, especially a grizzly bear, is bad news. This can occur when members of a group, whose numbers ought to give them a high degree of safety, become separated. A bear fleeing from an encounter with one part of the group and running into the other might feel trapped, and attack defensively. There is some safety in numbers, and some park jurisdictions now restrict human access in places where there is potential for human–grizzly bear conflict to groups of six or more people, who must stay within a certain distance of each other.

So what should you do if you encounter a bear? If you come across a bear that has seen you, and if you think you are within its "personal zone," one strategy is to hold your ground, analyze your options quickly and prepare your defenses—bear spray, air horn, bear banger, or firearm. If the bear advances toward you, continue to do the same thing. If the bear stops advancing, take the opportunity to retreat without running. If the bear advances again, stop and hold your ground. If the bear advances calmly and purposefully, making no attempt to avoid eye contact, and showing no sign of stress, it may be predacious. In this case, be prepared to act more assertively, and if necessary to fight for your life with whatever is at hand. If the bear attacks suddenly and you believe that the behaviour is defensive such as when protecting its cubs or food, fall to the ground at the last possible moment with your face and stomach down and your hands behind your neck to protect your head, neck, and vital organs. Spread your legs to make it harder for the bear to roll you over, and if it does succeed in doing this, try and complete the roll to end up face down again. Do not give the bear your pack—keep it on to help protect your back. Stay very still and quiet until you are sure the bear has left the area. If the attack becomes predacious, you must fight for your life. Perhaps the ultimate nightmare is an attack at night when you are in your tent. To prepare for this eventuality, it's best to take bear spray into the tent, and be prepared to fight for your life if you are attacked there, keeping in mind the effect of the spray on you as well as the bear in the confined space of the tent. Both grizzly and black bears attacking a tent at night are likely to become predacious, even if it is an opportunistic response to stumbling into your camp.

Ultimately there are no hard and fast rules and every situation has to be assessed and acted upon according to your knowledge and experience, and the situation. Usually this means getting a sense of what the bear is going to do before you react. In general, avoid direct eye contact and aggressive body language unless you are dealing with a predatory bear (usually a black bear), and retreat slowly when you have the opportunity. There are, however, some things one can do to help avoid conflict in the first place. They include making a lot of noise, preferably by talking or singing. Personally I dislike the noise of bear bells disturbing the natural sounds of the woods, although that might be preferable to someone's rendition of opera. If bells are your choice, lower pitched cowbells carry for a long distance and they avoid the suggestion some have made that higher pitch bells might arouse a bear's interest—dinner bells as the joke goes. If you travel with a party of around six or more people, you will naturally make so much noise that your chance of any kind of wildlife encounter is vanishingly small. Statistically, two people seem to be the most vulnerable sized group, possibly because two are likely to be less aware of their surroundings while not offering much more deterrence than a person alone.

On encountering fresh bear sign take a different route, if possible. One summer, in the Chilcotin Mountains, I was a member of a group of five hikers (one shy of the magic number of six) when we ignored fresh grizzly sign. We eventually walked into a blond-coloured grizzly that was feeding at the head of a lush, hanging valley, where, in our heat-exhausted state, we were determined to camp regardless of what the sign was telling us. In withdrawing, we walked through the bear's daybed in full sight of its owner. We had cornered the bear in its kitchen and had retreated through its bedroom, a situation that could have been entirely avoided if we had reacted sooner and more appropriately to the abundant sign it had left. This was a situation where the unspoken peer pressure to push on during a hot bushwhack put us in a dangerous situation. That being said, a judicious retreat worked for us then as it has for me on several occasions with both grizzly and black bears. A bear that shows no fear may simply be curious, or perhaps it is sizing you up, but either way it may become opportunistic if you stick around too long. Leaving may return control to you before the bear has made up its mind. If the bear follows, you may have to consider other tactics including deterrence.

Other safety tips include camping away from fresh bear sign. Avoid arranging tents in a circle such that an intruding bear might feel trapped. Cook well away from tents and avoid getting any food odours on either tents or clothes. Store food and white gas securely and well away from the tents. If you are travelling with a dog, keep it on a leash and tied up in camp. A dog in camp might be beneficial in deterring a bear from entering, or at least in raising the alarm. A free running dog is a considerable liability to other wildlife and can bring a bear back to you. Just before the first of the three grizzly bear encounters at the mountain pass described earlier, I had put my dog on a leash to stop him from chasing ground squirrels— a fortunate act that may have saved our lives.

Most people now carry bear spray, and the statistics citing its effectiveness, especially against grizzlies, suggest good (although far from certain) deterrent value. Practice when you get the chance, for example by discharging a recently expired canister so that your actions are instinctive in a real situation. Do not keep the product past its expiry date; it will lose effectiveness over time, especially in cool temperatures. Don't think in terms of throwing out a perfectly good $30 canister when it is three-years old. Think instead of depreciating it at a cost of $10 per year and anticipate the day when you and your partner can practice with it. The same principle applies to other deterrents that have shelf lives, such as bear bangers. Keep the bear spray handy at all times—it won't do you much good in your pack. Do not discharge the spray on your clothes or tent as a preventive measure—it doesn't work that way and there have been suggestions that the active ingredient may serve as a food attractant. If you get a chance, back up against, or better, get behind, a tree or a large rock so that the bear has to slow its charge before reaching you. Remember that the spray has a very limited range of up to four metres, and that many grizzly bear charges are initiated as a bluff or just as a means to find out what you are.

Another defensive option to consider is the use of bear bangers, especially to deter a bear that is showing an unhealthy interest, or is intent on stalking you. There are, however, some pitfalls to consider with this option. The main one is that a grizzly bear may attack in response to the sound of the launch and/or subsequent explosion, as happened to a forestry worker in the mountains east of Prince George in 2003. And even when a bear is scared by the sound of a bear banger, there is little control over the direction in which it will run, particularly if you drop the charge behind or above the bear instead of in front of it—both are easy to do. Conversely, don't fire it into the ground in front of the bear—I tried this once and the charge didn't explode. Bear bangers require safe storage and handling, and you need to check cartridges for discolouration that could result in a premature explosion and injury or fire. Transporting bear spray and bear bangers in chartered bush planes and helicopters requires special safety considerations, and is of course not allowed in scheduled commercial aircraft. Do not transport the repellents in the aircraft cabin—use the cargo compartment of a helicopter, or the pontoon of a floatplane. Aircrew will usually advise you of the requirements for safe carriage, but in case they don't, it is as well to be familiar with safety rules and insist that they be followed, as your life is on the line as well as theirs. Safety guidelines for using bear bangers indicate the need to hold the launcher at arms-length and above the head when firing, and to never screw a cartridge into the launcher until ready to use. This last suggestion, of course, would limit its effectiveness in a sudden bear encounter, so use your judgement on this. I usually arm my bear banger only while travelling in what I consider to be a high risk of encounter situation. An alternative sound deterrent is a horn powered by a small cylinder of compressed gas. I have seen one of these used effectively against an overly curious black bear that had approached a group of hikers who were sitting eating lunch on the bank of the Willow River. A gas horn is safer to handle and probably less likely to trigger the attack you are trying to prevent than a bear banger.

Should you carry a firearm? If you are hiking in a national park the question is moot since they are not allowed there. (There might be exceptions in the high Arctic in polar bear country.) But if you are travelling in an area where firearms are permitted, consider the following. Is it likely in the event of a sudden bear attack that you will have time to use a firearm effectively? How competent and practiced are you with the firearm in a moment of sudden and extreme stress? Will a warning shot from a firearm or bear banger provoke a violent response from a bear? Bears can be hard to stop even with a firearm.

What is the likelihood that you will wound a bear or cause an attack that wasn't going to happen? Are you prepared for the moral and legal implications of killing or wounding an animal that may be considered a member of a species at risk when bear spray, or simply retreating, might have sufficed? Have you considered the danger to human life of carrying a possibly loaded firearm in the group? Do you mind carrying an extra three or four kilos of weight? Yet, having said all this, there are situations where a firearm may be the only thing that might save your life, and I have heard of several such circumstances since coming to Prince George. I have carried a firearm in a few situations, but these are rare exceptions, and for my money, carrying a gun changes the dynamic between man and bear and is much more likely to cause a problem than to be of any real help. So in summary, learn about bears, take reasonable precautions, and prepare yourself for an experience that is as old as mankind!

Face to face

We stood very still, a tight group of three people. The object of our attention walked purposely toward us, large head swaying from side to side, muscles visible under its thick coat. We were three hours into a 12-day backpacking trip and were utterly absorbed in our situation—a Zen Master could not have achieved more presence. We were in the Spectrum Range, on the south boundary of Mount Edziza Provincial Park in northwest B.C., facing a grizzly.

Most of us today dwell in urban settings where we don't have much opportunity to meet wild animals in their natural environment. Yet living in a northern city, the wild side of life is never far away. The trick is to simply spend enough time in the outdoors to experience much of what Northern B.C. has to offer. Perseverance, patience, and letting go of expectations bring their rewards and are a metaphor for life. The unexpected is often a big part of wildlife encounters. A few years ago I was walking near Stone Creek, off Highway 97 a few kilometres south of Prince George, when suddenly three black bears came bounding around the bend in the trail ahead of me. I had a split second in which to decide what to do, and all I could think of was to throw up my arms and yell, "STOP!" That I am here to write about it suggests that this was a good choice—the sound and large appearance of me gave the playful siblings an instant of their own to look up and veer off the trail to run past me instead of over me.

Back in the Spectrum Range, Josette Wier, Lyle Daly, and myself assessed our combined arsenal of two cans of bear spray and one bear banger and, wisely, we chose to retreat.

Readiness for the Outdoors

We all hear of tragic events occurring in the outdoors, yet when we put things into perspective, we understand that the risks inherent in backcountry recreation are really no worse than those of everyday living. We have some wonderful backcountry close to Prince George, and the opportunity to experience it is one of the main benefits of living in this northern community. Today, there is hardly a workplace without a safety program, and outside the work environment we are all familiar with the constant emphasis on highway safety. Some accidents are bound to happen, but through awareness and training they can be kept to a minimum. In the same way, there are many opportunities to learn to do outdoor recreation safely through local training courses and by joining knowledgable groups. We can manage risk as we continue to enjoy the backcountry, just as we do on the highways. We must look at risks objectively—just because something has never happened to us doesn't mean it won't happen tomorrow, and just because it could happen doesn't mean that it will. We must anticipate the unexpected and consider the possible consequences of each action that we are about to undertake. Then, while we may still decide to cross a steep rock or snow slope, we can choose to minimize the risk by exposing only one person at a time; or we might pick a different route, or simply turn around and go home. And most importantly, in assessing the risk we must think not only of ourselves, but also of any less experienced people who may be travelling with us, and especially of those who are waiting at home for our safe return.

Have you taken an avalanche course before setting out into the winter mountains?

Preparedness

The first requirement of any outdoor activity is to try to prepare for whatever eventuality might happen. This usually means acquiring knowledge through some sort of training, and then developing and applying that knowledge through practice. Whether you are a joiner or not, a good way to start is to participate with an organized group or club to gain the basic experience that you will need before striking out on your own. Higher risk sports such as caving should always be done through a reputable organization—underground is never a place to go without experienced companions. Prince George has hundreds of clubs of all kinds and there is almost no reason why anyone has to learn an outdoor pursuit the hard way. For visitors and others who don't have the time or inclination to join a club, there are also a number of commercially guided outdoor recreation opportunities in the area.

As well as gaining knowledge, preparedness means thinking through the "what ifs." What if there is an injury, or signs of hypothermia or heat exhaustion? What if you are lost or have underestimated the time that is required to return before dark? What if you meet a bear on the trail, capsize a canoe on a lonely stretch of river, or if a member of your party is trapped in an avalanche? Do you have the self-rescue gear that you might need? Have you made sure that a reliable person at home has your itinerary and a list of participants? Does someone in the group have first aid skills and equipment? Does everyone in the party have enough raingear and extra warm clothes to spend one or two nights out? Does your daypack contain the basic essentials—raingear, extra warm clothing, fire-starters, a first aid kit, food, and water? Technology is changing too, with the advent of synthetic clothing and gadgets such as geographic positioning systems, as well as cell phones and satellite phones. The latter should be viewed as tools of last resort and should not be a substitute for common sense and the ability to self-rescue.

I once witnessed two people setting off up a steep trail on mountain bikes, wearing very lightweight riding gear. This was a real mountain, not just a mountain bike trail, and they had almost nothing with them save tiny micro-packs strapped to their backs. They were equipped for an optimum, all-out cardiovascular effort as if they were at a gym in town. They had made scant provision of any kind that I could see for an injury that might occur while riding in the mountains, an undertaking that could hardly be considered low risk. On the same trail a few years earlier I witnessed a young woman badly sprain both ankles just walking, having earlier resisted suggestions that her footwear was inadequate.

There is no substitute for experience, and I highly recommend that anyone who spends time in the backcountry also take a survival course that includes spending one, or better two, nights out in the bush. The psychological pressure faced in an unexpected overnighter and how

Dehydration and heat exhaustion? Time to ensure sufficient water intake and supplies.

you deal with it will make the difference between an adventure that builds confidence, and a frightening experience that you may or may not survive. I can attest from personal experience from unplanned bivouacs in the mountains, that prior practice in a safe setting made all the difference for me after I made the psychologically difficult decision to stop. I knew, then, that I had the skills to do what I had to do instead of worrying or panicking about it. The same is true for first aid training, especially all of the practice that goes with it. A wilderness first aid course is best because of its emphasis on improvisation. However, any first aid training is worth having and the principles involved in the priority assessment of an injured person can be applied to assessing almost any emergency situation.

Assessing the situation

Despite best efforts, something unexpected has happened to you or to your party in the outdoors, and you must now deal with it. The first, and very natural reaction is often fear, or even a sense of rising panic particularly if you are lost or in a circumstance that has life-threatening implications. Paradoxically, one of the fears that can arise is that of work or other commitments that you might have the next day, or of people at home worrying about you, or initiating some kind of emergency response that could be embarrassing. That can cause you to push on dangerously, when all you really need to do is to stop and wait for morning. "Get-home-itis" has killed many private pilots in this mountain province when they have pushed on into worsening weather, instead of simply turning around. A similar type of syndrome can arise on the ground.

The first consideration in assessing a situation is whether you or your companions are in immediate danger, and if so, taking urgent steps to minimize that exposure. Assessing a situation is always worth doing in order to help you select the most effective action, and it can be as short as taking a few seconds to scan the scene while walking toward it. Next, deal with any medical or first aid requirements, or urgent rescue such as the recovery of someone from an avalanche or river. The initial first aid assessment and response starts with the ABC's of airway, breathing, and circulation, and using a triage approach if there is more than one victim. Follow this with a more complete assessment, comforting the patient and making them secure, warm, and dry while starting any treatment. Assess the equipment that the group is carrying, as well as any natural materials at hand that could be used for making splints, building a fire, or constructing a shelter. Review what skills the group has, and how they can be applied to the situation. Once any immediate threats have been taken care of, it is usually best to sit down and think through the problem, assessing the options that are available. It is generally not a good idea to rush into action unless it is imminently life-threatening, or is a clearly defined situation that you have prepared for.

Leadership

The leader of an outdoor activity is anyone who, by virtue of their level of knowledge and experience, is presumed to be guiding the group. Sometimes in a small group of peers there might be a consensus arrangement, and some clubs use the concept of a trip coordinator in order to lessen their perceived liability. Either way, it is essential that whoever is in this role carefully monitor each participant as to their equipment, knowledge, preparedness, and their progress during the journey, and ensures that the experience is enjoyable and educational for all. The leader must discourage anyone from participating who is unlikely to be able to do so safely, but having accepted them, must ensure that the activity is conducted according to the abilities of the weakest and/or the least experienced member of the group.

Be prepared through knowledge and practice, and try to anticipate what could go wrong. Have at least some basic first aid experience, and carry extra clothing and good equipment. If you are taking children into the backcountry, make sure that you have the necessary skills and knowledge of the area that you are going to, and remember that the standard of care expected of you is much higher when dealing with minors. Understand the principles of good leadership, and practice assessing situations that might arise. Leave a detailed itinerary with a reliable person at home. Prepare for bad weather, and be ready for one or two nights out if necessary. Expect the unexpected, use your head, and be especially alert for the syndrome "it can't happen to me."

Technology in the backcountry

We have reached a turning point in the story of human wilderness experience. Lightweight, affordable communication devices are making it possible to remain in contact with the outside world wherever we are in the outdoors. The adventure of being completely on one's own for an extended period in the backcountry is now a thing of the past for anyone who values the peace of mind of friends and family left behind. Yet paradoxically, a big part of the wilderness experience for me has been the ability to get away from civilization and to immerse myself in a primal experience where I am a part of the

Technology toys of the well-equipped backcountry traveler may include GPS, satellite phone, altimeter wristwatch, and bear repellents!

landscape with all its joys and occasional sublime terrors. Although advantaged by lightweight modern gear, once embarked on any trek through the mountains I was as alone and vulnerable as my distant ancestors might have been as I faced the terror of a stalking grizzly bear or unstable terrain. I'm glad to have experienced this type of unbridled primitive travel, but it is getting harder to justify not taking advantage of satellite technology on an extended wilderness trek.

There have, of course, been communication options available for many years. Emergency locator transmitters designed for use on downed aircraft, and more recently personal locator beacons provide an alarm to a satellite surveillance system. The problem with these devices is that they are non-discriminatory, and if deployed will result in a full-scale, expensive emergency response that may take hours to get underway. Satellite phones are becoming more widely available and affordable. Unlike the personal locator beacon, a telephone or two-way radio is a highly selective device enabling precise information to be passed on in the event of a problem, or simply to update one's emergency contact with inevitable changes to travel itineraries. The trick while on a wilderness vacation is to resist the temptation to check the latest news, weather, investments, or business consultations. The key, in my view, is to be fully prepared with one's backcountry skills, and if you want that get-away experience then carry, but don't use, the satellite phone unless you must.

Preparing for the backcountry

Preparing for a major backcountry trek can be a year long endeavour that starts with the previous year's trip. Returning from such a trip, there are photographs to organize, presentations to give, and of course, the all-important party in which to relive one's adventures. And that inevitably leads to the question, "Where shall we go next year?" Serious planning starts in late winter so that everyone can arrange vacation time. Having a group that is reasonably well-matched is essential for a hike that involves travelling and moving camp every day in a remote area. It is important in that situation that the group stays together and that nobody get frustrated with a pace that's too slow or too fast. Next comes the task of short-listing areas, buying maps, choosing a destination, investigating logistics, and researching the wildlife, vegetation, geology, anthropology, and history of the area in order to get the most out of the time spent there. Some of my longer trips have been accessed by vehicle or by helicopter, but most have been by fixed-wing aircraft. A floatplane usually offers a cost-effective way to get to a remote place in the hinterland of B.C.. The charter is best booked early in the season, with most bush operations that I have dealt with taking a telephone booking followed by payment at time of flight.

A few weeks before departure and it is time to check equipment. Are any major new purchases needed such as sleeping bag, tent, backpack, or boots? It is important to break new equipment in well before a big trip to become familiar with it, make any necessary adjustments, and to generally avoid unpleasant surprises on the trip. There are quality outdoor stores in Prince George and it pays to buy good stuff. If you are new to the game, try to buy one major item each year and start with shorter trips. It doesn't take too many years before you are both mentally and physically ready and well-equipped for a longer trip. The next consideration is food. I have found that home-dried food is the best way to eat well, and pack light. Because the drying process can be lengthy, it's best to get that done a few weeks before you leave. (See following section.)

A week before departure is a good time to assemble all the food and equipment, to test stoves and put new batteries in headlamps and other gadgets. I use a checklist developed from previous trips, and I refine it each year—all the time learning, and refining such things as types and quantities of food. If this is a first trip, consult an experienced friend, or read a book on backpacking. An interesting paradox has arisen with modern backpacking equipment. As technology improves and equipment gets lighter, the overall weight seems to go up. The problem is that there are seemingly endless new gadgets to take along if you are not selective. First there are water filters—remember when mountain water was safe to drink? Next, a hand-held geographic positioning system will provide endless entertainment, and perhaps even help you to find your way in conditions where a map and compass are not sufficient. Then do you rent a two-way radio, satellite phone, or personal locator beacon? And who, now, would be without bear spray? Flares, bear bangers, headlight, camera, interpretive guidebooks, stoves and fuel, stainless steel pots instead of aluminum; the list goes on. Since there is clearly no limit to man's ingenuity to invent new toys, the problem is going to get much worse before it gets better. But perhaps it's not such a long leap from trekker to "trekky." So I'm waiting for a hand-held device that will allow me to beam down all the food and shelter I need each night, preferably already cooked and served with a bottle of fine wine. Then, the rest of the time I can hike with a lightweight daypack!

Food and food dehydrating

An essential part of a successful wilderness backpacking trip is tasty, nutritious food that is light to pack and easy to prepare. "Outdoors cooking doesn't have to be dull" recipes may work for a weekend at the lake or for the relative luxury of canoe tripping, but for an extended backpacking trip where weight is paramount, my philosophy is to keep it simple. The food must be substantial, nutritious, enjoyable, and easy to prepare in one pot in 15 minutes or less by people who are tired and hungry. Another key concern is that food in bear country has to be nearly odourless when packaged.

Breakfast is key to fueling the activities of the day. Mostly, I use large whole oat flakes, multi-grain cereals and granola with skim milk powder, home-dried fruit and brown sugar. This breakfast is high in carbohydrates and has good staying power. During the day, an occasional snack of trail mix and home-dried fruit provides an important boost between meals.

Lunch is an interesting challenge on a long trip. How do you replace all the sandwiches, bagels, and fruit etc. that one normally takes on a day or weekend hike? A combination that works for me is to use crisp-bread style crackers on which to put cream cheese, or peanut butter and jam. I avoid buying low fat fixings, since on a diet of dried food, you generally need all the fat per food weight ratio that you can get while in the outdoors. I complete the meal with more home-dried fruit, the equivalent of at least two apples. Cured meats are delicious in the outdoors, but I tend to avoid them because of the preservatives used and the risk of attracting unwanted dinner guests with the inevitable strong odour.

I usually begin supper with dried soup mix to provide needed salts and liquid, and as a psychological bridge while waiting for dinner. The main course must be filling, with lots of protein and carbohydrate. One of my favorites is pre-cooked extra lean ground beef with onions, red peppers, garlic, spices, and tomato sauce, dried for 10 to 12 hours in a food dehydrator and packaged in doubled, heavy-duty zippered plastic food bags. I've found that it keeps well on the trail for two weeks or more. Rehydrating and cooking can take as little as 15 minutes and it can be served with freshly cooked pasta and rehydrated vegetables. Dessert can be as simple as a few pieces of chocolate: something to sweeten the meal. Add lots of water and non-caffeinated tea throughout the evening for rehydration. An alternative dessert can be a pre-mixed bannock, baked in a small frying pan and topped with jam or freshly picked berries. The frying pan is an extra utensil to carry, but it can be considered group equipment and can double for pancakes to vary the breakfasts. On a group hike, take turns preparing breakfasts and dinners for the group, and take individual snacks and lunches. Consider dividing a larger party into three or four-person cooking groups each with its own single burner stove.

A food dehydrator will dry a wide range of foods. The results are generally tastier, more nutritious, and have fewer preservatives than if you bought commercially dried foods. Staples like pasta, rice, lentils, beans, and milk powder are taken just as they come from the store, but are best repackaged into meal-sized portions according to needs. I always dry a large quantity of fruit, starting with good-quality apples, peeled and sliced a quarter of an inch thick. To this can be added just about any other kind of fresh dried fruit, including mangos, kiwis, strawberries, bananas, oranges, as well as canned goods such as sliced pineapples. Canned baked beans are easy to dry, and rehydrate quickly to supplement any meal. The same applies to most vegetables, either lightly cooked or the frozen variety. All the foods can be dried, packaged, and if necessary, frozen a few weeks before the trip so that you are not faced with an impossible task a few days before leaving. Experiment with different foods, and try them first at home. Of course, as good as all this gets in the wild, there's nothing like that first cheeseburger with pie and ice cream as soon as you hit a restaurant at the end of the trip!

Northern Light

In this book, I have discussed many ideas for exploration and discovery in the outdoors around Prince George based on my own quarter-century of experience here. I couldn't possibly cover everything that I've done during that time, and there is much that I have not seen and will never see. But it's important for the human psyche, or my psyche at least, just to know that there are such places left to find. Each person undergoes their own journey of discovery, and every new place or insight is as valid for them as it was for the first people to walk this land.

Many people travel afar to seek new experiences and gain a well-rounded worldview. Yet there are more opportunities awaiting locally than one person can possibly cover in a lifetime, including the chance to tread where no one has likely gone before. I hope I have inspired you to undertake your own journeys of exploration, both to some of the places described in the book, as well as to the countless other possible destinations that exist near Prince George. If in the end you realize, as I have, what a truly amazing area this is, I will have succeeded. Prince George has become for me a place of light, and has provided an inspiration for some of the ideas and images in the book, and for these concluding words.

Webster's dictionary defines "light" as electromagnetic radiation, illumination, dawn, colour, enlightenment, and spiritual awareness. With its two places of higher learning, Prince George attracts students and teachers from around the world, as well as providing opportunities for knowledge and enlightenment for people throughout the region. The city is home to diverse religions and other opportunities for mind–body–spiritual well-being such as fitness or yoga classes, or simply a contemplative walk in the outdoors that surrounds us.

Because of our geography, sunsets are a feature of Prince George. A cloud base overhead, and clearing on the southwestern horizon is a signal for a fine sunset to come, as our setting star paints the clouds beneath with many varied forms and colours. In the winter, add to this a few days of cold, clear weather to build up hoarfrost crystals on the trees, and the stage is set for dramatic effect. Such is often the case toward year's end, with lovely midwinter sunsets over Summit Lake, across the Prince George Bowl, and unexpected light shows on the city's northern hilltops. One notable day, when trees and bushes on Pilot Mountain were heavily laden with ice crystals, the setting sun appeared below the clouds to produce a dazzling golden display. As I looked down the hill at golden treetops and across the Interior Plateau, the light was in a constant state of change. When I thought I had seen its peak, it kept evolving into something better—a kaleidoscope of light, colour, and space, with the lengthening shadow of the earth slowly consuming the alpenglow on the distant mountains.

During midwinter, the low-angle sun shines nearly horizontally through leafless glades. Pastel colours reflect off birch and aspen trees, and patches of light invite a path through the forest. Backlit draperies of caribou moss decorate the conifers of a black spruce swamp and a subalpine forest better than ornaments on any Christmas tree. Settling into a sunny spot for lunch in a snowy mountain meadow, the long shadow of a subalpine–fir soon reminds me what season it is. Then from the mountaintop, a vertical column of light materializes as tiny, airborne, plate-like crystals of ice refract the sunlight behind.

On a midsummer evening, an immense rainbow column of light rises from the Rocky Mountain Trench and inspires the lone occupant

Summer sunset in the Dezaiko Range of the Rocky Mountains.

Winter sunset in the Dezaiko Range of the Rocky Mountains.

of an alpine camp. Clouds and rain showers to the east, with a bright setting sun on the other horizon, create a brilliant triple rainbow over a downtown grocery store—sunlit against a jet-black sky.

Prince George in the fall has vast displays of yellow, gold, and green, with splashes of red and rust underbrush. Perhaps disappointing to someone transplanted from the maple forests of eastern Canada; after a year or two it will win over the senses. Fall, for many, is the best time of year to be in the outdoors—there are few bugs, the temperature is agreeable for exercise, and nature's colours are at their best.

When the light of day fades into evening, the show is not necessarily over. The cycle of the moon, visiting comets, lunar eclipses, and the aurora borealis can light up the night sky. Go to a place like the McGregor Valley, away from the haze and light of town, and four hundred billion stars wheel overhead in the clear dark sky. Looking up, there is the same sense of wonder that Alexander Mackenzie must have felt travelling through in 1793. And we have the added knowledge of our place in a quiet suburb of a remarkable galaxy, bathed in the northern light of Prince George's outdoors.

Index

Adolphus Lake 163
Akeley, Carl 230
Akeley, Mary Jobe 230
Alaska Highway 66, 69, 74, 96
Alberta Speleological Society 173, 189
Alexander Mackenzie Heritage Trail 145
Alexandra Falls 232
Aleza Lake Research Forest 165-166
Alpine Club of Canada 35, 121, 187, 191, 229-230
alpine tundra 83
American kestrel 178
American pipit 249-250
ancient forest 11, 128
Andrews, G.S. 73
Angel Peak 74
Archibald, S.W. 73
Arctomys Cave 251
Association of BC Forest Professionals 26-27, 280
Aubrey, Elisabeth Spaude 132
avalanche 74, 83, 120, 129, 132-133, 137, 149, 159, 169, 171, 175, 183, 195, 211, 237, 263, 265
avalanche lily 129, 132, 195
Azouzetta Lake 62-64
B.C. Express 92, 198-199
B.X. 199
Baker Creek 150, 202
Baldy Hughes 199-201, 240
bald eagle 11, 40, 45, 129, 209
Banff 11, 44, 143, 163, 186, 191
Barbara Lake 236
Barkerville 52, 143-145, 202-203
Barton, Tom 173
basaltic columns 58, 204
Bastille Creek 185, 188, 196
BC Rail 18, 38
Bearpaw Ridge 94, 113, 133, 174, 242-243, 257
bear banger 257, 259-261, 269
Bear Glacier 71
Bear Lake 39, 59, 61-62, 215, 224
bear spray 66, 254, 257, 259-261, 269
Beaumont Provincial Park 226
Beaver Falls 151
Begbie (Judge) 206
Begbie Lookout 206
Bella Coola 145, 200
Bell Mountain 147
Bend 134
Bennett, W.A.C. 51, 239
Berg Lake 151, 157, 162-163, 196
Bess Pass 143, 151, 229
Big Mountain 187, 230
Blackwater LRUP 201
Blackwater Road 197, 199-201, 240
black bear 7, 11, 28, 40-43, 61, 65, 75, 81, 145, 149-150, 167, 184, 209, 256-261
black flies 41, 121
black spruce 58, 85, 88, 93, 272
Bloody Tower 73
blowdown 57, 166, 235
Blunderbuss 232-233
Bobtail Mountain 216-217

Bob Harkins Library 15
bog orchid 109
Boone and Crockett 234-235
Boudreau, Jack 10, 129
Boulder Mountain 144,
Bowron, John 145
Bowron Forest Service Road 82, 131, 167
Bowron Lake Provincial Park 139, 145, 203
Bowron River 134
Bowron Valley 82, 107, 133
Bow Lake 214-215
Broadview Mountain 188
Browne, Capt. O.F. 198-199
Bucey (Captain) 92
Buchanan, Don 217
Buchanan Creek 188, 196
Bulkley Valley 201
bull trout 145
Burns Lake 78, 227, 239-240, 241
Burnt Bridge Creek 200
Caledonia Nordic Ski Club 39, 46, 77, 121
Caledonia Ramblers Hiking Club 63, 65, 85, 116-117, 121, 158
Camp Lake 214-215
Canada geese 228
Canadian National Railway 129, 131, 142
Canadian Nature Federation 227
Canadian Pacific Railway 185, 190
Canadian Rocky Mountains Expedition 72
Canis lupus columbianus 78
Captain Creek 176
Cariboo Mountains 11, 33, 39, 83, 85, 89, 125, 132, 140, 143, 149, 151, 153, 155, 188, 244, 251
caribou 12, 65-66, 68-69, 71-72, 74-75, 83, 89, 91, 105, 107-109, 111, 119-121, 127, 140, 163, 168, 174, 183-184, 189, 222-223, 253-254, 272
Caribou Meadows 108-109, 111
Carrier 145, 185, 200
Carrie Jane Grey Park 17
Cataline 231
Catfish Creek 134, 137, 140
Cathedral Grove 127
Caux, Jean 231-232
centennial project 28
Chalco Creek 143
Chappise, Sam 73
Chilako River 216
Chinook salmon 145
Christmas bird count 47
Chuchi Lake 222
Churchill Mine Road 67, 71
Circle Route 66
citywide trails 19-20
Close to the Edge 181, 247, 249
Cluculz Lake 225
Coffeepot Mountain 55-56, 58-59, 61, 224, 233
Coleman Glacier 163
College Heights 44, 46
College of New Caledonia 11, 13, 26, 139, 202
Collins Telegraph Trail 144, 201, 231
Columbia University 229

community gardens 23
Connaught Hill 15, 20
cornices (snow) 159, 187
Cottonwood Canyon 198
Cottonwood House 203
Cottonwood Island Nature Park 15, 24, 35, 37, 44-45, 117, 210
cougar 25, 28, 42, 76, 217
cow parsnip 21, 139, 195
Coxson, Darwyn 128
Craighead, Frank and John 194
Craighead, Lance and April 194
Cranbrook Hill Greenway 17, 19, 21, 28, 39, 42, 44-47, 207
Cree 73, 185, 187, 239
Crescent Spur 130, 132, 134, 137, 143, 144
Crooked River 39, 50, 53, 55, 59, 61-62, 233
cross-country ski 8, 30, 36, 39, 54, 77, 105, 171, 197, 211, 213-214, 237
Croydon 151, 155-156
Crystal Lake 61
Daly, Lyle 249, 255, 261
Dawson Creek LRMP 184
deer 11, 25, 40, 75, 120, 150, 222
devils club 43, 113, 125, 127, 167
Devils Fence Posts 204
Dezaiko Range 175, 181, 183, 249, 254
Dimsdale, H.G. 236
Dimsdale Lake 189, 236
DNA 188, 194
dog 105, 111, 132, 203, 206, 214, 259
Dome Creek 20, 82, 125, 130, 134, 193, 234
Dore River 134
Douglas fir 28, 30, 56, 76, 82, 155
Draper, Robin 42
Driftwood Forest Service Road 221-222
Driscoll Creek 124, 134
Driscoll Ridge 122, 124-125, 129
Ducks Unlimited 228
Dunn, Alice and Fred 190
Dunster 75, 142, 145, 152, 154, 156
Dunster Ice Cream Social 152
Dunster Trail 153-154, 156
Eaglet Lake 130, 165-167
East Twin Creek 143
Edmonton 7, 11, 190, 214, 236
Elk Mountain 203
entomologists 181
equinox 14, 94, 169
Erg Mountain 116, 135, 138-140, 252
Eskers Provincial Park 35, 39, 46, 211, 213, 215
Evanoff, Craig 188
Evanoff, George 10, 18, 117, 171-173, 179, 188, 191, 217, 237, 244-245, 251, 254, 257
Evanoff Provincial Park 117, 172, 250, 256
Evans, Jack 238
Evans Creek 238
Fallis, Mary 35
fall colour 29, 138, 237
Fang Cave 174, 179, 244-245, 251
Fang Mountain 174
farmers market 112
Fay, S. Prescott 187
Federation of B.C. Naturalists 227
Federation of Mountain Clubs of B.C. 117, 280
Ferguson Lake 37-39
Finlay 50, 235
firearm 257, 260
fire lookout 125, 131-132, 147, 205, 219
first aid 52, 93, 263, 265-266, 280
floatplane 189, 260, 268
flowstone 245, 248
food 31, 67-68, 89, 111, 122-123, 162, 177, 192, 195, 221, 234, 255-256, 258-259, 264, 268-270
food dehydrating 269, 270
Footner, Hulbert 232, 233
Forests for the World 17, 21, 28-34, 41-44, 47, 117
forest certification 26, 59
Forlorn Gorge 66, 72
Fort Fraser 112, 224-225
Fort George 15, 18, 20, 43-44, 45, 53, 87, 91, 190, 197, 199, 210
Fort George Canyon 197, 199
Fort George Park 15, 18, 20, 45, 210
Fort McLeod 233
Fort Nelson 66
Fort Prince of Wales 7
Fort St. James 50, 112, 203, 211, 218-219, 221
fossil 189, 245, 248
Fox, Terry 157, 159-160
Framstead 176-179, 181, 183
Framstead Creek 176, 177-178, 183
Fraser Headwaters Alliance 155
Fraser Lake 218, 224-227
Fraser Mountain 112, 218, 224-226
Fraser River 15, 18, 23, 30, 44, 46, 48, 53, 75, 83, 85, 88-91, 93, 95-96, 131, 133-134, 143-144, 145, 147, 149, 152, 154, 156, 162, 176, 188, 194, 197, 200, 202, 204, 210, 232, 234, 242, 280
Front Ranges 184
Fusilier Creek 74
Fusilier Glacier 74
Garvin Creek 35, 46, 211
geographic centre 227
geographic positioning system 264, 269
Giguère, Jean-Jaques 32
Gilmour, Andrew 188
Ginter, Ben 21-22, 31, 47
Giscome 48, 52, 130, 165, 167, 243
Giscome Portage 48, 52, 232-233
glacier 11, 35, 73, 137, 182, 186, 190, 230
Goat Island 23
Goat River 134, 137, 139, 143-146
Goat River Trail 143-145
golden eagle 11, 159-160, 175, 177-178
gold fields 87, 145, 201, 205
gold rush 53, 202, 206, 238
Gold Rush Trail 144
gour dam 245
Grand Canyon of the Fraser 83, 85-86, 89, 93, 96, 107, 232-233, 242
Grand Reo 218, 226
Grand Trunk Pacific Railway 232
Grand Trunk Pacific Railway Company 18
Gray, Prentiss Nathaniel 10, 234, 235-236
Gray, Sherman 234-236
Gray Pass 189, 234, 236
Grease Trail 145, 200

Greens Rock 85, 87
Green Mountain 76, 79
Gregg Creek 216-217
grizzly bear 7, 11, 51, 61, 65, 75, 79, 82-83, 91, 113, 116, 125, 134,137-140, 150, 173, 177, 181, 184, 188, 194-195, 224, 232, 252-255, 256-257, 259-261, 267
grizzly bear den 181
Grizzly Bear Mountain 129
Grizzly Den 26, 83, 107, 118-121
Groundhog Lake 203
Groveburn Road 77
Gunn, Luther Collins 18, 23
Gunn Trail 17, 18, 20, 23, 38
Hagen Peak 121
Haiku 132
Hanington 190
Hansard Bridge 131, 167
hantavirus 122
Hardin, Joel 199, 240
harlequin ducks 145
Hart Highway 36, 46, 48, 54, 211
Hart Ranges 176, 182, 223
Harvard Mountaineering Club 190
Hazelton 201, 231
Hedrick Creek 181, 249
helicopter 56, 76, 88, 122, 151, 160, 169, 176-177, 181-183, 217, 235, 237, 260, 268
helicopter logging 76
helictites 245
Hepburn, Sandra 128
Heritage Park 21
Heritage River Trail 15, 18-20, 24, 34, 37, 44-46, 89
Herrero, Stephen 256
Herrick Creek Local Resource Use Plan 27, 176, 178, 183
Herrick Forest Service Road 182
Herrick Valley 176-177, 183, 250
Highway 16 18, 42, 71, 75, 77, 80, 82-83, 85-86, 90-91, 93, 105-106, 110, 112, 119, 123-124, 128, 130, 134, 137, 140, 142-145, 147, 149, 150-152, 154, 156-157, 163, 167, 185, 188, 197, 216, 218, 224-227, 239
Highway 5 157, 159, 163
Highway 97 37, 45, 48, 50-51, 54, 55, 59, 62-64, 144, 202, 206, 261
Hike Canada En Marche 142
Hinton 163
History of the Northern Interior 87, 91, 200
hoarfrost 118, 272
hoary marmot 65, 105, 141, 150, 163
Holliday Creek 150-151
Holmes River 143, 151-152, 229
Hooge, Bonnie 188
horseflies 121
Horsefly 204-205
Horsefly Lake 205
Houston 240
Howard, Roy 10, 145, 154
Huble Homestead 48, 52, 233
Hudson Bay 7, 10, 17, 204, 210
Hudson Bay Company 204
Hudson Bay Slough 17, 210
Hudson Hope 234-235

Hughes, Jim 239
Hungary Creek 83, 118-119, 122, 134
Hunter, Dan 79, 191
Hutton 83, 86, 106, 119
Hyder 71
ice fishing 215
Ice Mountain 107
Important Bird Area 227
Indata Lake 222
independent power plant 135
Inside Passage 8
interior cedar-hemlock 122-123
interior cedar–hemlock 83, 105, 122
Interior Plateau 8, 20, 48, 51, 55, 165, 200, 206, 216, 219, 224-225, 272
interior wet belt 130
Interprovincial Boundary Survey 231
Iroquois 75, 185
Jackpine Pass 151, 229
James Creek 176
Jarvis, Edward William 185, 190, 214
Jarvis Creek 189
Jarvis Lakes 185, 189, 191
Jarvis Pass 189
Jasper 11, 75, 143, 151, 162-163, 186, 191, 229-230, 239
Jasper National Park 143, 151, 162-163, 229
Jean de Brebeuf Park 46
Jobe, Mary 129, 187, 229-231
Jones, Captain M.F.R. 72, 74
Joule Mountain 139
Kabuki 243
Kain, Conrad 230
Kakwa 10, 125, 129, 184-186, 188-189, 191-192, 194-196, 229-231, 234, 236, 250
Kakwa Pass 188
Kathie Lake 213-215
Kearney, Jack 240
Keen, Clive 174, 248-249
Kenneth Creek 85-86, 88, 90, 93, 134
Kidprice Lake 238
Killoren Crescent 21
Killy, Ivor 38
King, Dave 113, 115-117, 158
Kinney, Reverend George 187, 230
Kinney Lake 162
Kinsey, Sandra 57, 128
Kinuseo Falls 235
Kitchi Creek 187
Kitwancool 71
Kiwa 155
Kiwi Mountain 74
Knudsen Lake 183
Koeneman Park 156
Kootenays 26, 185
Kopas 144
Kruger Lake 146
Kuzkwa River 221
Lakes Country 241
Lake St. Sepulchre 74
Land and Resource Management Plan 27, 58, 83, 89, 116, 135, 166, 183-184, 211, 216, 221, 249, 280
Last Call Lake 67, 69, 74

Latrobe Park 46
La Glace Lake 188, 192
Leo Creek Forest Service Road 221
Leprechaun 119-120
Lett, Judy 10, 169, 204
Lewis and Clark 186
lichen 56, 111, 121, 123-124, 128, 222
Likely 204
Little, J.D. 25- 28
Littlefield Creek 146
Livingstone Springs 57, 61
llama 188, 191
Local Resource Use Plan 176
Long, Gordon 231
Longworth 95, 96, 125, 130-131, 133, 167
Longworth Lookout 130-131, 133
Lucille Mountain 147
lynx 43, 76
MacDonald Creek 67, 69, 71, 74
Mackenzie 50, 62, 186, 200, 210
Mackenzie, Alexander 145, 186, 200, 210, 273
Mackenzie Heritage Trail 200
Malton Airport 237
Mariel Lake 189, 192, 196
marten 83
Massey Stadium 17, 22, 45
Mastodon 87
McBride 75, 82, 88, 134, 138, 142, 145, 147-151, 156, 160, 188, 229
McBride Peak 147, 149
McCaulay, Alex 239
McCrory, Wayne 188, 194
McCullagh Pass 179
McGregor, Captain James Herrick 176
McGregor Model Forest 167
McGregor Mountains 110, 130, 165, 167-169, 256
McGregor Pass 188, 192, 196
McGregor River 26, 176-177, 181, 187-188
McKirdy, Margaret 238-239
McMillan Creek 36-37
McMillan Regional Park 37, 45-46
Mercers Peak 73
Merchant Taylors Peak 73
Metis 185, 238-239
Milk River 144-145
Ministry of Sustainable Resource Management 128
Mitchell Range 222
Miworth 8, 40, 42, 207, 209-210
MOJO 132
Monkman Park 235
Monroe, Everett 193
Monroe, Ian 193
Monroe, Stanley James 149
Montreal 236
moonmilk 245
Moon River Cave 189
Moon Valley Cave 189
Moores Meadow 20, 24, 34-36, 45, 89, 211
moose 11, 25, 28, 30, 41-42, 51, 57, 65, 75, 78-79, 80, 83, 91, 94, 105, 109, 145, 184, 188, 192, 217, 222
Moose Lake 232
moose viewing area 80
Morice 92, 200

Morice, A.G. 87, 91, 200
Morkill River 231
mosquitoes 41, 85, 91, 121, 148, 154, 232
Mountainview Road 147-149
mountain caribou 57, 76, 89-90, 111, 121, 123, 145, 168, 177, 223
Mountain Equipment Co-op 155
mountain goats 145, 150, 160, 163, 189, 195
Mountain Pine Beetle 13, 58-59, 177, 223, 227
Mount Agnes 203
Mount Alexander 187
Mount Awasie 190
Mount Begbie 206
Mount Begbie Lookout 206
Mount Cross 188
Mount Edziza 201, 261
Mount Fitzwilliam 163, 238
Mount Hammell 139
Mount Holmes 151-152, 229
Mount Ian Monroe 193
Mount Ida 120, 185-186, 190-191
Mount Jarvis 189
Mount Jobe 231
Mount Kitchi 187, 230
Mount Knudsen 178
Mount Koona 190
Mount Monroe 149
Mount Murray 62-65, 203
Mount Nechamus 182
Mount Netim 189
Mount Ovington 182
Mount Pearson 182
Mount Plaskett 182
Mount Pope 112, 219
Mount Resplendent 251
Mount Robson 72, 75, 142, 151-152, 157-158, 162-163, 187, 196, 229-232, 238-239, 251
Mount Ruth 188
Mount Sir Alexander 107, 120, 129, 140-141, 186-188, 191, 230
Mount St. Andrews 189
Mount St. George 67
Mount St. Magnus 74
Mount St. Sepulchre 74
Mount Stalin 73
Mount Terry Fox 75, 116, 157, 159-160
Mount Walrus 190
Mueller, Louisa 242-243
Mueller, Ray 87, 242-243
Murch Lake 211
Murtha, Mike 10, 235
Muskwa 68, 95
Muskwa-Kechika 71
Mystic, Connecticut 230-231
Narraway River 184, 189
Nass 123
National Hiking Trail 10, 142-145, 200
Nation Lakes 221, 222
Nation Mountain 222
natural arch 150
Nature Trust 38
Nautley River 226
Nechako Ridge Trail 45

Nechako River   8, 15, 24, 35-37, 40, 43-46, 207, 209-211, 218, 226
Nechako River Bird Sanctuary   226
Nechako River Park   45-46, 207
Nelson, Bob   116, 139-140
Ness Lake   206, 211, 213
Northern Rocky Mountains 50, 71, 83, 109, 125, 182, 184, 191, 230, 231
Northwood   25, 26, 27, 88, 121, 216
North Bastion   68, 72
North Bastion Mountain   68, 72
North Boundary Trail   151, 162
North Nechako   46
Nuxalk Carrier Grease Trail   145, 200, 201
official community plan   19
old-growth   36, 46, 83, 112, 123-124, 128, 130, 132, 138, 148, 166, 181, 183
Old-growth Management Area   128
Ootsa Lake   239-240
orchid   35
Ormond Creek   218, 225-226
Ormond Creek Canyon   226
Ormond Lake   226
Otway cross-country ski centre   207
Otway Road   39, 46, 207
Overlanders   87, 91, 154
Overlander Falls   162
Ovington Creek   177, 183
Paddle Wheel Park   18, 210
Paradise Ridge   148-150
Parkridge Creek   44, 46
Parsnip River   48, 50, 52, 62, 233
Pass Lake   133, 167, 169, 171-172, 175, 177
Pass Lake Forest Service Road 133, 167, 170, 175
Peace River   50, 232, 234-235
Penny   26, 88, 124-125, 129-131
personal locator beacon   267, 269
phreatic tubes   249
Pidherny Recreation Area   46
Pilot Mountain   39, 205, 272
Pinchi Creek   221
Pinchi Fault   221
Pinchi Lake   221
Pinnacles Provincial Park   202
pin lichen   123, 128
Plenk, Joe   88
Plug Creek   68, 72, 74
Pope Mountain   218-219, 221
porcupine   66, 185
Powder King   62, 64
Premier Range   155-156, 158-159
Price, Kid   238
primordial   128
Prince George Astronomical Society   197
Prince George Naturalists Club   31, 38, 47, 121, 129, 227
Prince George Search and Rescue   239-240
Prince George Secondary School   22
Prince Rupert   7, 11
prostitutes   92
protozoan   123, 213
Ptarmigan Creek   116, 134-135, 13-140, 142, 188, 252
Ptarmigan Falls   135

pulp mill   32
Punchaw Lake   200
Purden Lake   82, 85, 123, 131, 167
quartzite mine   188
Quesnel   144, 198-199, 201-204, 231
Quesnel River   202
radio collar   89
railway and forestry museum   13, 15, 20, 24
Rainbow Falls   147
Raush Valley   10, 152, 154-156
Raven Lake   26, 83, 107, 118-119, 121
Rearguard Falls   162
Redemption Cave   244-245, 247, 248-249
Red Mountain   125, 129
Reef Icefield   163
Reflection Lake   21, 32
Rennie   92
Research Forest   166
Richfield Courthouse   203
Ridgeview Lake   213
Rivers Committee   18, 27, 38, 44
River Road   24, 37, 44-45, 144
Roberge, Luc   183
Robson Valley   75, 116, 142-143, 152, 238
Rocky Mountains 8, 11, 17, 21, 27-28, 30, 50, 59, 62, 77, 107, 113, 129, 140, 143, 156, 161, 165, 167, 175-176, 185-186, 214, 234, 244, 247, 249, 254-255
Rocky Mountains World Heritage Site   185
Rocky Mountain bighorn sheep   184, 234
Rocky Mountain Trench   11, 75, 82-83, 85, 90, 95-96, 105-106, 109, 113, 122, 124, 129-130, 132, 134, 140, 142-144, 147, 150-151, 155-156, 232, 272
Rouchon, Claude   171, 251
Royal Fusiliers   72
Rutherford, Bob   248-249
Safford, Kirk   247, 249
Salmon River   48, 51-52
satellite phone   264, 267, 269
scrub birch   69, 74
search and rescue   199, 240, 280
seasonal affective disorder   24
serpentine   213, 216
Shane Lake   21, 28, 31, 43
Sheep Pass   187
Shelford, Cyril   239, 241
Shelford, John   240-241
shelterwood   166
Sherman, General William Tecumseh   234
Sherman, Laura   234
Sherman Lake   236
Simon Fraser Bridge   18, 23
Sinclair Mills   27, 85, 87, 131, 242-243, 257
Skeena   123
Slim Creek   82, 122, 125, 128, 134
Smith, Cyndi   230
Smithers   8, 224, 226, 238
Smoky River   151, 229
Snowbird Pass   163
snowmobiling   12, 186, 203
snowshoe   77, 79, 91, 105, 110-111, 113, 129
Snowshoe Creek   134
Snyder, Harry   235
soda straws   245, 248

Sons of Norway Ski Club 77, 121
Southern Chilcotin Mountains 79
South Bastion Mountain 72
South Fort George 17, 18, 37, 199
Spahl, Randy 173
spiritual 32, 271
Stellako River 226
Stewart 71
Stikine River 201
stinging nettle 139
stone arch 150-151
Stone Bay Road 219
Stone Mountain 66, 67, 71, 74
Strathcona 17, 23
Strider Adventures 79, 188, 191, 194
strike-slip fault 75
Stuart Eskers 35, 211
Stuart Lake 50, 219, 221
Sugarbowl-Grizzly Den Provincial Park 26, 76, 83, 90, 112, 121
Sugarbowl Creek 85, 90, 93, 113, 134
Sugarbowl Mountain 107-109, 113
Sugarbowl Ridge 83, 85, 91, 105, 110, 113, 117, 125
Summit Lake 48, 50, 53-56, 59, 66, 67, 71, 112, 232-233, 272
Swift Current Creek 238-239
Tabor Lake 77
Tabor Mountain 30, 76-77, 79-80, 112, 130, 167
Tachick Lake 218
Tachie 221
Takla 44, 210, 222
Takla caribou herd 222
Takla Road 44, 210
Taylor, William 230
Tchentlo Lake 221-222
Teapot Mountain 54-55, 112, 233
Teare Mountain 147-148
Teepee Creek 158
Telegraph Creek 201
Terry Fox Day 157, 160
Tête Jaune Cache 75, 87, 91, 142, 154, 157, 162-163, 238
Tezzeron Lake 219, 221
The Burn 167-170
The Farm 169-171
Three Sisters 185, 190
Tintina Trench 75
Toronto 7, 47, 236-237
Torpy 117, 172, 174, 256
Tower of London Range 74
Trans-Canada Trail 145
Triassic fish fossils 184
Trudeau, Pierre Elliott 23, 73, 236-238
trumpeter swan 61, 209, 227
Tsayta Lake 222
Tumbler Ridge 235
Two Rivers Art Gallery 13, 15
UNBC Outdoors Club 121
University of British Columbia 113, 166

University of Northern British Columbia 11, 13, 17, 21, 26, 28, 30, 35, 42-44, 46, 51, 121-122, 127-128, 166, 174, 235, 280
University Way 17, 21, 28, 40, 46
Upper Fraser 130, 165, 167, 242
Upper Herrick Creek 183
Valemount 142, 157-160, 163
Vama Vama Creek 134
Vanderhoof 218, 224-227
Van der Post, Fred 79
Viking Ridge 83, 89, 91, 105-106, 108-111, 117, 125
visual quality 58, 76, 176, 179, 183
Vreeland, Frederick 188
walkabout 20
Walker Creek Forest Service Road 135, 185, 188, 196
walkway 23, 24
Wansa Creek 134
Wapiti Lake 235
Wapiti River 230
Watson Lake 69
Waverly Hut 203
Wells 202-203
Wenzel, Jan-Udo 21
West Lake 197
West Lake Provincial Park 197
West Twin Creek 134
West Twin Provincial Park 144, 146
whirlpool 88, 92
Whitehorn 158-159, 162
Whitestone Ridge 74
White Tower 68, 72
Wild Bird Trust of B.C. 227
Wild Kakwa Provincial Park 184
Wilkins Regional Park 207, 209
Williams, Ted 51
Williams Lake 204
Williston Lake 233
Willmore Wilderness Provincial Park 143, 151, 184, 229
Willow Canyon 80, 81
Willow River 81, 130, 134, 150, 167, 260
Wilson, Gerda 231
Wilson Park 24, 44, 210
Winnipeg 7, 27
winter solstice 30, 31, 213-214
Wishaw Glacier 188
Wishaw Lake 188, 196
Wishaw Mountain 188
Wokkpash 10, 66, 67-69, 71-74
wolf 74, 76-79, 83, 88, 91, 94, 105, 108, 111, 132, 145, 159, 200, 217, 222, 223, 240
wolverine 65, 105, 109, 140, 145, 222
Wolverine addition 145
Wolverine caribou herd 222
Yellowhead Bridge 18, 23, 76, 85, 210
Yellowhead Highway 17, 37, 75, 142, 163
Yellowhead Pass 87, 154
YMCA 15, 45
Yukon 66, 69, 85, 116, 201

About the author

Mike Nash has been a backcountry recreation enthusiast for 35 years, most of it in Northern British Columbia. During this time he has written over three hundred articles on B.C.'s outdoors and outdoor safety that have appeared in newspapers, magazines, books, and newsletters. Mike has participated for 15 years in public land use planning initiatives, including the protected area recommendations of the Prince George Land and Resource Management Plan. From 2002 to 2004, he was a lay member of the governing council of the Association of B.C. Forest Professionals, and he has been a member of various local and provincial government, industry, and university advisory committees. In the early 1990s, Mike chaired the City of Prince George's Nechako and Fraser River Valleys Committee and helped to develop a 10-year strategic plan for the riverside trails and parks in Prince George. During that same period, he represented the Federation of Mountain Clubs of B.C. in the development of the province's first commercial recreation policy. Mike has guided many hiking and backpacking trips, often including historical and natural history interpretation, and he has presented slide shows

on backcountry recreation themes in Prince George and elsewhere in B.C. Soon after arriving in Prince George, Mike spent several years as a volunteer search and rescue leader. He went on to pursue industrial and wilderness first aid training; became involved with health and safety in the workplace; and taught outdoor safety in the community, and through UNBC. Together, this background has given Mike Nash a unique opportunity to present what he feels is one of the world's remarkable places in this, his first full-length book.